Decolonization, Development and Knowledge in Africa

This provocative book is anchored o[illegible]surgent and resurgent spirit of decolonization in the twenty-first century. The author calls upon Africa to turn over a new leaf in the domains of politics, economy, and knowledge as it frees itself from imperial global designs and global coloniality.

With a focus on Africa and its Diaspora, the author calls for a radical turning over of a new leaf, predicated on decolonial turn and epistemic freedom. The key themes subjected to decolonial analysis include: (1) decolonization/decoloniality – articulating the meaning and contribution of the decolonial turn; (2) subjectivity/identity – examining the problem of Blackness (identity) as external and internal invention; (3) the Bandung spirit of decolonization as an embodiment of resistance and possibilities, development and self-improvement; (4) development and self-improvement – of African political economy, as entangled in the colonial matrix of power, and the African Renaissance, as weakened by undecolonized political and economic thought; and (5) knowledge – the role of African humanities in the struggle for epistemic freedom.

This groundbreaking volume opens the intellectual canvas on the challenges and possibilities of African futures. It will be of great interest to students and scholars of Politics and International Relations, Development, Sociology, African Studies, Black Studies, Education, History, Postcolonial Studies, and the emerging field of Decolonial Studies.

Sabelo J. Ndlovu-Gatsheni is Professor/Chair of Epistemologies of the Global South with Emphasis on Africa at the University of Bayreuth in Germany. He formerly worked as Research Professor and Director of Scholarship in the Department of Leadership and Transformation (DLT) in the Principal and Vice-Chancellor's Office at the University of South Africa (UNISA) and was 2019 Visiting Professor at the Johannesburg Institute for Advanced Study (JIAS) at the University of Johannesburg. He is a leading decolonial theorist and historian with over 100 publications, including eight sole-authored and nine edited books. His most recently published book is *Epistemic Freedom in Africa: Deprovincialization and Decolonization* (Routledge, 2018).

Worlding Beyond the West

Series Editors:
Arlene B. Tickner, *Universidad del Rosario, Colombia,*
David Blaney, *Macalester College, USA and*
Inanna Hamati-Ataya, *Cambridge University, UK*

Historically, the International Relations (IR) discipline has established its boundaries, issues, and theories based upon Western experience and traditions of thought. This series explores the role of geocultural factors, institutions, and academic practices in creating the concepts, epistemologies, and methodologies through which IR knowledge is produced. This entails identifying alternatives for thinking about the "international" that are more in tune with local concerns and traditions outside the West. But it also implies provincializing Western IR and empirically studying the practice of producing IR knowledge at multiple sites within the so-called 'West'.

21 **NGOs, Knowledge Production and Global Humanist Advocacy**
The Limits of Expertise
Alistair Markland

22 **Theory as Ideology in International Relations**
The Politics of Knowledge
Edited by Benjamin Martill and Sebastian Schindler

23 **International Relations from the Global South**
Worlds of Difference
Edited by Arlene B. Tickner and Karen Smith

24 **Making Global Knowledge in Local Contexts**
The Politics of International Relations and Policy Advice in Russia
Katarzyna Kaczmarska

25 **Decolonization, Development and Knowledge in Africa**
Turning Over a New Leaf
Sabelo J. Ndlovu-Gatsheni

For more information about this series, please visit: https://www.routledge.com

Decolonization, Development and Knowledge in Africa

Turning Over a New Leaf

Sabelo J. Ndlovu-Gatsheni

Routledge
Taylor & Francis Group
LONDON AND NEW YORK

First published 2020
by Routledge
2 Park Square, Milton Park, Abingdon, Oxon OX14 4RN

and by Routledge
605 Third Avenue, New York, NY 10017

First issued in paperback 2022

Routledge is an imprint of the Taylor & Francis Group, an informa business

Publisher's Note
The publisher has gone to great lengths to ensure the quality of this reprint but points out that some imperfections in the original copies may be apparent.

British Library Cataloguing-in-Publication Data
A catalogue record for this book is available from the British Library

Library of Congress Cataloging-in-Publication Data
A catalog record has been requested for this book

ISBN: 978-0-367-50595-0 (pbk)
ISBN: 978-0-367-46693-0 (hbk)
ISBN: 978-1-003-03042-3 (ebk)

DOI: 10.4324/9781003030423

Typeset in Times New Roman
by codeMantra

Contents

Tables

but they have been
<u>trained</u> /taught to think
that way for years - like being
dependent on the West for support /aid
or not having their own
agency... it's a psychological
shackled behaviour they
have to come out of which
takes time & a new
way of thinking

Turning over a new leaf Africa – Foreword

Alfred Babatunde 'Tunde' Zack-Williams
Emeritus Professor of Sociology, University of Central Lancashire, United Kingdom
President of the United Kingdom African Studies Association (ASA-UK) (2006–2008)
Member of British Academy Africa Panel

Professor Sabelo J. Ndlovu-Gatsheni's call for Africa to 'turn over a new leaf' (TOANL) is a welcomed reaction to the failure of African leaders to muster both human and physical resources within the continent for the task of nation-building and economic development, and thus free Africa from global imperial designs and global coloniality. In this *tour de force*, Professor Ndlovu-Gatsheni points out that the expression was first used by the Martinique revolutionary Frantz Fanon in describing his experiences of the Algerian revolution and the failure of African leaders to implement policies for radical transformation of their economies and societies in order to rid the continent of its status as the backwater of neo-colonialism and economic backwardness. The author, like Fanon, is calling for a different approach to development and world-making in order to put an end to estrangement.

Professor Ndlovu-Gatsheni, a leading African thinker and decolonial theorist, calls on African leaders to implement radical transformative policies to liberate the continent from all forms of oppressions, domestic and external, which made the lot of the African masses unbearable. In his magnum opus, *The Wretched of The Earth*, Fanon warned of the danger of the emerging culture of leadership embedded in the personality cult, which was distancing the leadership from the masses they sought to serve, whilst for him the true culture that could liberate the African masses from economic and social misery is that of revolutionary culture, which is constantly being produced by the workers and peasants in their struggles against domestic oppression and imperialist subjugation.

This book, in spite of its seeming 'starchiness' in parts (largely as a result of its engagement not only with complex ideas of postmodernism and postcolonialism but with complex archives and paradigms over a longue durée), is not designed simply for 'academic consumption.' It is a brave and noble project, which must trigger reactions as it raises an important question: 'which way Africa?' This question was also posed by Basil Davidson, one of the doyens of African history. Whilst the book is mainly concerned with Africa's past, present, and future, the role and the history of the African diaspora in championing the cause of the 'motherland' is never far from the mind of Professor Sabelo Ndlovu-Gatsheni; indeed, it cannot be otherwise for, whilst those in the diaspora hanker for recognition and respect, continental Africans yearn for freedom and relief from hunger and disease – thus the call for TOANL. According to Professor Ndlovu-Gatsheni, this process by necessity inculcates a pan-Africanist perspective, drawing on the ideas of such luminaries as Frantz Fanon, Walter Rodney, C. L. R. James, W. E. B Du Bois, Aime Cesaire, Marcus Garvey, and Kwame Nkrumah; Marxist and radical writers, such as Ngugi wa Thiongo; and black consciousness thinkers like Steve Bantu Biko as well as inculcating the lessons to be learned from the Haitian Revolution (1791–1804), 'which occupies a place of pride at the centre of black people's re-membering,' as Prof Ndlovu-Gatsheni points out.

Whilst Professor Ndlovu-Gatsheni's interests mainly lie with continental Africa, he draws attention to the fact that the concerns of Africa and its diaspora cannot be treated as separate (see Zack-Williams 1995). This is clear from the six forms of dismemberment that Professor Ndlovu-Gatsheni identified as relating to the humanity of black people and the intervention of Blackness: enslavement, commodification, and fragmentation of black people; the European scramble for, and partitioning of, Africa at the Berlin Conference; theft and usurpation, erasure, and silencing of African history so as to deny its existence; and the production and reproduction of patriarchy by dismembering African women from power. For example, with regards to one of the biggest developments in the diaspora, the Haitian Revolution, Professor Ndlovu-Gatsheni points to the enormous significance of this event to both diasporian and continental Africans. Thus he points out:

> The most important but silenced significance of the Haitian Revolution is that it led to the collapse of the entire system of slavery and constituted a major chapter in the history of 'remembering' of black people.

Professor Ndlovu-Gatsheni points out that in spite of this famous victory won by enslaved black people in Haiti, emancipation was a pipe dream for large number of black people, whose lives were plagued by racism, capitalism, colonialism, and patriarchy. This concern led Professor Ndlovu-Gatsheni to theorise what he refers to as 'Blackness.' In his view the question of Blackness:

> …emerged first as an invention within the politics of governing what it meant to be a human being. It is an existential question. It is a problem

> created by racism. Blackness is best understood as a problematic state of being. When it mutated into an identity, it became part of assertion of humanity and a de-colonial declaration: I am a human being.

Professor Ndlovu-Gatsheni correctly draws our attention to the fact that the triumph of Haiti did not reduce white racism towards black people. Indeed, it created the bifurcation of 'blackism' and 'whitism,' with the latter being fuelled and justified by what he calls 'dismemberment.' As he puts it, 'Racist configuration of the world is the fuel and justification for the dismemberment.' Drawing on the work of C. L. R. James (1994) and Eric Williams (1938) the author draws our attention to how the invention of blackism on a global scale was inextricably intertwined with the unfolding of the capitalist economic system, the modern patriarchal system, and indeed the modern colonial system. Professor Ndlovu-Gatsheni warns that '"Re-membering" continues to elude Africa and Africans. Consequently, the "postcolonial" and indeed the "post-racial" is yet to be born.'

In looking at the political economy of Africa, Professor Ndlovu-Gatsheni draws on the work of the radical Kenyan scholar Ngugi wa Thiong'o's concept of the four journeys of capital: namely the slave trade, the slave plantation system, colonialism, and the debt slavery to explicate how Africa increasingly became entrapped in global coloniality, further fortifying its dependence on the global capitalist order. According to Professor Ndlovu-Gatsheni, after 1945, we witnessed the growth of 'subliminal Euro-centric institutionalism,' within which scientific racism was de-escalated but never expunged from the structures and institutions of the modern world system. Thus, according to him, there was a move from direct colonialism to global coloniality, 'rather than from colonialism to post-colonialism.' Professor Ndlovu-Gatsheni alerts us to the fact that the notion of resurgent Africa (Africa Rising) is 'intertwined with the third scramble for Africa.'

Professor Ndlovu-Gatsheni examined the notion of the 'African Renaissance,' which is associated with former South African President Thabo Mbeki, and the concept of 'Africa Rising,' an idea associated with *The London Financial Times*, by referring to the growth of local entrepreneurship in Africa. The crucial point is that this momentum has now been submerged and subdued by the dynamism and the new language of neo-liberalism. The latter, under the rubric of structural adjustments, which was imposed on virtually all African countries, thanks to the 'Washington Consensus,' has fuelled the destruction of many 'infant industrial nuclei' on the continent, which were impelled to open their industries to unfair competition from the more mature Western manufacturing centres, with the result that virtually all the 'infant industries' established after independence have folded.

Anti-state and pro-market philosophies such as neo-liberalism brought misery to the people of Africa, whose governments were pushed to become observers as local industries were hived off to foreign multinationals or simply destroyed through unfair competition because their governments were prevented from intervening to save their industries or to spend on social welfare provisions. Subsidies were removed from essential commodities, and teachers and civil servants had to go months without salaries. These self-destructive policies led to political instability, conflicts, and civil wars, which, in turn, negatively impacted on the economy. Unsurprisingly, then, the period of International Monetary Fund (IMF) structural adjustment programmes was accompanied by poverty and widespread conflicts, and, in some countries, civil wars.

In the final chapter of the manuscript, Professor Ndlovu-Gatsheni discussed the issue raised by Dipesh Chakrabarty (2000) about coming to terms with European domination of socio-political-economic space and the need to 'provincialise Europe.' Professor Ndlovu-Gatsheni points out that the best de-colonial strategy is to 'delink from the colonial matrices of power.' Africa would signal its intention to put an end to 'provincialization' via each African state investing heavily in education at all levels, consolidating the proposed Africa Continental Free Trade Agreement and thereby demonstrating to the rest of the world that Africa is fighting to turn over a new leaf and will not be a spectator watching things unfold in the era of the fourth Industrial Revolution.

Acknowledgements

The most fortuitous moment during the writing of this book was when I met Emeritus Professor Alfred Tunde Zack-Williams from the University of Central Lancashire at the Edinburgh Catalyst Fellows Workshop (22–26 July 2019) at the University of Edinburgh in Scotland, and we began to talk about early African educated elite from Sierra Leone and how they agitated for indigenous African universities. I took advantage of my meeting with this senior African scholar to invite him to write a foreword for this book. He graciously agreed. I would therefore like to express my gratitude to Professor Zack-Williams for the intellectual conversations and the foreword.

Professor Finex Ndhlovu from the University of New England in Australia read the whole manuscript and provided useful feedback. This work would not have materialised without the support of my wife Pinky Patricia Ndlovu-Gatsheni. My daughter Nobuntu Anaya Ndlovu-Gatsheni and my son Langelihle Vulamazulu Ndlovu-Gatsheni always wanted my attention, so they tried all their tricks on me and taught me how to divide time and attention. My eldest son, Vulindlela Kings Ndlovu-Gatsheni, always drove me to wherever I was invited to deliver lectures and keynotes, and I am very grateful for that support as it enabled me to test the ideas that constitute this book.

I owe a load of thanks to Professor Morgan Ndlovu, Professor Last Moyo, Professor Tendayi Sithole, Professor Zodwa Motsa, Dr William Mpofu, and Dr Eric Nyembezi Makoni, with whom I consistently shared ideas on decolonization/decoloniality. Emily Ross and Jessica Holmes at Routledge developed an interest in my work when it was still an idea and facilitated the review of the manuscript by four anonymous reviewers, right up to its acceptance for publication under the Worlding Beyond the West Series.

I remain responsible for all the ideas expressed in this book.

1 Introduction

Beyond the European game

As an African decolonial 'writer in politics,' in addition to my desire to 'write what I want' (to exercise epistemic freedom), I strive to produce liberatory knowledge subversive of the Eurocentric epistemology of concealment of crimes of racism, slavery, colonialism, patriarchy, sexism, and capitalism. Ngugi wa Thiong'o, in his *Writers in Politics: A Re-Engagement with Issues of Literature and Society* (1997: xvi), delineated key characteristics of such writers, noting that their works 'reflect one or more aspects of the intense economic, political, cultural and ideological struggles in a society.' Writers on politics do not merely write 'about politics.' They take clear sides 'in the battle field' of ideas, where the oppressed and violated (the people) confront the oppressors and their well-crafted systems, structures, institutions, strategies, and 'games' of oppression, exploitation, and dehumanization. Decolonial writers in politics are never 'neutral,' as Ngugi wa Thiong'o (1997: xvi) explained: 'What he or she cannot do is to remain neutral.' Born in Africa, which experienced slavery and colonialism, I cannot 'remain neutral' either. As a product of a dehumanizing modernity/coloniality and its 'European game,' I seek decolonization, deimperialization, depatriachization, debourgeoisefication, decorporatization, deracialization, detribalization, and democratization as the broader 'will to live' rather than 'will to power' (Ndlovu-Gatsheni 2019; see also Dussel 2008). As a product of and as someone employed by the 'westernized modern university,' I strive to liberate myself from 'miseducation' (unlearning impositions of colonialism/coloniality), and I am consistently 're-educating' myself (relearning). My entry point is rethinking and unthinking thinking itself because it is in the epistemic domain that the sources of systemic, structural, and institutional crises are resident (see Hoppers and Richards 2012; Ndlovu-Gatsheni 2018b). My target is what Frantz Fanon (1968) called the 'European game.'

At the centre of the 'European game' which Fanon urged the colonized to abandon is epistemic and ideological trickery. This is fundamentally a game founded on the epistemological invasion of the mental universe of its targets (coloniality of knowledge), the transhistoric expansion of imperial/colonial/capitalist/patriarchal heterosexual power (coloniality of power/coloniality of gender), the social classification and racial hierarchization of world population (coloniality of being human itself), conceit, and seduction (rhetoric of modernity). In all this, Eurocentric epistemology actively worked and continues to work as the primary and active enabler of planetary European hegemony. As understood and defined by Samir Amin (2009: 154), Eurocentrism is 'a theory of world history' which puts Europe at the centre of the idea and philosophy of human history, and which is a cultural expression of Euromodernity, mediated by the inferiorization of others and the superiorization of Europeans. Teshale Tibebu, in *Hegel and the Third World: The Making of Eurocentrism in World History* (2011: xxi), identified Georg Wilhelm Friedrich Hegel (1770–1831) as one of the key articulators of Eurocentrism and concluded that 'All Eurocentrism is thus essentially a series of footnotes to Hegel.' Hegel embodied Eurocentric epistemology and the 'geo-culture' of Euromodernity. He was not alone. They were many other philosophers of Euromodernity and Eurocentrism, including David Hume and Rene Descartes.

The key logic at the centre of Euromodernity was a radical shift from a 'God-centred' society to a 'science-centred' society, whereby those who claimed and monopolized being complete human beings (Europeans/Cartesian subjects) simultaneously claimed to be creators of human history and innovators who conquered and reordered the world, in the process redefining human life itself as they disregarded traditions and religion. Fanon (1968: 252) explained why the 'European game' has to be abandoned in the following strong words:

> When I search for Man in the technique and style of Europe, I see only succession of negations of man and an avalanche of murders. The human condition, plans for mankind and collaboration between men in those tasks which increase the sum total of humanity are now problems, which demand true inventions. Let us decide not to imitate Europe; let us combine our muscles and our brains in a new direction. Let us try to create the whole man, whom Europe has been incapable of bringing to triumphant birth. Two centuries ago, a former European colony decided to catch up with Europe. It succeeded so well that the United States of America became a monster, in which the taints, the sickness and inhumanity of Europe have grown to appalling dimensions. Comrades, have we not other work to do than to create a third Europe?

The 'technique' and 'style' of Europe is carried by Eurocentric epistemology. The primacy of epistemology and indeed the entanglement of knowledge and ontology features even in the widely read book called *The Bible*. Knowledge is invoked at the very myth of the foundation and genesis of the universe. In the Book of John, the Bible says that at the beginning was the 'word.' Western secular philosophers have interpreted the 'word' as *logos*, which is a key element in modern epistemology (way of knowing). The key point here is that epistemology is the primary domain within which ontology emerges (is created and articulated). One can therefore posit that epistemology enabled God (the creator) to envision the universe before practically creating the world in seven days. This means that the world is an epistemic creation. Walter D. Mignolo and Cathrine E. Walsh (2018: 135) give credence to this proposition:

> What matters is not economics, or politics, or history, but knowledge. Better yet, what matters is history, politics, economics, race, gender, sexuality, but it is above all the knowledge that is intertwined in all these praxical spheres that entangles us to the point of making us believe that it is not knowledge that matters but really history, economy, politics, etc. Ontology is made of epistemology. That is, ontology is an epistemological concept; it is not inscribed in the entities the grammatical nouns name.

Mignolo and Walsh (2018: 136) elaborated that 'It is knowledge weaved around concepts such as politics and economy that is crucial for decolonial thinking, and not politics and economy as transcendental entities.' Perhaps it was for this reason that God planted the 'Tree of Knowledge' at the centre of the Garden of Eden. When Eve and Adam ate the fruits from this tree, it is said that they immediately realized they were naked (reality dawned on them). In other words, they became aware of themselves. This proposition resolves the long-standing egg-chicken conundrum in the knowledge/epistemology-reality/-ontology dialectic. What is therefore emphasized in this book is that the modern world system and the global order are epistemic creations. Such spheres of life as society, politics, and economy are also epistemic creations. The 'European game' is a secular invention of the modern world in the image of Europe, claiming that only Europeans are creators and rendering 'Others' as imitators. At the centre of the 'European game' is Euromodernity as a broad discursive formation enabled by the invasion of the earth through the colonization of knowledge (coloniality of knowledge), which, in turn, enabled the colonization of time, space, nature, and people.

Euromodernity materialized through the colonization of time (rupture and difference) in the first instance. It is driven by the racial, imperial/colonial, capitalist, and hetero-patriarchal logics of domination, exploitation, and dehumanizing experienced by all those rendered as 'pre-modern.' But to legitimate itself Euromodernity's rhetoric of salvation, social evolution, progress, civilization, rationality, scientism, emancipation, modernization, development, and liberalism was laid out. Its horizon is universalism, with Europe and North America at the centre. Even today, those who are enchanted by Euromodernity continue to push the colonial struggle of completing the 'unfinished project of modernity' as a guarantor of human freedom and human flourishing (Habermas 1996). This is why one finds such leading African philosophers as Olufemi Taiwo writing books like *Africa Must Be Modern: A Manifesto* (2014: xii), in which he posits that 'modernity is life,' and its key tenet is 'the open future' (see Taiwo 2014: 185). This enchantment with Euromodernity is understandable. It comes partly from a strong belief in its claims and promises to overcome all human problems through the deployment of enlightened secular thinking and modern science in order to deliver a brave new world, and partly from its effective strategies of seduction and a concealment of 'coloniality' (its underside/its negative side) (see Quijano 2000).

However, to be enchanted by Euromodernity is to fall headlong into the logics and traps of the 'European game,' where even enslavement and colonization were articulated as part of the discourse of progress and salvation. Defining the 'European game' from the perspective of decolonization, it is a terrain of racism, domination, exploitation, and dehumanization for those who experienced negative modernity, and were targeted for enslavement and colonization. On the other hand (and read from a Eurocentric perspective), the 'European game' is a triumphant story of the successful delivery of the gifts of salvation, progress, civilization, rationality, scientism, emancipation, liberalism, and development. Euromodernity is defined as a gift. Of course, Europe and North America benefited materially from the 'European game' through the slave trade, colonialism, and capitalism. Meanwhile, Africa suffered due to the slave trade, colonialism, and capitalism. Inevitably, the Eurocentric perspective urges Africa to imitate and emulate Europe and North America in its search for liberation and development.

The key problem with the Eurocentric perspective is that it conceals the 'underside' (violence and violations) of Euromodernity known as 'coloniality' (negatives of Euromodernity) (see Quijano 2000). Tibebu (2011: xvi) posits, 'There are three pillars of negative modernity: the American holocaust, New World slavery, and colonialism.' Colonialism is succeeded by coloniality. This is the term for the transhistoric expansion of racist logics which enabled inimical processes of enslavement, racial capitalism, colonial domination, hetero-normative patriarchal domination, and their perpetuation into the present (see Quijano 2000; Morana et al. 2008). Even the post-Cold War emergent ideas of multiple, plural, and trans-modernities have not adequately resolved the dirtiness of the concept of modernity and its Eurocentrism. Gurminder K. Bhambra (2007: 1) revealed the *modus operandi* of Euromodernity as '*rupture* and *difference*—a temporal rupture that distinguishes a traditional, agrarian past from the modern, industrial present; and a fundamental difference that distinguishes Europe from the rest of the world.'

The push for the completion of the 'unfinished business of modernity' is countered by the decolonial perspective, driven by an effort to complete the incomplete decolonization/decoloniality. At the centre of the contemporary decolonial struggles are such targets as racism, enslavement, imperialism, colonialism/coloniality, capitalism, and patriarchy. The envisioned horizon is that of a pluriversity in which many worlds fit, and ecologies of knowledges strive (Santos 2007; Escobar 2018; Reiter 2018). The proposed turning over of a new leaf for Africa is directly informed by decolonization. The call comes from the Caribbean revolutionary Frantz Fanon: 'For Europe, for us, and for humanity, comrades, we must turn over a new leaf, we must work out new concepts, and try to set afoot a new man.' The expansive and revolutionary process of turning over a leaf for Africa entails a radical negation of racism, enslavement, colonialism/coloniality, capitalism, and patriarchy in their past and contemporary forms. It means abandoning the 'European game' on the grounds that it is dehumanizing and dismembering other human beings.

These inimical processes are enabled by the paradigm of difference predicated on religious and pseudo-racial scientific thought constitutive of the unfolding of Euromodernity. The consequence has been the social classification and racial hierarchization of humanity in accordance with invented differential ontological densities. Europeans arrogated to themselves the category of 'modern humans' and relegated others into the status of 'primitive/pre-modern sub-humans' as they colonized time itself. Thus, to Fanon, Europe, though it invoked the idea of the human throughout its history, failed to create common humanism. Rather, through such inimical processes as enslavement (turning African people into commodities/things and trafficking them in the world market), genocides (physical liquidation/final solutions), colonization (taking over space and domination and exploitation of people/dehumanization), and epistemicides (theft of knowledge and history, appropriation, and displacement of endogenous knowledge), Europe declared war on humanity and displayed its barbarism on a world scale. This reality led Aime Cesaire (2000: 31) to depict European civilization as 'decadent,' 'sick,' 'de-civilizing,' and 'dying.' Thus, one can delineate key drivers of the 'European game': the paradigm of difference (racism), the will to power (the urge to conquer/I conquer, therefore I am), and the paradigm of war (*homo polemos*/warrior tradition).

The radical shift from the logics and practices of the 'European game' is what is rendered here as the turning over of a new leaf for Africa. It is a double act of decolonizing and making a new humanism (another possible world). Growing a 'Decolonial Tree of Knowledge' (DKT) at the centre of the modern world is an ideal beginning of decolonization. Those who partook of its decolonial fruits would immediately realize that they are naked (walking lies, liminal subjects, and indeed a people who are not only denied humanity but also pushed to into a colonial limbo). The metaphor of nakedness encapsulates self-realization and self-knowledge. For example, those who suffer from an imposed inferiority complex and therefore feel they have been reduced to a sub-human category would immediately arise from this form of coloniality. Those who have been elevated into superior human beings above all other beings would immediately realize the lie of racism. Thus, the turning over of a new leaf by Africa must begin in the knowledge domain and entails the process of producing new knowledge and working out new concepts that liberate human genius rather than imprisoning it.

Inevitably, the revolutionary act of invention of new humanism must be carried out through a protracted decolonization struggle and process. Decolonization, to Fanon, was not reduced to the attainment of political independence. Genuine decolonization entailed a planetary revolution underpinned by abandonment of Europe (deimperialization). Deimperialization and decolonization further entail revolutionary transformation of the very immanent logics of Euromodernity, including colonialism, capitalism, and patriarchy, that were sold to the world as progress, civilization, emancipation, modernization, and development. Deimperialization, decolonization, and depatriachization have to create something new—a new world, free from the paradigm of difference which enabled enslavement, colonial exploitation, and racist domination—beyond all forms of dismemberment and dehumanization.

In her recent book, *Worldmaking After Empire: The Rise and Fall of Self-Determination* (2019), Adom Getachew posited that anti-colonial nationalism and decolonization were fundamentally about 'nation-making' and 'worldmaking' as simultaneous tasks. Getachew (2019: 2) emphasized that 'decolonization was a project of reordering the world that sought to create a domination-free and egalitarian international order.' Thus, such anti-colonial nationalist leaders as Kwame Nkrumah and Julius Nyerere are credited for laying out three different decolonial projects, 'the institutionalization of a right to self-determination at the United Nations, the formation of regional federations, and the demand for New International Economic Order,' as they sought to 'overcome the legal and material manifestations of unequal integration and inaugurate a postimperial world' (Getachew 2019: 2). Getachew (2019: 3) challenged those who critiqued nationalism as 'parochial and anti-universal' as well as those who reduced African nationalism to a derivative discourse and anti-colonialism to a mere 'transfer of power.' In the scholarship of Getachew (2019: 3), anti-colonial nationalists like Nkrumah and Nyerere were 'worldmakers rather than solely nation builders.' This argument resonates with that of Paul Tiyambe Zeleza (2003), who depicted decolonization of Africa as the 'proudest moment in African history' because it contained historic and humanistic agendas of the African nationalist project: namely nation-building, socio-economic development, and pan-African unity.

This means that decolonization/decoloniality must not be reduced to post-Enlightenment Eurocentric historicism predicated on linear notions of social evolution, progress, civilization, emancipation, modernization, and development. It was not and is not about 'incomplete modernity' as a key problem. It was and remains an original African liberatory initiative, which must not be equated with ideas of 'transition from empire to nation and the expansion of international society to include new states' (Getachew 2019: 14). It is not reducible to the liberal project, although it embraced some of its claims. Decolonization/decoloniality continues to be 'a radical rupture—one that required a wholesale transformation of the colonized and a reconstitution of the international order' (Getachew 2019: 17). Thus, to Nkrumah, it was a 'hurricane of change' rather than a 'wind of change' (Getachew 2019: 17). Under decolonization, Euromodernity was openly questioned and challenged, the imposed inferiorization of the colonized was rejected, the invented superiority of Europeans was questioned and rejected, the sovereign humanity of the colonized was asserted, and the denied agency and genius of the colonized was reasserted. Thus, the turning over of a new leaf by Africa lies not in completing the 'incomplete project of modernity' but in the 'incomplete project of decolonization' predicated on the decolonization of the very concept of being human (see Maldonado-Torres 2017).

However, the decolonization/decoloniality movement continues to be haunted by the gender question. The dominance of male figures in the struggles for decolonization/decoloniality revealed the patriarchal structure of coloniality of power which privileged European males as well as African males, albeit differently. The introduction of the concepts of 'coloniality of gender' and the 'modern/colonial gender system' by Maria Lugones (2007, 2010) allowed for a historical articulation of the impositions of gender as an organizing principle and paradigm of difference, resulting in the dehumanization of the targets of colonization. Lugones (2007) explained how colonial subjection of both men and women resulted in the complicity of colonized and racialized men in the 'modern/colonial gender system' and their indifference to systemic violence inflicted on what she termed 'women of colour.' If one reads Lugones's ideas together with the interventions of 'African feminism' the 'modern/colonial gender system' is brought to the centre of decolonization struggles. African feminism correctly brought to the fore another interpretation of the 'woman question' and gender issues, taking into account African histories and cultures, and thus recovering matriarchal systems of power that existed in the pre-colonial period, and even the existence of societies where gender was not the organizing principle (Oyewumi 1997). Taken together with Lugones's systemic analysis, what is revealing is how the 'modern/colonial gender system' invented gender, which subordinated European bourgeois women to European men, on the one side, and dehumanized the colonized into 'bestial and thus non-gendered, promiscuous, grotesquely sexual, and sinful' non-beings, on the other side (see Lugones 2010: 743). The colonized were not even included in the 'gender' but reduced to creatures of 'sex' as part of colonial animalization. For more details on the coloniality of gender, 'modern/colonial gender system' and 'African feminism,' see Chapter 2 of this book.

It is sufficient to say that turning over a new leaf for Africa entails depatriachization as a key aspect of the decolonization struggles and processes. Thomas Sankara (1990: 11) laid out the key contours of depatriachization as a form of decolonization and indeed anti-capitalist and anti-imperialist revolution in these revealing words:

> The women and men of our society are all victims of imperialist oppression and domination. That is why they wage the same struggle. The revolution and women's liberation go together. We do not talk of women's emancipation as an act of charity or out of a surge of human compassion. It is a basic necessity for the revolution to triumph.

Alas, the decolonization of the twentieth century did not deliver a new humanism and a depatriarchized postcolonial and postracial world. This failure is partly explained by the deep interpellation of decolonization by the immanent logics of colonialism. The very process of decolonization was held hostage by the 'cognitive empire'/'metaphysical empire' (the empire of the mind) (see Ndlovu-Gatsheni 2018a, 2018b; Santos 2018). This dangerous empire operated through the infection of the mental universe of its victims, which amounted to the removal of the hard disk of previous endogenous knowledge and downloading into the African minds of the software of European knowledge and languages (Ngugi wa Thiong'o 1986; Ngugi wa Thiong'o 2009a). It committed such heinous crimes as theft of history, ontocides, epistemicides, linguicides, and cultural imperialism. Inevitably, the decolonization of the twentieth century assumed a reformist, rather than maintaining a revolutionary anti-systemic, character.

Eventually, the signs and symbols of being decolonized included invitation and accommodation of the so-called 'independent African states' into the lowest echelons of the United Nations Organization (UNO), in which they had no veto power. However, according to Getachew (2019: 14–15), anti-colonial nationalists used the UNO as a forum to radicalize the liberal reformist notion of 'self-determination' into a 'human right' in the process of securing the passage of the General Assembly Resolution 1514, known as the 'Declaration on the Granting of Independence to Colonial Countries and Peoples.' Despite these inroads the UNO remained a key institution of the post-1945 world order and world system, which remained hierarchical in configuration. In the resilient Western tradition, being invited into the UNO was nothing but accommodation into a modern system of power that emerged in 1492 and was consolidated at Westphalia in 1648. The system gave itself a new lease on life by including the previously excluded non-Europeans into a modern sovereignty system. This was the case partly because the erstwhile colonial powers always wanted to emerge still powerful, in charge, and in control of the modern world system and the world order, and partly because the 'indigenous' African elites produced by colonialism itself were at the helm of the struggles for decolonization of the twentieth century. However radical, many of these elites displayed problematic colonial consciousnesses, which haunted their liberatory initiatives and projects. Of course, there were exceptions, such as Nkrumah, Amilcar Cabral, and Thomas Sankara, who continuously fought and agitated for genuine liberation, a deimperialized world system, and a decolonized world order as well as depatriarchized mindsets, social orders, and institutions.

The problems of the 'indigenous' African elites on the continent and in the Diaspora were well articulated by William E. B. Du Bois and Fanon. Du Bois identified the problem of double-consciousness (two souls/two strivings in a single body), and Fanon explained the pitfalls of such consciousness (see Fanon 1968; Du Bois 1986). Along the same vein, Ali A. Mazrui (1978) spoke of cultural schizophrenia. As products of seductive colonialism, with its rhetoric of progress, civilization, emancipation, and development, most of the 'indigenous' African elites were enchanted and seduced, to the extent that they suffered from racial melancholia (wishing to be white). Thus, to most of the 'indigenous' African elites decolonization was a vehicle to enable them to simply replace white foreign elites and continue where these people left off. Fanon depicted this as the desire to join the racket. Indeed, many of the elites became notorious accomplices in neo-colonialism and facilitated the continuation of the underdevelopment of Africa. The example of Mobutu Sese Seko of Zaire, who became a puppet of the United States of America, comes immediately to mind, as does that of Paul Biya of Cameroon, who controls his country mainly from France. Worse still, even radicals such as Robert Gabriel Mugabe of Zimbabwe still suffered from the same pitfalls of consciousness, with their Europhobia (fixation with Europe, especially after being sanctioned by it) acting as a cover-up for their Europhilia (love for everything European). Africa's turning over of a new leaf must not exhaust itself in Europhobia or Europhilia but impact the world beyond Europe via the recovery of those visions of the world that Europe denied and repressed (see Dabashi 2019: 132–134).

However, like all true ideas of liberation, decolonization has refused to die. There is hope that its resurgence and insurgence in the twenty-first century will, this time around, enable a genuine process of turning over a new leaf by taking advantage of hindsight. At the core of the process of turning over a new leaf are four important steps. The first is the urgent task of restoring deprived ontology (subjecthood/humanhood) to a people who had been pushed out of the human ocumene (human family/zone of being) and relegated to sub-humanhood (zone of non-being). This second step is to turn the colonized men and women into craftsmen and craftswomen (geniuses and inventors) as creators of their own futures and in charge of their destinies (Fanon 1968). They must emerge as inventive human beings with regained agency. The third move is to reject mimicry and subvert the colonial law of repetition. This will enable African people to radically break from the immanent logics of colonialism (freedom from repetition without change). The fourth move is to negate colonial time—to rebel against the theft of history, against being thrown out of civilization and out of time—so as to relocate themselves into human history as sovereign subjects. Taken together, all these initiatives involve casting Africa as the centre, not the periphery, of the world. This is possible today because Europe and North America, which previously cast themselves as the centre of the world, are experiencing degradation, manifesting itself as fortressing, walling, nativism, and xenophobia. Brexit and Trumpism are symptoms of this degradation and inward-worlding (narrow nationalism). Africa has to open up and occupy the centre instead. As Achille Mbembe (2017: 1) put it, 'Europe is no longer the centre of gravity of the world. This is the significant event, the fundamental experience of our era.'

The resurgent and insurgent decolonization of the twenty-first century is built upon a strong foundation, laid out by such freedom fighters and visionary leaders as Kwame Nkrumah, Steve Bantu Biko, Samora Machel, Thomas Sankara, and Amilcar Cabral. Because these leaders displayed a deeper understanding of the dirty *modus operandi* of imperialism, colonialism, and neo-colonialism, they became victims of sponsored military coups and assassinations. But their spirit of struggle and visions of liberation continue to inspire the resurgent and insurgent decolonization of the twenty-first century. These are the giants on whose shoulders such student-led formations as the Rhodes Must Fall and Fees Must Fall movements stand. What is distinctive about these movements is that they emerged within the centre of what Julie Cupples (2019: 2) termed 'the westernized university' as

> a site where learning and the production, acquisition and dissemination of knowledge are embedded in Eurocentric epistemologies that are posited as objective, disembodied and universal and in which non-Eurocentric knowledges such as black and indigenous knowledges are largely ignored, marginalised or dismissed.

The 'westernized university' is a globalized institution and exists in Africa and the rest of the world as the 'Tree of Coloniality' (TC). Those who eat its fruits immediately speak in European colonial tongues.

Thus, this book is anchored on the resurgent and insurgent decolonization of the twenty-first century. At its centre is the task of re-humanizing the dehumanized. This process entails picking up fragments, known as re-membering after centuries of dismemberment, to borrow an argument from Ngugi wa Thiong'o (2009a, 2009b). What cuts across and connects the eight chapters is the spirit of resurgent and insurgent decolonization, which has the potential to enable Africa to turn over a leaf. At its deepest conceptualization, decolonization entails a re-writing of human history as opposed to a re-interpretation (same facts of history)—bringing forth 'new facts,' 'new voices,' and fundamentally opening up 'new possibilities for mutual learning and new beliefs and actions' (Bhambra 2007: 155). What is envisioned is another possible world, with a different ethics of living together.

Therefore, at the ontological level, decolonization has the outstanding task of resolving the processes of the colonization of the human ('coloniality of being,' as Nelson Maldonado-Torres termed it in 2007). The degradation of those classified as 'slaves,' 'natives,' 'blacks,' and 'females' into a sub-human category continues to be a key existential concern today. This is so because the social classification and racial hierarchization of human beings continues to determine intersubjective relations. They are still divided into races, in spite of the fact that scientific racism has been discredited. The upsurge in discourses on human rights and their norming under the Universal Declaration of Human Rights in 1948 did not resolve the long-standing question of who is the 'human' in the human rights discourse. When a person who has been rendered as native and black travels across the world, he or she confronts the whiteness of the world in its most detestable forms, particularly when its hidden anti-blackness rears its head at borders and airports. Today, this anti-blackness is also hidden in biometric instruments of surveillance, control, and exclusion. The black migrant and the Muslim symbolize blackness on a world scale (see Mbembe 2017). Thus, the long-standing problem known as 'Negrophobia' becomes conjoined with 'Islamophobia.' Trumpism is the latter-day storm trooper and representative of the perpetrator of anti-black violence; Donald Trump's obsession with building a wall at the Mexican border is a testimony to a mindset guided by the paradigm of difference and notions of an 'impossibility of co-presence,' as Boaventura de Sousa Santos (2007) calls it.

At the political level, the notion of national sovereignty has remained hollow in Africa. Neo-colonialism and neo-liberalism have combined to produce global coloniality and a global financial empire which subverts the sovereignty of other states (see Gildea 2019). Such institutions as the World Bank, World Trade Organization, and International Monetary Fund are constitutive of the powerful financial empire and enable its global coloniality. At the centre of this are resilient asymmetrical power relations cascading from the time of enslavement and colonial conquest. The decolonization of the twentieth-century was not successful in de-structuring and deimperializing the modern world system. The post-1945 world order is characterized by four major global colonialities: the Cold War coloniality, neo-colonialism, the 'imperialism of decolonization' (Eurafrica/Francafrique), and the neoliberal market coloniality (financial republic with its market fundamentalism) (Ndlovu-Gatsheni 2015; Gildea 2019). The so-called 'newly independent African states' were submerged under these global colonialities. The truth of the matter is that anything amounting to 'African states' is yet to be born; those that exist now are outward-oriented and very predatory 'states in Africa' created by colonialism. Such leaders as Julius Kabarage Nyerere, through such initiatives as the Arusha Declaration, tried to decolonize the very constitution of the political and to re-invent the state as a truly African institution in the service of African people. But active global colonialities torpedoed these liberation initiatives. Thomas Sankara tried to do the same in Burkina Faso and was physically and violently eliminated. After seeing how global powers dealt with Robert Mugabe of Zimbabwe when he attempted to institute a compulsory fast-track land reform programme, the leaders of other former settler colonies, like Namibia and South Africa, became fearful of directly addressing skewed land holdings.

At the knowledge level, the cognitive empire maintained a strong grip on epistemology. Because epistemology always frames ontology, there was no way that the empire would not intervene directly in the knowledge domain (see Mignolo and Walsh 2018). Epistemology was deployed strategically to colonize the minds of Africans. This was possible because it always frames ontology. Eurocentric epistemology was and continues to be used effectively in the invasion of the African mental universe (Ngugi wa Thiong'o 1986; Ndlovu-Gatsheni 2018b). Thus, such African nationalist-inspired initiatives as deracialization and Africanization did not successfully uproot the Euro-centric epistemology from the African knowledge domain. Deracialization and Africanization, while very necessary, only dealt with surface appearances/the symptoms of the problem. Inevitably, the only thing that changed were the players in a European game; the rules remained unchanged. We are called upon as African people to change the rules, if not to totally abandon the European game. This requires what Cathrine Odora-Hoppers and Richard Howard (2012) aptly described as 'rethinking thinking' itself. For example, in the field of historical studies, we must pose deeper questioning of the idea and philosophy of history to get to the issue of how 'African' is the recognized and disciplinary African history taught in the academy. Yes, if indeed colonialism invaded the entire mental universe of the African people, decolonization must be an expansive liberation initiative, dealing with psychological, aesthetic, ideological, epistemic, institutional, social, economic, political, cultural, and other aspects of African life. It must be restorative of what was lost and inventive of the new.

The second chapter introduces the concept of the 'decolonial turn' and directly addresses various topical issues in decolonization/decoloniality debates, in the process revealing and explaining inevitable tensions in a knowledge produced on the battlefields of human history. The question of how different decolonization/decoloniality is from postcolonialism and postmodernism is directly confronted, taking into account Pal Ahluwalia's argument that some versions of postcolonialism and post-structuralism have Maghrebian roots (African roots). The chapter also pitches decolonization/decoloniality at the planetary level as it strives to provide a deeper and expansive genealogy as well as an explanation of how the African and Latin American conceptions of decolonization/decoloniality overlap and influence each other, even though they draw from different geo-political constructions and divergent colonial experiences. Insights from decolonial feminism and African feminism are deployed to further explicate and expand the scope of decolonization/decoloniality. The 'decolonial turn' is presented as a compass directing African people into a possible and better world, characterized by pluriversality.

The third chapter turns to the 'Bandung spirit of decolonization,' re-reading it back into the *longue durée* of African and black history of resistance, such as the anti-enslavement revolts and the 'primary resistance' movements of the nineteenth century, and, more importantly, connecting it with the paradigmatic Haitian Revolution (1791–1804) as its precursor, on the one hand, and with the current efforts of 'dewesternization' symbolized by such formations as BRICS (Brazil, Russia, India, China, and South Africa), on the other. While 'dewesternization' may not be synonymous with decolonization/decoloniality, mainly because it does not radically delink from capitalist logics, it still forms part of the struggle against Euro-North American hegemony. The chapter demonstrates the connections between African and black struggles for liberation, and the solidarities created while documenting efforts at re-making a modern world order that is domination-free.

The fourth chapter deals with the cross-cutting and complex identity question while examining the politics of elevating whiteness to a badge of full humanity and superiority, and rendering blackness a sign of subhumanity and inferiority. The problem of blackness stands at the centre of the unfolding of colonial processes of dismemberment, on the one hand, and the African struggles and initiatives aimed at re-membering Africa, on the other. In a modern world system that has remained imperial and a global order that is resiliently colonial, the problem of racism continues to haunt humanity, with those rendered as black being the main victims. As Africa fights to turn over a new leaf, the existential question of blackness must be resolved and never taken as a sign of inferiority. Building on the most recent work of Kehinde Andrews *Back to Black: Black Radicalism in the 21st Century* (2019) this chapter re-articulates blackness not only as a problem but also as embodying potential for liberation.

The fifth chapter is concerned with how the journey of capital across space and time since the fifteenth century resulted in the entrapment of Africa in a web of colonial matrices of power, resulting in enduring dependence and underdevelopment. What is brought into the debates on African political economy is the fundamental issue of knowledge, resulting in a critique of economic theory and economic thought, which tends to create the false idea of an economy that is not entangled in colonial matrices of power and other complex hetararchies constitutive of the modern world system. Building on the epistemic question, the chapter proceeds to subject to critical analysis those anti-colonial initiatives aimed at liberating Africa from the bonds of capitalist entrapment and the concomitant development pathways that were chosen. What emerges poignantly is the poverty of epistemology which produced such weak responses to the Eurocentric world system and weak initiatives haunted by what Fanon termed 'repetition without change.' The key thesis of the chapter is that what appears as the problem of political economy and as a 'development impasse' is, in reality, an epistemic crisis. The debates on African economic liberation are discussed, up to the current issues of creating the African market zone, the adoption of ECO as a pan-Africa currency for the Economic Community of West African Sates (ECOWAS), and the struggles by Francophone Africa to liberate itself from Communaute Financiere Africaine/African Financial Community (CFA)monetary imperialism. To move forward, we must rethink thinking itself so as to build a future beyond the straitjacket of developmentalism. However, France continues to intervene in West African affairs, hijacking the initiatives, which indicates the urgent necessity for deimperialization and decolonization.

The sixth chapter revisits the African Renaissance, beginning with how Africa, during the second evolutionary/development period prior to the fifteenth century, was a world leader, with its own universities in Egypt,

Morocco, and Mali, and boasting of the most expansive civilizations in Egypt and Great Zimbabwe. This means that through the African Renaissance, Africa is striving to re-emerge after its trajectory was disturbed by a period of kidnapping (the slave trade) and colonialism. It proceeds to highlight how such African scholars and leaders as Cheikh Anta Diop, Nnamdi Azikiwe, and Pixley Ka Isaka Seme laid the foundational thought on the regeneration of Africa, a theme which was later embraced by leaders like Thabo Mbeki of South Africa. The Arab Spring is included in the chapter as another attempt to renew Africa. The African Renaissance remains an important terrain of struggle, within which Africa fights to turn over a new leaf, but again, the epistemological crisis weakens it. This is why new movements like Rhodes Must Fall are very critical: because they take the issue of epistemic freedom very seriously, as an essential pre-requisite for other freedoms.

The seventh chapter is focussed on decolonization of knowledge in general as well as African humanities. Its central thesis is that at the centre of the unfolding of humanities has always been the changing idea of the human. Therefore, any decolonization of knowledge in general, and decolonization of humanity in particular, requires a shift from the European conceptions of human which reduce African people to a sub-human species. The chapter details previous continent-wide initiatives predicated on deracialization and Africanization, and explains how they fell short of genuine decolonization. The Rhodes Must Fall movement symbolizes the resurgence and insurgence of decolonization, which gives African humanities a new lease on life as the soul of the very process of rehumanization.

The concluding chapter not only draws together the various strands of arguments cascading from the seven chapters but also highlights Africa's concerted efforts to turn over a new leaf during the Fourth Industrial Revolution. The chapter highlights some of the other key contemporary challenges facing Africa, such as the resurgence of military interventions intervening in civilian politics and thwarting possibilities of democratic transitions in countries like Egypt, Zimbabwe, Algeria, and Sudan, and revealing how liberal democracy itself is in trouble. Liberal democracy for instance has been used by racists, populists, and xenophobes to ascend to power in the United States, Brazil, and other places. Because liberal democracy has failed to resolve inequalities and poverty on a world scale, the chapter makes a strong case for decolonization as a better path into the future. It also documents the noticeable and commendable initiatives, such as the agreements on the creation of the African Continental Free Trade Area (AfCFTA), adoption of common currency for the Economic Community of West African States (ECOWAS) known as 'eco,' and the escalating struggles and attempts by some activists from Francophone African states to liberate themselves from the neo-colonial reality of CFA franc (monetary slavery/monetary imperialism). In summary, the book underscores the fact that decolonization is the most legitimate vehicle available for Africa to utilize in turning over a new leaf. The concept of turning over a new leaf for Africa is presented as a revolutionary call, one that was also made eloquently in 1963, by Kwame Nkrumah at the formation of the Organization of African Unity (OAU), during which he underscored the imperative of African unity. *Africa Must Unite* is still as revolutionary and necessary as it was in 1963. Without pan-African unity, there is no way Africa will ever be able to turn over a new leaf. Disunity is the staple of colonialism/coloniality (paradigm of difference), while unity is the nerve centre of decolonization/decoloniality (the will to live). There is '*amandla*' (power/strength) in unity. There is revolutionary spirit in unity. There is relationality in unity. There is future in unity (pluriversality).

References

Amin, S. 2009. *Eurocentrism: Modernity, Religion, and Democracy: A Critique of Eurocentrism and Culturalism*. Translated by Russel Moore and James Membrez. New York: Monthly Review Press.

Andrews, K. 2019. *Back to Black: Black Radicalism for the 21st Century*. Second Edition. London: Zed Books.

Bhambra, G. K. 2007. *Rethinking Modernity: Postcolonialism and the Sociological Imagination*. New York: Palgrave Macmillan.

Cesaire, A. 2000. *Discourse on Colonialism*. Translated by Joan Pinkham. New York: Monthly Review Press.

Cupples, J. 2019. 'Introduction: Coloniality Resurgent, Coloniality Interrupted.' In J. Cupples and R. Grosfoguel (eds.), *Unsettling Eurocentrism in the Westernised University*. London and New York: Routledge, pp. 1–22.

Dabashi, H. 2019. *Europe and Its Shadows: Coloniality after Empire*. London: Pluto Press.

Du Bois, W. E. B. 1986. 'The Conservation of Races.' In N. Huggins (ed.), *Du Bois: Writings*. New York: Library of America, pp. 815–826.

Dussel, E. 2008. *Twenty Theses on Politics: Translated by George Ciccariello-Maher*. Durham, NC and London: Duke University Press.

Escobar, A. 2018. *Designs for the Pluriverse: Radical Interdependence, Autonomy, and the Making of Worlds*. Durham, NC and London: Duke University Press.

Fanon, F. 1968. *The Wretched of the Earth*. New York: Grove Press.

Getachew, A. 2019. *Worldmaking after Empire: The Rise and Fall of Self-Determination*. Princeton, NJ and Oxford: Princeton University Press.

Gildea, R. 2019. *Empires of the Mind: The Colonial Past and the Politics of the Present*. Cambridge: Cambridge University Press.

Habermas, J. 1996. 'Modernity: An Unfinished Project.' In M. P. d'Entreves and S. Benhabib (eds.), *Habermas and the Unfinished Project of Modernity: Critical Essays on the Philosophical Discourse of Modernity*. Cambridge, MA: Polity Press, pp. 38–58.

Hoppers, C. O., & Richards, H. 2012. *Rethinking Thinking: Modernity's 'Other' and the Transformation of the University*. Pretoria: UNISA Press.

Lugones, M. 2007. 'Heterosexualism and the Colonial/Modern Gender System.' *Hypatia*, 22(1), pp. 186–209.

Lugones, M. 2010. 'Towards a Decolonial Feminism.' *Hypatia*, 25(4), pp. 742–759.

Maldonado-Torres, N. 2007. 'On the Coloniality of Being: Contributions to the Development of a Concept.' *Cultural Studies*, 21(2–3), pp. 240–270.

Maldonado-Torres, N. 2017. 'On the Coloniality of Human Rights.' *Revista Critica de Ciencias Sociais*, 114 (Decembro), pp. 117–136.

Mazrui, A. A. 1978. *Political Values and the Educated Class in Africa*. Berkeley and Los Angeles: University of California Press.

Mbembe, A. 2017. *Critique of Black Reason*. Durham, NC and London: Duke University Press.

Mignolo, W. D., & Walsh, C. E. 2018. *On Decoloniality: Concepts, Analytics, Praxis*. Durham, NC and London: Duke University Press.

Morana, M., Dussel, E., & Jauregui, C. A. (eds.). 2008. *Coloniality at Large: Latin America and the Postcolonial Debate*. Durham, NC and London: Duke University Press.

Ndlovu-Gatsheni, S. J. 2015. 'Genealogies of Coloniality and Implications for Africa's Development.' *Africa Development*, XL(3), pp. 13–40.

Ndlovu-Gatsheni, S. J. 2018a. 'Metaphysical Empire, Linguicides and Cultural Imperialism.' *The English Academy Review: A Journal of English Studies*, 35(2) (October), pp. 96–115.

Ndlovu-Gatsheni, S. J. 2018b. *Epistemic Freedom in Africa: Deprovincialization and Decolonization*. New York and London: Routledge.

Ndlovu-Gatsheni, S. J. 2019. 'Empire, Decolonization and Development in Africa.' Annual Hormuud Lecture Delivered at the 62nd Annual Meeting of the African Studies Association (ASA), Boston, Massachusetts, United States of America, 23rd November.

Ngugi wa Thiong'o. 1986. *Decolonizing the Mind: The Politics of Language in African Literature*. Oxford: James Currey.Ngugi wa Thiong'o. 1997. *Writers in Politics: A Re-Engagement with Issues of Literature and Society*. Oxford: James Currey.

Ngugi wa Thiong'o. 2009a. *Something Torn and New: An African Renaissance*. New York: Basic Civitas Books.

Ngugi wa Thiong'o. 2009b. *Re-Membering Africa*. Nairobi, Kampala, and Dar es Salaam: East African Educational Publishers Ltd.

Oyewumi, O. 1997. *The Invention of Women: Making an African Sense of Western Gender Discourses*. Minneapolis and London: University of Minnesota Press.

Quijano, A. 2000. 'Coloniality of Power, Eurocentrism, and Latin America.' *Nepantla: Views from the South*, 1(3), pp. 533–579.

Reiter, B. (ed.). 2018. *Constructing the Pluriverse. The Geopolitics of Knowledge*. Durham, NC and London: Duke University Press.

Sankara, T. 1990. *Women's Liberation and the African Freedom Struggle*. New York and London: Pathfinder.

Santos, B. de S. 2007. 'Beyond Abyssal Thinking: From Global Lines to Ecologies of Knowledges.' *Review*, XXX(1), pp. 45–89.

Santos, B. de S. 2018. *The End of the Cognitive Empire: The Coming of Age of Epistemologies of the South*. Durham, NC and London: Duke University Press.

Taiwo, O. 2014. *Africa Must Be Modern: A Manifesto*. Bloomington: Indiana University Press.

Tibebu, T. 2011. *Hegel and the Third World: The Making of Eurocentrism in World History*. New York: Syracuse University Press.

Zeleza, P. T. 2003. *Rethinking Africa's Globalization: Volume 1: The Intellectual Challenges*. Trenton, NJ: Africa World Press.

2 The decolonial turn

Introduction

The radical decolonial turn is part of the long-standing decolonization process in which Africa is enabled to turn over a new leaf. At the core of the radical decolonial turn are struggles for the completion of the 'unfinished business of decolonization' as opposed to the colonial/imperial/capitalist/patriarchal/liberal bourgeois drive towards the completion of the 'unfinished business of modernity.' Frantz Fanon (1968) captured the radical spirit of the decolonial turn, and indeed the necessity of worlding beyond Europe, when he declared, 'Let us decide not to imitate Europe and let us tense our muscles and our brains in a new direction. Let us endeavour to invent a man in full, something which Europe has been incapable of achieving.' However, the decolonial turn has never been a unified, univocal, and singular movement, partly because colonial experience itself and its practices were never the same across geo-spatial constructions and cartographies—Africa, Asia, Latin America, Caribbean, and others—and partly because decolonization/decoloniality is born out of struggles in different battlefields of history, with enslaved, racialized, indigenous people; women and feminist formations; peasants; workers; decolonial intellectuals; and even native elites of the Global South acting as the storm troopers. Inevitably, the turning over of a new leaf has never been a coherent or homogeneous movement of liberation. As Audre Lorde (1984: 138) warned, 'there is no such thing as a single-issue struggle because we do not live single-issue lives'; therefore, decolonization/decoloniality is multi-vocal and tension-ridden, reflective of the plethora of issues it is confronting.

This chapter returns to the complex and rich anti-colonial and decolonial archive as it deals with some of the key questions, misunderstandings, tensions, and logics in the understandings of colonialism/coloniality, on the one hand, and decolonization/decoloniality, on the other. What is brought to the centre of the discourses of colonialism/coloniality and decolonization/decoloniality are three empires (physical, commercial, and cognitive/metaphysical) in an endeavour to effectively make sense of the challenges facing contemporary struggles for liberation and freedom. What is also addressed are the complex convergences and divergences of decolonization/decoloniality and postcoloniality/postcolonialism as the chapter underscores the 'decolonial turn' as a discursive terrain of liberation and a foundation for pluriversality (a world in which many worlds strive, unencumbered by racism). This chapter also introduces decolonization/decoloniality as both a political and an epistemological movement gesturing towards the attainment of ecologies of knowledges and pluriversality, and deepens and widens the decolonization/decoloniality perspectives, offering additional insights from decolonial feminism and African feminism.

Knowledge born in the battlefields of history and struggle

It is not surprising that the militant and subversive works of Aime Cesaire, *Discourse on Colonialism* (1950[2000]); Frantz Fanon, *Black Skins, White Masks* (1952[1967]) and *The Wretched of the Earth* (1968); Kwame Nkrumah, *Neo-Colonialism: The Last Stage Imperialism* (1965); Walter Rodney, *How Europe Underdeveloped Africa* (1972[1973]); Cheikh Anta Diop, *Nation, Negres at Culture* (1954), *The African Origins of Civilization* (1974a), and *Precolonial Black Africa* (1974b); Steve Biko, *I Write What I Want* (1978), Samir Amin, *Delinking: Towards a Polycentric World* (1990); and Ngugi wa Thiong'o, *Decolonizing the Mind: The Politics of Language in African Literature* (1986), among others, laid a solid foundation for a decolonial turn. These texts picked up the key existential questions from the vantage point of the colonized, exploited, and dominated (the wretched of the earth) as the departure point for unmasking colonialism as a death project, on the one hand, and proposing decolonization as the basis for envisioning new humanism and another world, on the other.

Some of the earlier permutations of the decolonial turn emerged as 'a critique of empire as a form of enslavement' in the Black Atlantic world (Getachew 2019: 80). This critique is represented by such texts coming from the stable of what Cedric Robinson (1983) called the 'black radical tradition.' The key texts of this tradition included *Black Reconstruction in America 1860–1880* (1935) by William E. B. Du Bois, *The Black Jacobins: Toussaint L'Ouverture and the San Domingo Revolution* (1938) by Cyril L. R. James, *Capitalism and Slavery* (1944) by Eric Williams, and the trilogy by Oliver Cox: *Caste, Class and Race* (1948), *The Foundations of Capitalism* (1959), and *Capitalism as a System* (1964). In many respects, this archive is important in laying the groundwork for the decolonial turn. First, it established the importance of slavery in the construction of a racially hierarchized modern international. Second, it enabled the anti-imperial/colonial narrative of the empire as a form of enslavement of the colonized. Third, it challenged and successfully rejected a Eurocentric moralizing narrative of the abolition of slavery that privileged Europeans like William Wilberforce and highlighted the agency of the enslaved in fighting for emancipation (see Getachew 2019: 80). Thus, while the Eurocentric articulation of historical consciousness and struggles for emancipation and liberation highlight the liberal-capitalist bourgeois consciousness, nationalist consciousness, class consciousness, and feminist consciousness, they also ignore the earliest form of liberatory consciousness, represented by enslaved people and slave revolts (see Robinson 1983).

At another level, such works as *Postcolonial Thought in the French-Speaking World* (2009), edited by Charles Forsdick and David Murphy; *African Art as Philosophy: Senghor, Bergeson and the Idea of Negritude* (2011) by Souleymane Bachir Diagne; *Freedom Time: Negritude, Decolonization and the Future World* (2015) by Gary Wilder; and *Return to the Kingdom of Childhood: Re-envisioning the Legacy and Philosophical Relevance of Negritude* (2014) by Cheikh Thiam, among many others dealing with struggles against French colonialism, highlight other strategies of decolonization that have been informed by the realities of operations and practices of French colonialism and its assimilationist ideologies. There is clear emphasis on the links between politics, poetics, aesthetics, and culture in the anti-colonial struggles and decolonial imaginations. One can notice the drive to re-make the post-war world through reconciliation of the colonized and the colonized, predicated on strong ideas of universal humanism denied by French colonialism and the push for self-determination without falling into the prison-house of the nation-state but through realization of a democratic transnational French citizenship for all (Wilder 2015). The emphasis on cultural aspects of freedom might have emerged from the French colonial aggression towards African culture in its assimilationist colonial politics and policies. This is why Wilder (2015: 1) posited that:

> Decolonization raised fundamental questions for subject peoples about the frameworks within which self-determination could be meaningfully pursued in relation to a given set of historical conditions. These were intertwined with overarching temporal questions about the relationship between existing arrangements, possible futures, and historical legacies. The year 1945 was a world-historical opening; the contours of the post-war order were not fixed, and a range of solutions to the problem of colonial emancipation were imagined and pursued. At the same time, the converging pressures of anticolonial nationalism, Euro neocolonialism, American globalism, and UN internationalism made it appear to be a foregone conclusion that the post-war world would be organized around territorial national states.

A different take on decolonization/decoloniality emerges in the work of Caribbean scholar Edouard Glissant, namely *Poetics of Relation* (1997) and *Caribbean Discourse: Selected Essays* (1989), and in An Yountae's *The Decolonial Abyss: Mysticism and Cosmopolitics from the Ruins* (2017), in which there is emphasis on these questions:

> How to gather the self after a history of suffering, transportation, discontinuity, slavery, and death? In other words, how is selfhood possible for a colonized subject whose very horizon of existence is breached by

> the ongoing effects of 'coloniality'? What happens when the abyss is not merely a metaphysical figure but a social, historical, and political one that emerges from the terrain marked by coloniality? In what ways and in which directions do theological and political concerns evolve when we relocate the account of the self to the colonial abyss?
>
> (Yountae 2017: 13)

In thinking about decolonization and liberation from the Caribbean experience, Glissant and Yountae posit the Caribbean as a site of 'nonhistory,' 'no collective memory,' and 'no sense of a chronology,' which make it a 'ruin' and an 'abyss' (Glissant 1989; Yountae 2017). This is possible because of colonial genocide and the trafficking of Africans into the Caribbean as slaves. Compared to those African people who remained on the African continent, those in the Caribbean have both history and memory of genocides, the middle passage, the sea, and the plantation. As Yountae (2017: 142) put it, 'As we stare at the abyss and as the abyss stares back at us, we lose ourselves for a creolized self yet to be created on the ever-unfolding horizon of the groundless middle.'

Depatriachization and even 'degenderization,' 'defeminisation,' and 'desexualisation' are key aspects of decolonization/decoloniality. This is necessary because, as proven by Ifi Amadiume (1997), Oyeronke Oyewumi (1997), and Paula Allen Gunn (1986), there were African societies and indigenous societies in the Americas and Africa that were not organized along the lines of gender prior to colonization. Thus, when the often-ignored voices, eyes, and perspectives of women thinkers, scholars, theorists, and feminists are brought into the decolonization/decoloniality struggles, the tensions and convergences are accentuated at the same time that the canvas of complexities, blind spots, collaborations, and solidarities are widened. Women and female fighters for liberation are not themselves reducible to a singular body of thought because their knowledge is also born in the battlefields of history and struggles against heterosexual patriarchism, capitalism, and colonialism, but their insights still enrich and advance the decolonization/decoloniality struggles, particularly in the direction of depatriachization. The work of Maria Lugones (2007, 2008, 2010) gifted us with the concepts of 'coloniality of gender,' 'decolonial feminism,' and the 'modern/colonial gender system.' While she is in agreement with the overall modernity/coloniality school of thought, she also raises sharp criticism of Anibal Quijano (who is credited with coining the concept of 'coloniality of power') on the questions of gender and women. Lugones's first line of critique is that Quijano's assumption of patriarchal and heterosexual oppression mediated by disputes over control of sex, its resources, and products is considered too narrow and therefore serves to 'veil the ways in which "non-white" colonized women were subjected and disempowered differently from the white bourgeois women by the same "modern/colonial gender system."'

Lugones (2008) posits that it is necessary to 'understand differential gender arrangements along "racial" lines so as to highlight the two sides of the 'modern/colonial gender system." The 'light' side represents oppression, along the lines of gender privileging white bourgeois men over their white bourgeois women but without reducing them to the status of non-beings (Lugones 2008). The 'underside' or 'darker side' represents dehumanization and animalization, to the extent that the colonized men and women are subjects not of 'genderization' but of mere crude 'sexualisation' into female and male non-beings (Lugones 2010). Building on this analysis, Lugones (2010: 752) pushes for 'decolonial feminism,' whose departure point is a re-reading of the modern capitalist colonial modernity itself, and 'takes the global designs for racialised female and male energy and, erasing the colonial difference, takes that energy to be used towards the destruction of the worlds of meaning of our possibilities.'

In summary, Lugones's critique of Quijano's conception of gender is fourfold. The first argues that his approach presupposes sexual dimorphism where none existed. The second is that it naturalizes heteronormativity without taking into account that there were societies and cultures that were not organized by the gender line and did not deem homosexuality either a sexual or a social transgression. The third is that his approach to the gender and woman question is still trapped in biological determinism and thus is not totally free from Eurocentrism. The fourth is that it presumes a patriarchal distribution of power, even in societies and cultures which were socially egalitarian, to the extent of not using gender as a dividing line and organizing principle (Lugones 2007, 2008, 2010; Mendoza 2016).

The divergences in womanist and feminist struggles gifted us with the useful concept of 'intersectionality' (Kimberle 1995), which highlighted the intersections of race, class, gender, and sexuality in the oppression and exploitation of black women in particular. However, the decolonial power of the concept of intersectionality is weakened by its appropriation by liberal, white, bourgeois feminists and when it is allowed to degenerate into an 'olympics' of oppression, pitting the racialized, colonized, and feminized against each other, with the result of blocking possibilities for collaboration and solidarity (see Lugones 2003 on resistance, collaborations, and solidarities). On the divergence scale, there is also 'African feminism,' which has been pushed forward by such African feminists as Morala Ogundipe-Leslie (1994) and Nnaekema Obiama (1997). The emphasis here is on history/ethnography, colonialism, culture, tradition, ethnicity, context, and social change as resistance against Western feminist domination, without ignoring patriarchy and sexism in Africa (Mikell 1997). African feminism has produced such feminist scholars as Oyeronke Oyewumi (1997), who posed a successful intellectual challenge to Western gender discourses (as a part of the Eurocentric discursive empire) and rejected the universalization of gender as an organizing principle across space and time. These divergences do not dilute the struggles for decolonization/decoloniality; instead, they provide the necessary nuances, complexity, depth, and expansion.

But what is distinctive about these subversive and decolonial texts is well articulated by Hamid Dabashi (2019: 124–126). These are text from the 'battlefields of history.' They are 'written with blood and tears.' They are subversive. They are unruly. They are disruptive. They are renegade texts. They are defiant. They do not belong to any particular field or academic discipline. According to Dabashi (2019: 125) they

> habitually defy and misbehave whenever you place and expect them to behave and yield or serve one discipline or another. These texts disallow themselves to be appropriated and put into work for any disciplines or academic disposition that expects them to forget their militant origin and defiant dispositions.

Instead of these texts being 'incarcerated inside syllabi and libraries,' 'They need to be read in streets, back alleys, open squares, and mountain-tops' (Dabashi 2019: 125). Finally, the texts carry 'pains and sufferings, hopes and aspirations, of nations, of people brutalized by those empires and their colonial holdings into our conditions of coloniality' (Dabashi 2019: 127).

Diop confronted and challenged Eurocentric history and laid a foundation for the denied African history. As noted by Dani Wadada Nabudere (2007: 6), Diop also contributed to a scientific understanding of ancient African history, race, and the study of culture. Cesaire and Fanon grounded their interventions on the essence of colonialism and its impact on the humanity of both the colonizers and the colonized; using this analysis they were able to lay bare the 'fact of blackness' in an anti-black, white-dominated modern world. Nkrumah, Rodney, and Amin focussed on how imperialism survived the dismantlement of direct colonial administrations and exposed the ways in which colonial-like relations of exploitation and domination (neo-colonialism) continued to leave Africa underdeveloped and to tighten the grip of a dependent relationship. Biko, building on the work of Fanon as well as the Black Power movement, turned to the question of the psychological impact of colonialism/apartheid and expressed his epistemic refusal through writing what he wanted.

A closer reading of these decolonial texts reveals a concerted effort to shift the very constitution of the political from its foundation on the paradigms of difference, war, and the 'will to power' (which enabled racism, patriarchy, enslavement, genocides, and colonization) to the 'will to live,' justice, and peace. This emerges clearly from Cesaire's dismissal of colonialism's rhetoric of salvation, civilization, progress, emancipation, and development, and his revelation that Eurocentric conceptions of being human in both its Christian and its bourgeois iterations never disconnected from dirty paradigms of difference, war, and the discourses of the 'will to power' which enabled Europe to dominate people outside of Europe. The antennae of Eurocentric humanism only piqued when Adolf Hitler of Germany began using the colonial procedures of genocide and deadly gas chambers of reserved for the colonies in Europe itself.

These realities make decolonization/decoloniality to remain necessary idiom and expression of current struggles for liberation and freedom. If global coloniality continues to wreak havoc across the world, we must remain attuned to decolonization/decoloniality, which will enable confrontation of enslavement and domination. The resurgence and insurgence of decolonization/decoloniality in the twenty-first century is directly ranged against the violence of modernity, colonialism, imperialism, and neo-colonialism. Such violence is systemic, structural, institutional, symbolic, and physical. As such, it results in genocides, poverty, epistemicides, culturecides, ecocides, linguicides, and even ontolocides.

Decolonization/decoloniality constitutes a legitimate mode of turning over a new leaf, enabling a shift from colonialism/coloniality to liberation and freedom. It is, therefore, not surprising that the 'wretched of the earth,' scattered throughout different constructed geo-political locales, are becoming increasingly attracted by the insurgent and resurgent spirit of decolonization/decoloniality on a world scale. For example, the long-standing Latin American and African discourses on decolonization/decoloniality are converging in many ways in the intellectual/academic sphere. The writings of such African thinkers/scholars/activists/freedom fighters, such as Kwame Nkrumah, Steve Biko, Ngugi wa Thiong'o, Samir Amin, Chinweizu, Claude Ake, and many others, are increasingly read alongside those of Latin American thinkers/scholars, such as Enrique Dussel, Anibal Quijano, Walter D. Mignolo, Ramon Grosfoguel, Nelson Maldonado-Torres, Maria Lugones, Cathrine E. Walsh, and many others. The same is true of the seminal works of black American scholars/activists like William E. B. Du Bois and Caribbean philosophers/thinkers/scholars, like Marcus Garvey, Eric Williams, Cyril L. James, Aime Cesaire, Frantz Fanon, Walter Rodney, Lewis R. Gordon, and Henry Paget. These works converge on concerns about the long-term impact of enslavement, colonial genocides, being black in an anti-black white world, and how colonialism/coloniality continues to be the source of many modern problems as well as the possibilities of liberation and freedom predicated on decolonization/decoloniality. However, decolonization/decoloniality has never been perfected as a theory because it was born from the battlefields of history. The resurgence and insurgence of decolonization/decoloniality today is explained by Isaac Kamola (2019: 68):

> There are good reasons for this return. These voices are poetic yet strident, theoretical but immediately practical to the particularities of struggle. These writings on colonialism, race, class, violence, and governance avoid abstract musing—and the polish and perfection of argument that goes along with it. Instead there are timely statements made with great urgency. The assumed audience of African anticolonial thought was often not scholars, but rather one's immediate and intimate comrades. The horizon of these texts and arguments often contain futures filled with possibility, even if the specific outlines are not entirely discernible in the present moment.

In *Politics of African Anticolonial Archive* (2017), Shiera S. El-Malik and Isaac A. Kamola delved deeper into the heterodox group of anti-colonial scholars who produced the African anti-colonial archive on which the decolonial turn was founded. At its centre, to borrow a concept introduced by Boaventura de Sousa Santos (2007, 2014), are 'ecologies of knowledge,' which speaks to the recognition of the diverse ways of knowing by which people across the human globe provide meaning to their existence and understanding of the world. This thinking dovetails with the decolonial concept of pluriversality, which directly challenges the 'one-dimensional solutions to diverse problems and impositions of universal claims to the very nature of humanity' (Reiter 2018b: 1). Pluriversality underscores a world governed by relationality and transcendence over the bourgeois values, knowledge, economic logics, and political perspectives masquerading as scientism and rationality imposed on the rest of humanity (Escobar 2018). The concept of pluriversality originates from indigenous movements in Latin America, especially the Zapastista, with their vision of a world in which many worlds coexist in a pluriverse (see Mignolo 2002; Escobar 2018; Reiter 2018).

The decolonial turn, which is an encapsulation of the technologies of turning over a new leaf by a colonized, dehumanized, and dismembered people, is enabled by the definitive entry of these people into the realm of thought and politics at previously unknown institutional levels, carrying with them the scars of racism, patriarchy, colonialism, and underdevelopment (see Maldonado-Torres 2008). Their definitive entry inevitably stirs the toxic pond of colonialism/coloniality to the boiling point, with the formerly enslaved and colonized people vehemently refusing to accept imposed inferiority. As such, the decolonization/decoloniality of the twenty-first century draws from many sources and schools of thought, though it should not be confused with postmodernism, post-structuralism, or postcolonialism, which have their own genealogies, including the powerful Euro-North American academies giving birth to such influential schools as the South Asian Subaltern Studies collective (see Guha 1982; Lyotard 1984; Spivak 1985; Bhabha 1994; Cook et al. 2008).

While Frantz Fanon gifted us with the decolonial concept of 'the wretched of the earth,' the South Asian Subaltern Studies collective popularized Antonio Gramsci's concept of the 'subaltern.' Many of the members of the South Asian Subaltern Studies collective were Marxist in ideological orientation, and the 'subaltern' was a form of unearthing another important class beyond Karl Marx's 'working class,' which he claimed were responsible for leading the proletarian world revolution and who he designated as the inheritors of the earth. The South Asian Subaltern collective took a postcolonial and postmodernist turn when such members as Gayatri Spivak (1985) and Dipesh Chakrabarty (2000) dealt with the colonial question, the problems of Eurocentric historicism, and the invisibilization of women and other poor people in India in particular and Asia in general. The fiercest and widest-ranging critique of the collective's work, including its reduction to 'postcolonial theory' and 'cultural studies,' however, comes from Vivek Chibber's *Postcolonial Theory and the Specter of Capital* (2013), in which Chibber discusses restoring universalizing Eurocentric thought as planetary thought. Because of his Eurocentric epistemological gaze, he failed to see any paradigmatic shift in the South Asian Subaltern Studies and dismissed it as derivative.

What distinguishes resurgent and insurgent decolonization/decoloniality is its drive for connections rather than differences. Colonialism/coloniality is driven by paradigms of difference rather than connections. However, decolonization/decoloniality can be easily and seamlessly conflated with postmodernism and postcolonialism, creating an urgent need for further clarification of concepts. For example, Pal Ahluwalia, in *Politics and Post-Colonial Theory: African Inflections* (2001) and *Out of Africa: Post-Structuralism's Colonial Roots* (2010), highlighted the African roots (Maghreb region) of postcolonialism and post-structuralism as he grappled with the writings of Jacques Derrida and Helene Cixous (born in French-colonial-Algeria) as well as Michel Foucault (who spent time in Tunisia). He noted that 'some of the most profound contemporary French theorists who have challenged the very precepts of modernity' 'have been deeply affected in some way by France's Africa colonial project' (Ahluwalia 2010: 2). His (2010: 3) position is that postcolonialism is 'counter-discourse that seeks to disrupt the cultural hegemony of the West, challenging imperialism in its various guises, whereas post-structuralism and postmodernism are counter discourses against modernism that have emerged within modernism itself' (see also Ahluwalia 2001).

While geographical location is not the most important determiner of epistemic location, it cannot be ignored. Perhaps what is poignant is that while postcolonialism and postmodernism have multiple valences, the former is used mainly with reference to the 'non-Western' world, and the latter is used mainly with reference to the 'Western/white world' (Adesanmi 2011: 74). Pius Adesanmi (2011: 74) depicted postcolonialism and postmodernism as products of 'the suffocating influence of North American high theory over the global production of meaning and identity.' Postmodernism and postcolonialism challenged not only grand/meta-narratives but also transcendental cultural commonalities and transcendental identities, created by such movements as Ethiopianism, Garveyism, Negritude, the Harlem Renaissance, pan-Africanism, African nationalism, and other black consciousness- and identity-forming projects. Decolonization/decoloniality returns to the violence of Euromodernity and underscores coloniality (the transhistoric expansion of colonial domination and the perpetuation of its effects in contemporary times) as a key problem in the modern world (see Morana et al. 2008: 2).

While postcolonialism and postmodernism underscored the 'cultural turn,' decolonization/decoloniality is predicated on the 'decolonial turn,' which is traceable to what Robinson (1983) termed the 'radical black tradition' and politically linked to the Haitian Revolution of 1791–1804, which was ranged against racism, enslavement, and colonialism (dehumanization) (for details, see Chapter 3 of this book). Its intellectual genealogy embraces Diaspora pan-African movements, such as Garveyism, as well as early black consciousness iterations, such as Ethiopianism, the Black Power Movement, the Harlem Renaissance, African Personality, Negritude, Pan-Africanism, African nationalist anti-colonial thought, Black Marxist thought, Black feminist thought, and Nkrumah's ideas of neo-colonialism; Fanonian decolonization thought; Walter Rodney's ideas on how Europe underdeveloped Africa; Albert Memmi, Ngugi wa Thiong'o, and Chinweizu's ideas on how Europe invaded the mental universe of Africa, resulting in the colonization of the minds of the African people; Cheikh Anta Diop and Molefi Asante's Afrocentricity; Africana existential philosophy; Mahmood Mamdani's thinking on how Europe ruled Africa and the long-term consequences of colonialism on postcolonial Africa; and Achille Mbembe's postcolonial thought on how Africa ruled/governed itself and the current Latin American modernity/coloniality/decoloniality (Ndlovu-Gatsheni 2018, 2019). This is why Nelson Maldonado-Torres (2011) defined decoloniality as a 'family' of thought that identified modernity/colonialism/coloniality as the foundation of some of the major problems haunting the modern world.

The intention of colonialism was to destroy rather than blend other civilizations with those of the colonizer, but this failed because colonial encounters became a site not only of contestation but also of blending. This blending is well articulated by Dipesh Chakrabarty (2000: xiii–xiv), who demonstrated how European ideas intersected with Indian ones to reinforce the notion of pluralizing reason and concluded that 'To provincialise Europe was then to know how universalistic thought was always and already modified by particular histories, whether or not we could excavate such pasts fully.' Chakrabarty's position is that of postcolonialism and its emphasis on co-invention of the modern world by the colonizers and the colonized. However, colonialism predicated on the paradigms of 'difference' and 'war' engaged in the redefinition of human species by socially classifying and racially hierachizing rather than inventing a common humanity. Inevitably, what emerged were two zones of being—the zone of being for the colonizers and the zone of non-being for the colonized (Fanon 1968; Santos 2007; Grosfoguel 2019). It is therefore not surprising that the return, resurgence, and insurgence of decolonization/decoloniality have once again placed the problem of colonialism and coloniality at the centre of global studies as that discursive terrain which makes it impossible to construct a postcolonial and post-racial world.

Besides the identification of modernity/colonialism as the fundamental problem, decolonization/decoloniality challenges the present globalization and its pretensions of universalism, which hides the reality of the Europeanization and Americanization of the modern world. While colonialism and imperialism embarked on an aggressive destruction of existing diverse worlds, they have also been equally aggressive in denying common humanity, inventing all sorts of pseudo-scientific discourses to divide people racially across the planet as well as notions of stages of developmentalism to push other human beings below the invented 'human line' (Fanon 1968; Santos 2007; Grosfoguel 2019). What is emerging poignantly today is the knowledge that decolonization is a much more profound process than simply obtaining political independence; it is a condition of possibility to start a new thinking and doing aimed at a re-humanized world (Maldonado-Torres 2017).

Framing the issues and opening the canvas

The modern world is facing a triple crisis, which is systemic, epistemic, and ideological in character. At the systemic level, one witnesses a global capitalism that is haunted by a terminal crisis, a planetary ecological/environmental crisis, and exploding social divisions. It was these realities that led Slavoj Zizek (2011) to write about 'living in the end times.' At the epistemic level, there is clear exhaustion of a once hegemonic knowledge that has been dominant for over 500 years. This epistemic crisis was well captured by Immanuel Wallerstein (2004: 58):

> I believe we live in a very exciting era in the world of knowledge, precisely because we are living in a systemic crisis that is forcing us to reopen the basic epistemological questions and look to structural reorganization of the world of knowledge. It is uncertain whether we shall rise adequately to the intellectual challenge, but it is there for us to address. We engage our responsibility as scientists/scholars in the way in which we address the multiple issues before us at this turning point in our structures of knowledge.

The epistemic crisis is a product of the 'epistemicides' (killing and displacement of other knowledges) which made the Global North lose 'the capacity to learn from the experiences of the world' and fail to learn 'in noncolonial terms.' There is a glaring loss of 'critical nouns' in conventional Eurocentric critical epistemology, which explicitly signifies an epistemic crisis. This point is delivered more powerfully by Boaventura de Sousa Santos (2014: 33):

> There was a time when Eurocentric critical theory 'owned' a vast set of nouns that marked its difference from conventional or bourgeois theories. These nouns included socialism, communism, revolution, class struggle, dependency, alienation, fetishism of commodities, and so on. In the past thirty years the Eurocentric critical tradition seems to have lost 'its' nouns and now distinguishes itself from conventional or bourgeois theories by the adjectives it uses to subvert the meaning of the proper nouns it borrows from such theories. Thus, for instance, if conventional theory speaks of development, critical theory refers to alternative, integral, inclusionary, democratic, or sustainable development;

> if conventional theory speaks of democracy, critical theory proposes radical, participatory, or deliberative democracy.

Perhaps Frantz Fanon (1968: 78) saw this epistemic crisis coming when he urged humanity to 'turn over a new leaf,' 'work out new concepts,' and 'try to set afoot a new man.' With regard to the ideological crisis, Michael Neocosmos's *Thinking Freedom in Africa: Towards a Theory of Emancipatory Politics* (2016: xiii) posed important questions:

> How are we to begin to think human emancipation in Africa today after the collapse of Marxist, the Third World nationalist as well as the neoliberal visions of freedom? How are we to conceptualize an emancipatory future governed by a fidelity to the idea of a universal humanity in a context where humanity no longer features within our ambit of thought and when previous ways of thinking emancipation have become obsolete?

It is mainly because of these systemic, epistemic, and ideological crises that decoloniality has emerged as a long-standing but suppressed political and epistemological movement, aimed at the liberation of (ex-)colonized peoples from global coloniality. It emerged as a way of thinking, knowing, and doing. It is part of marginalized but persistent movements that have emerged from struggles against the slave trade, imperialism, colonialism, apartheid, neo-colonialism, and underdevelopment as constitutive negative elements of hegemonic Euromodernity. As an epistemological movement, decoloniality has always been overshadowed by hegemonic intellectual thought and social theories. It speaks to the resurgence and insurgence of decolonization movements in those spaces, sites, and locales that experienced racism in its most detestable forms: the slave trade, imperialism, colonialism, apartheid, neo-colonialism, and underdevelopment.

Latin America and Africa are good examples of sites currently experiencing resurgences and insurgencies of decoloniality. This is mainly because, in the domains of culture, the psyche, the mind, language, aesthetics, religion, and many others, coloniality continues to wreak havoc. At one level, decoloniality calls on intellectuals from imperialist countries to undertake 'a deimperialization movement by re-examining their own imperialist histories and the harmful impacts those histories have had on the world' (Chen 2010: vii). At another, it urges critical intellectuals from the Global South 'to once again deepen and widen decolonization movements, especially in the domains of culture, the psyche and knowledge production' (Chen 2010: vii). This takes us to the discussion of colonialism and coloniality, making clear their differences and convergences.

Modernity/colonialism/coloniality

The Latin American modernity/coloniality school of thought departs from the premise that the colonization of the Americas laid the foundation for the rise of Euromodernity and the existing capitalist world economy. This view is well expressed by Anibal Quijano and Immanuel Wallerstein (1992: 549): 'The Americas were not incorporated into an already existing capitalist world-economy. There could not have been a capitalist world-economy without the Americas.' Colonialism/coloniality constitutes the discursive terrain within which many forms of domination and exploitation rest. Thus, as concepts, colonialism and coloniality have to be clearly understood. Without the reality of colonialism and coloniality there is no need for decolonization and decoloniality.

For analytical purposes, and to gain a deeper appreciation of colonialism and coloniality, Sabelo J. Ndlovu-Gatsheni (2018) introduced the notion of three empires: the physical empire, the commercial non-territorial empire, and the cognitive empire. The physical empire is the easiest to identify because it concretized itself through physical conquest and the open administration of conquered territories. Even the 'direct' and 'indirect' modes of rule left the physical empire exposed (on 'direct' and 'indirect' rule, see Mamdani 1996, 2013). From Mahmood Mamdani's (1996) work emerged the details of how Europe ruled Africa; earlier on, Walter Rodney (1973) had explained how Europe underdeveloped Africa.

Kwame Nkrumah (1965) argued that the commercial non-territorial empire operated through 'neo-colonialism.' This was one of the earliest names for the continuation of domination after the end of direct administrative colonialism. The concept of neo-colonialism underscored the continued economic exploitation of the resources of the newly 'independent' African states by the empires within an undecolonized world economic order.

The commercial non-territorial empire and the cognitive empire are inextricably intertwined. The cognitive empire/metaphysical empire operates through the invasion of the mental universe of its victims, in the process emptying the hard disk of African memory and downloading into African minds the software of European memory (see Fanon 1968; Memmi 1974; Chinweizu 1975; Chinweizu and Madubuike 1980; Ngugi wa Thiong'o 1986; Chinweizu 1987; Ngugi wa Thiong'o 2009a, 2009b). To borrow a concept from Ashis Nandy (1983), the cognitive empire lives and subsists within the victim's body and mind as 'the intimate enemy.'

Beyond theorization, African scholars have historicized colonialism in an attempt to highlight its depth and pervasiveness. Ali A. Mazrui (1986) argued that the long-term impact of colonialism on Africa can be understood from two perspectives. He designated the first perspective the epic school. This school underscored the fact that colonialism amounted to 'a revolution of epic propositions' (Mazrui 1986: 12). He further identified six deep implications and consequences of colonialism. First, colonialism and capitalism forcibly incorporated Africa into the world economy, beginning with the slave trade, 'which dragged African labour itself into the emerging international capitalist system' (Mazrui 1986: 12). African labour contributed immensely to the economic rise of a Euro-North American-centric trans-Atlantic commerce. Second, Africa, which had been excluded from the post-1648 Westphalian sovereign state system and physically partitioned after the Berlin Conference of 1884–1885, was later incorporated into the post-1945 United Nations sovereign state system. One can add that the fragmented and weak African 'postcolonial' states were admitted into the lowest echelons of the Euro-North American-dominated state system of the world (Clapham 1996).

Third, Africa was incorporated into a Eurocentric world culture and European languages. Fourth, it was also incorporated into a heavily Eurocentric world of international law. Fifth, as a consequence of colonialism, Africa was incorporated into the modern technological age, effectively being 'swallowed by the global system of dissemination of information' (Mazrui 1986: 12). Finally, Africa was dragged into a Euro-North American-centric moral order dominated by Christian thought. Mazrui's (1986: 13) conclusion was, therefore, that 'What Africa knows about itself, what different parts of Africa know about each other, have been profoundly influenced by the West.'

The epic school is countered by the episodic school. It posits that 'the European impact on Africa has been shallow rather than deep, transitional rather than long-lasting' (Mazrui 1986: 13). In fact, it was the Nigerian historian Jacob F. Ade Ajayi of the Ibadan nationalist school who depicted colonialism as 'an episode in African history' (Ajayi 1969). He elaborated that:

> In any long-term view of African history, European rule becomes just another episode. In relation to wars and conflicts of people, the rise and fall of empires, linguistic, cultural and religious change and the cultivation of new ideas and new ways of life, new economic orientations [...] in relation to all these, colonialism must be seen not as a complete departure from the African past, but as one episode in the continuous flow of history.
>
> (Ajayi 1968: 78)

This argument amounts to a very complacent view of colonialism as a system of power. African institutions and African leadership were destroyed by colonialism, then the colonialists invented their own versions and called them African institutions, traditions, and customs (see Ranger 1983). At another level, although the episodic school was correct in underscoring the longevity of African history pre-dating the time of colonialism and in articulating the African factor in the making of human history, there is danger in its decoupling of colonialism from the broader wave of Euromodernity that radically transformed human history. From this perspective, colonialism cannot be understood as an event/episode. It was a major part of what Walter D. Mignolo (2000) referred to as the 'global designs' that became entangled with 'local histories.'

At the University of Ibadan itself, where Ajayi was based, the episodic school was heavily challenged by Peter P. Ekeh (1983). Ekeh understood colonialism to be 'a social movement of epochal dimensions' (Ekeh 1983: 4). He (1983: 5) noted that colonialism 'constitutes an epochal era in Africa' and that it introduced 'massive and enduring social formations' (Ekeh 1983: 8). According to him, colonialism directly transformed pre-colonial indigenous social structures, making them serve the colonial capitalist project of domination and exploitation. Even more profoundly, colonialism introduced what he (1983: 9) described as 'migrated social structures and constructs' 'literally parcelled from metropolitan centres,' and these were 'engrafted onto the new colonial situation.' At another level, colonialism invented what Ekeh described as 'emergent social structures,' which were 'not indigenous to Africa' or 'brought from outside'—rather, 'They were generated, born that is, from the space-and-time span of colonialism' (Ekeh 1983: 9).

Latin American theorists' introduction of the concept of coloniality in order to name the continuation of colonialism beyond its physical dismantlement has effectively countered the episodic school. The thesis of coloniality's advocates even argues convincingly that the decolonization of the twentieth century failed to destroy colonialism as a system of power. What was delivered was far from a 'postcolonial world'; rather, as noted by Ramon Grosfoguel (2007), global coloniality ensued. Global coloniality cannot be separated from Euro modernity. Today, African leaders continue to manage and maintain the global system, even after replacing direct colonial rulers. Mabel Morana, Enrique Dussel, and Carlos A. Jauregui (2008: 1–2) write about 'colonialism and its replicants,' relating that:

> In the particular case of Latin America, a discussion of *post*-or *neo*-colonialism—or that of *coloniality*, a term that encompasses the transhistoric expansion of colonial domination and the perpetuation of its effects in contemporary times—is necessarily intertwined with the critique of Orientalism and modernity, a critique that requires a profound but detached understanding of imperial rationality.

To Grosfoguel (2007), Euromodernity has to be broadly defined as a racially hierarchized, patriarchal, sexist, Christian-centric, hetero-normative, capitalist, military, colonial, imperial, and modern form of civilization. Grosfoguel (2007) used the term 'hetararchies' of power to underscore the complex vertical, horizontal, and crisscrossing invisible entanglements in the configuration of the modern global power structure that emerged from colonial encounters. The epic impact of colonialism led the leading decolonial theorist and poet Aime Cesaire (2000) to pose the question 'what, fundamentally, is colonialism?' Cesaire (2000: 32) understood colonialism to be a disruptive, 'decivilizing,' dehumanizing, exploitative, racist, violent, brutal, covetous, and 'thingfying' system.

Coloniality, therefore, names the various colonial-like power relations that currently exist in those zones that experienced direct colonialism. The concept of coloniality was introduced by the Peruvian sociologist Anibal

Quijano (2000) but was further elaborated by the Argentinean decolonial semiotician Walter D. Mignolo (2000) and others, such as Nelson Maldonado-Torres 2007). Quijano (2007: 173) identified four key levels of coloniality. The first is control of the economy. The second is control of authority. The third is control of gender and sexuality. The fourth is control of knowledge and subjectivity. Mignolo (2000) emphasized 'colonial difference' as a central leitmotif of coloniality. Coloniality is a name for the 'darker side' of modernity that needs to be unmasked because it exists as 'an embedded logic that enforces control, domination, and exploitation disguised in the language of salvation, progress, modernization, and being good for everyone' (Mignolo 2005: 6). Building on the work of Quijano and Mignolo, Maldonado-Torres (2007: 243) formulated a very useful definition of coloniality:

> Coloniality is different from colonialism. Colonialism denotes a political and economic relation in which the sovereignty of a nation or a people rests on the power of another nation, which makes such a nation an empire. Coloniality, instead, refers to long-standing patterns of power that emerged as a result of colonialism, but that define culture, labour, intersubjectivity relations, and knowledge production well beyond the strict limits of colonial administrations. Thus, coloniality survives colonialism. It is maintained alive in books, in the criteria for academic performance, in cultural patterns, in common sense, in the self-image of peoples, in aspirations of self, and so many other aspects of our modern experience. In a way, as modern subjects we breathe coloniality all the time and every day.

This definition converges with Ngugi wa Thiong'o's understanding of the psychological/epistemological, as well as cultural and linguistic, impact of colonialism on Africa. He (1986: xii) posited that 'The present predicaments of Africa are often not a matter of personal choice: they arise from an historical situation.' He elaborated that 'imperialism is not a slogan,' and 'It is real; it is palpable in content and form and in its methods and effects' (Ngugi wa Thiong'o 1986: 2). Ngugi wa Thiong'o detailed the workings of colonialism on the minds of its targets:

> The biggest weapon wielded and actually daily unleashed by imperialism against that collective defiance is the cultural bomb. The effect of a cultural bomb is to annihilate a people's belief in their names, in their languages, in their environment, in their heritage of struggle, in their unity, in their capacities and ultimately in themselves. It makes them see their past as one wasteland of non-achievement and it makes them want to distance themselves from that wasteland. It makes them want to identify with that which is furthest removed from themselves; for instance, with other people's languages rather than their own. It makes them identify with that which is decadent and reactionary, all those forces

> which would stop their own springs of life. It even plants serious doubt about the moral rightness of struggle. Possibilities of triumph or victory are seen as remote, ridiculous dreams. The intended results are despair, despondency and a collective death-wish. Amidst this wasteland which it has created; imperialism presents itself as the cure and demands that the dependent sing hymns of praise with the constant refrain: 'Theft is holy.' Indeed, this refrain sums up the new creed of neo-colonial bourgeoisie in many 'independent' African states.
>
> (Ngugi wa Thiong'o 1986: 3)

It would seem that, understood this way, colonialism and coloniality refer to the same situation. At the centre of coloniality is race as an organizing principle, which not only hierarchizes human beings according to racial ontological densities but sustains asymmetrical global power relations and a singular Eurocentric epistemology that claims to be universal, disembodied, truthful, secular, and scientific (Grosfoguel 2007: 303). Coloniality created what Frantz Fanon (1968) described as the 'wretched of the earth.' According to Mignolo (2000: 16):

> The wretched are defined by the colonial wound, and the colonial wound, physical and/or psychological, is a consequence of racism, the hegemonic discourse that questions the humanity of all those who do not belong to the locus of enunciation (and the geo-politics of knowledge) of those who assign the standard of classification and assign to themselves the right to classify.

This takes us to the analysis and explication of decolonization and decoloniality as efforts to transcend the present historical interregnum and registers of a post-globalist, post-neoliberal, and post-capitalist pluriversal future.

Decolonization/decoloniality

The decolonization of the twentieth century failed to deliver the expected postcolonial and post-racial world. Because of this, Latin American theorists introduced the concept of decoloniality to capture not only the continuation of colonialism beyond dismantlement of juridical colonialism but also its 'planetarinization' into global coloniality (Mignolo 2000; Quijano 2000; Grosfoguel 2007). Decoloniality is therefore different from the anti-colonialism that dominated the twentieth century. Anti-colonialism was largely an elite-driven project in which indigenous elites mobilized peasants and workers as foot-soldiers in a struggle to replace direct colonial administrators. For instance, the African anti-colonial struggles of the twentieth century did not produce a genuine 'postcolonial' dispensation marked by the birth of a new humanity, as demanded by Fanon. What was produced was a complex situation that Achille Mbembe (2001) termed 'the postcolony,'

Gayatri Spivak (1990) described as a 'postcolonial neo-colonized world,' and decolonial theorists understood as 'coloniality.' This situation was characterized by what Sabelo J. Ndlovu-Gatsheni (2013a, 2013b) termed the 'myths of decolonization.' But decoloniality materialized at the very moment in which the slave trade, imperialism, and colonialism were being launched as resistance, thought, and action.

As stated at the opening of this chapter, decoloniality is a broad church or family of all those initiatives formulated by the colonized, including intellectual-cum-political-cum-cultural movements, such as Ethiopianism, Negritude, Garveyism, the Black Consciousness Movement, and many others (Ndlovu-Gatsheni 2018). Nelson Maldonado-Torres (2011: 117) is correct in defining decoloniality as such:

> By decoloniality it is meant here the dismantling of relations of power and conceptions of knowledge that foment the reproduction of racial, gender, and geo-political hierarchies that came into being or found new and more powerful forms of expression in the modern/colonial world.

Decoloniality

> struggles to bring into intervening existence an-other interpretation that bring forward, on the one hand, a silenced view of the event and, on the other, shows the limits of imperial ideology disguised as the true (total) interpretation of the events in the making of the modern world.
>
> (Mignolo 1995: 33)

Decoloniality embraced the consistent push for shifting of geography of reason from the West as the epistemic locale from which the 'world is described, conceptualized and ranked' (Mignolo 1995: 33). Decoloniality names a cocktail of insurrectionist-liberatory projects and critical thoughts emerging from ex-colonized epistemic sites like Latin America, the Caribbean, Asia, the Middle East, and Africa as it seeks to make sense of the position of ex-colonized peoples within the Euro-American-centric, Christian-centric, patriarchal, capitalist, hetero-normative, racially hierarchized, and modern world-system that came into being in the fifteenth century (Mignolo 2000).

The core tasks of decoloniality are to unmask, unveil, and reveal coloniality as an underside of modernity and to problematize its rhetoric of progress, equality, fraternity, and liberty. It is a particular kind of critical intellectual theory as well as political project which seeks to disentangle ex-colonized parts of the world from coloniality (Mignolo 2011). What distinguishes decoloniality from other existing critical social theories is its locus of enunciations and its genealogy – which is outside of Europe. Decoloniality can be best understood as a pluriversal epistemology of the future – a redemptive and liberatory epistemology that seeks to de-link from the tyranny of abstract universals (Mignolo 2007). Decoloniality informs the ongoing struggles against the inhumanity of the Cartesian subject, 'the irrationality of the rational, the despotic residues of modernity' (Mignolo 2011: 93).

Born out of a realization that the modern world is an asymmetrical world order that is sustained not only by colonial matrices of power but also by pedagogies and epistemologies of equilibrium that continue to produce alienated Africans who are socialized to hate the Africa that produced them and like the Europe and America that reject them, decoloniality addresses the key issues of consciousness. Schools, colleges, churches, and universities in Africa are sites for a reproduction of coloniality. So far, we don't have African universities; instead, we have universities in Africa (Ndlovu-Gatsheni 2013a; Ndlovu-Gatsheni 2018). They continue to poison African minds with research methodologies and inculcate knowledges of equilibrium. These knowledges do not question methodologies or the current asymmetrical world order. In decoloniality, research methods and research methodologies are never accepted as neutral but are unmasked as technologies of subjectivation, if not surveillance tools that prevent the emergence of another-thinking, another-logic, and another-world view. Research methodologies are tools of gate-keeping.

One of the key concepts/units of analysis in decoloniality is *coloniality of power*. It helps in investigating how the current 'global political' was constructed, constituted, and configured into a racially hierarchized, Euro-American-centric, Christian-centric, patriarchal, capitalist, hetero-normative, hegemonic, asymmetrical, and modern power structure (Grosfoguel 2007). The concept of colonial power enables us to delve deeper into how the world was bifurcated into a 'Zone of Being' (the world of those in charge of global power structures and beneficiaries of modernity) and a 'Zone of Non-Being' (the invented world that was the source of slaves and victims of imperialism, colonialism, and apartheid) maintained as invisible by what Boaventura de Sousa Santos (2007) termed 'abyssal thinking.' Abyssal thinking, according to Santos, is informed by imperial reason and manifests itself in bifurcation of the world into 'this side' (the side of complete beings governed according to the rules of emancipation, law, and ethics) and 'that side' (the side of incomplete beings governed according to expropriation and violence) (Santos 2007: 45–46). In short, coloniality of power is a concept that decolonial theorists use to analyze the modern global cartography of power and how the modern world works.

Coloniality of knowledge, which focusses on teasing out epistemological issues, politics of knowledge generation, and questions of who generates which knowledge and for what purpose, is another key unit of analysis of decoloniality (Quijano 2007). Coloniality of knowledge is useful in enabling us to understand how endogenous and indigenous knowledges have been pushed to what are now understood as 'the barbarian margins of society.' Today, Africa is saddled with irrelevant knowledge that serves to disempower rather than empower individuals and communities. Claude Ake (1979) emphasized that Africa had to seriously engage in struggles to free itself from the 'knowledge of equilibrium,' that is, knowledge that serves the present asymmetrically structured world. On the sphere of knowledge, decolonial theorists are at the forefront of decolonizing what they have termed 'Westernized' universities, which have been built throughout the world (Grosfoguel 2013).

The third concept is that of *coloniality of being*, which gestures to the pertinent questions of the making of modern subjectivities and issues of human ontology (Wynter 2003). African scholars engaged with the question of coloniality of being from the vantage point of what they termed 'African Personality' and 'Negritude,' among many other registers used in the African decolonial search for restoration of denied ontological density, sovereign subjectivity, and self-pride and self-assertion (Blyden 1967). Both 'African Personality' and 'Negritude' were concepts developed in the midst of struggle by Africans as they tried to make sense of their predicaments within a context of dehumanizing colonialism. Coloniality of being is important because it allows us to determine how African humanity was questioned as well as the processes that contributed to the 'objectification'/'thingification'/'commodification' of Africans (Ndlovu-Gatsheni 2013a). One of the continuing struggles in Africa is resisting the objectification and dehumanization of black people on a world scale. It is a struggle for (re)existence in the form of regaining lost subjecthood and citizenship.

Therefore, one grand proposition of decoloniality is that modernity unfolded as a Janus-headed process, characterised by rhetoric of salvation, civilization, progress, development and emancipation on the one side and on the other the reality of coloniality (Mignolo 2000). In decolonial thought, modernity is said to have unfolded as a phenomenon that colonized *time*, *space*, and *being* (Wynter 1991). This reality has taken decolonial thinkers into historical and philosophical mediations, which are beginning to reveal the 'under side' of modernity (Mignolo 2011).

Transcendence over narrow conceptions of being and consistent gesturing towards liberation from coloniality as a complex matrix of knowledge, power, and being is the core task of decolonial struggles. In this case decoloniality consistently reminds decolonial thinkers of 'the unfinished and incomplete twentieth-century dream of decolonization' (Mignolo 2000: 221). The 'decolonial turn' as a long existing 'turn' standing in opposition to the 'colonizing turn' underpinning Western thought is what decoloniality pushes for (Maldonado-Torres 2011). The 'decolonial turn' involves the 'task of the very decolonization of knowledge, power and being, including institutions such as the university' (Maldonado-Torres 2011: 1).

Decolonization/decoloniality versus postcolonialism/ postcolonial theory

To be overconcerned with the difference between human intellectual and academic traditions, rather than with their connections and convergences, is to fall into the problematic colonial paradigm of difference. While colonialism/coloniality was founded on the paradigm of difference, decolonization/decoloniality is about connections and convergences. This intervention does not authorize a simplistic conflation of human intellectual/academic productions and ideological ones. As noted in the introduction, decolonization/decoloniality is often confused with postcolonial theory. Decoloniality and postcolonial theory converge and diverge. On the convergence side, they both aim at dealing with the colonial experience. Ahluwalia (2001: 1) posited that 'Post-colonial theory has been characterised as being epistemologically indebted to both post-structuralism and postmodernism,' elaborating that 'Such a reading denigrates the authenticity of post-colonial theory and renders it subservient and theoretically venerable to charges levelled at post-structuralism and postmodernism.' While Ahluwalia invites us to 'differentiate between post-colonialism and other "post" phenomena'; Sabine Broeck and Carsten Junker (2014) effectively delineated converging and diverging positions, approaches, and trajectories of decoloniality and postcoloniality. Decoloniality and postcoloniality provide a range of critiques of modernity, but they diverge in their intellectual genealogy, trajectories, and horizons. Ahluwalia (2010: 3) insisted that 'postcolonialism is a counter-discourse that seeks to disrupt the cultural hegemony of the West, challenging imperialism in its various guises, whereas post-structuralism and postmodernism are counter discourses against modernism that have emerged within modernism itself.'

Genealogically, decoloniality, like postcoloniality, emerges 'from the receiving end of Western imperial formations' (Mignolo 2014: 22). However, decolonial theory is traceable to those thinkers from the zones that experienced the negative aspects of modernity, such as Aime Cesaire, Frantz Fanon, William E. B. Du Bois, Kwame Nkrumah, Ngugi wa Thiong'o, and many others; postcolonial theory, meanwhile, is traceable to post-structuralists and postmodernists like Jacques Derrida and Michel Foucault, and was later articulated by scholars such as Gayatri Spivak and Homi Bhabha (Grosfoguel 2007). Postcolonial theory and decolonial theory also differ in terms of where they begin their critique of modernity/coloniality. Decolonial theorists begin as far back as 500 years, covering Spanish and Portuguese colonialism. While it is clear that postcolonialism has different temporalities in its rendition of the impact of colonialism and imperialism, what emerges poignantly is its critique of the British colonization of India in the nineteenth century, in the process of which it ignored some 300 years of the unfolding of modernity/coloniality (Mignolo 2000; Grosfoguel 2007). Of course, Latin American postcolonialism does not begin with the British colonization of India.

Because of this, postcolonial theorists somehow try to decouple modernity and colonialism, in the process missing the fact that they are inextricably and paradoxically intertwined. While postcolonial theorists are concerned with dismantling meta-narratives, decolonial theorists push forward an analysis predicated on questions of power, epistemology, and ontology as foundational questions in the quest to understand the unfolding and operations of Euromodernity (Maldonado-Torres 2007). The postcolonial 'cultural turn' is different from the 'decolonial turn' because the former is located within a Euro-North American-centric modernist discursive, historical, and structural terrain, and the latter is born at the borders of Euro-North American-centric modernity and fuelled by a decolonial spirit of epistemic disobedience and delinking (Amin 1990; Mignolo 2008). Whereas postcolonial theorists' horizon is universalism and cosmopolitanism, decolonial theory gestures towards pluriversality and a new humanism. In short, one can say that postcoloniality and decoloniality converge and diverge across genealogies, trajectories, and horizons.

Postcolonial theorists, in particular, Achille Mbembe, are very critical of some forms of critique of modernity, colonialism, imperialism, and capitalism, such as Afro-radicalism and nativism. Mbembe's (2002b) critique is that these forms of resistance tend to be locked in what he terms a 'neurosis of victimhood' and 'narcissism of minor difference.' These analyses in Mbembe's critique are based on and informed by nationalism and Marxism, which Mbembe reduces to 'false philosophies' (Mbembe 2002a). These 'false philosophies,' according to him (1999), have been elevated into 'dogmas and doctrines' that have been 'repeated over and over again' by Afro-radical nationalists and Afro-Marxists. Those that Mbembe (2002b: 241) considers Afro-radical nationalists are accused of promoting a 'false belief that only autochthonous people who are physically living in Africa can produce, within a closed circle limited to themselves alone, a legitimate scientific discourse on the realities of the continent.' He also states that African scholarship that blames globalization is informed by 'a lazy interpretation of globalization' (Mbembe 2002b: 269).

Mbembe's critique provoked powerful responses from scholars like Paul Tiyambe Zeleza. Zeleza (2004) critiqued Mbembe for his uncritical celebration of the globalization and cosmopolitanism that underpin Eurocentric hegemony. Mbembe's call for 'internationalization' of African scholarship, which he presented as a way of 'getting out of the ghetto,' was equated with the 'globalizing tendencies of neo-liberal economic policies of liberalization' (Zeleza 2004). Zeleza (2004) reminded Mbembe that the domain of knowledge generation in and on Africa has never been 'ghettoized' as it has always been excessively exposed to external and imported Eurocentric paradigms.

Decoloniality is related to Afro-radical nationalist and Afro-Marxist thought, but it is also different. It is not only critical of these but also against facile essentialism and all forms of fundamentalism. This point is stated clearly by Grosfoguel (2007: 212):

> This is not an essentialist, fundamentalist, anti-European critique. It is a perspective that is critical of both Eurocentric and Third World fundamentalisms, colonialism and nationalism. What all fundamentalisms share (including the Eurocentric one) is the premise that there is only one sole epistemic tradition from which to achieve Truth and Universality.

Decoloniality is ranged against what Cesaire (2000) termed the European fundamental lie which states that 'Colonization = Civilization.' Thus, it enables the colonized peoples a space through which to judge Eurocentric conceit, deceit, and hypocrisy.

Conclusion

Decolonization/decoloniality identifies colonialism/coloniality as the progenitor of most modern problems. Colonialism/coloniality is thus isolated as the main source of the present historical interregnum, necessitating the resurgence and insurgence of the decolonization/decoloniality of the twenty-first century and its push for the decolonial turn. In hindsight, considering the limits of decolonization in the twentieth century, the current decolonization/decoloniality effort has been vigilant against being interpellated by the immanent logics of colonialism/coloniality. The decolonization of the twentieth century became entangled in the post-1945 colonialities of the superpower politics of empire-building and alliance-building (North Atlantic Treaty Organization (NATO) vs. Warsaw Pact); the United Nations Organization (UNO) rhetoric of being against war and being for national self-determination; the Universal Declaration of Human Rights and its pretensions of delivering a world in which all human lives mattered, and all human beings were equal; the Cold War coloniality, with its ideological divisiveness and sponsorship of hot wars in Africa; discourses on territorial nationalism and its universalization of the Westphalian modern nation-state template; Truman version of development and its claims of the 'white man's burden'; 'imperialism of decolonization' embodied by such discourses as Eurafrica; and finally, the emergence of the 'global financial empire' propagated by the World Bank and the International Monetary Fund (IMF), with their prescriptions of disastrous Structural Adjustment Programmes (SAPs).

The decolonial turn is predicated on epistemic freedom and a recognition of ecologies of knowledges, which form some of the essential ingredients for pluriversality (a world in which many worlds exists un-hierarchized). To realize this utopic imaginary, decoloniality lays out a multipronged attack on coloniality in the domains of knowledge, power, and subjectivity (being/ontology). It utilizes effective and consistent unmasking of what is hidden behind the rhetoric of Euromodernity as it exposes the fact that Eurocentric epistemologies are exhausted. It introduces what have been dubbed variously theories from the South, epistemologies from the South, and decolonial epistemologies from the South in an endeavour to attain cognitive justice as a pre-requisite for other forms of liberation—political, cultural, ontological, economic, and social (Ndlovu-Gatsheni 2013a, 2013b; Ndlovu-Gatsheni 2018). Santos (2014: x) defined the epistemologies of the South as 'a set of inquiries into the construction and validation of knowledge born in struggle, of ways of knowing developed by social groups as part of their resistance against systemic injustices and oppressions caused by capitalism, colonialism, and patriarchy' (see also Comaroff and Comaroff 2012: 1–2).

In terms of its horizon, decoloniality gestures towards the construction of the pluriverse as another possible world. The Global South is rich in resources for pluriversality. First, if one brings into the domain of knowledge the suppressed and displaced knowledges into the academy and general human life, a 'mosaic epistemology' conducive to the ecologies of knowledge begins to be constructed (Connell 2018). Mobilization and deployment of non-Western ways of thinking, doing, and acting are at the core of this construction, and different ontologies and epistemologies will be the order of the pluriverse. The problem constitutive of the present historical interregnum is not that of lack of ideas but that of taking ideas from a singular 'province' of the world and making them into universal knowledge, including its limits and its problems.

References

Adesanmi, P. 2011. *You're Not a Country, Africa: A Personal History of the African Present*. Cape Town: Penguin Books.

Ahluwalia, P. 2001. *Politics and Post-Colonial Theory: African Inflections*. London and New York: Routledge.

Ahluwalia, P. 2010. *Out of Africa: Post-Structuralism's Colonial Roots*. London and New York: Routledge.

Ajayi, J. F. A. 1968. 'The Continuity of African Institutions under Colonialism.' In T. O. Ranger (ed.), *Emerging Themes in African History*. Nairobi: Longmans, pp. 71–98.

Ajayi, J. F. A. 1969. 'Colonialism: An Episode in African History.' In L. H. Gann and P. Duignan (eds.), *Colonialism in Africa, 1870–1960: Volume 1*. Cambridge: Cambridge University Press, 69–89

Ake, C. 1983. *Colonialism and Social Structure: An Inaugural Lecture*. Ibadan: Ibadan University Press.

Ake, C. 1979. *Social Science as Imperialism: The Theory of Political Development*. Ibadan: University of Ibadan Press.

Amadiume, I. 1997. *Re-Inventing Africa: Matriarchy, Religion, and Culture*. London: Zed Books.

Amin, S. 1985. *Delinking: Towards a Polycentric World*. London: Zed Books.

Amin, S. 1990. *Delinking: Towards a Polycentric World*. London and New York: Zed Books.

Bhabha, H. K. 1994. *The Location of Culture*. London: Routledge.Biko, S. 1978. *I Write What I like: Steve Biko: A Selection of His Writings*. London: Bowerdean Press.

Blyden, E. W. 1967. *Christianity, Islam and the Negro Race*. Edinburgh: Edinburgh University Press.

Broeck, S., & Junker, C. (eds.). 2014. *Postcoloniality-Decoloniality-Black Critique: Joints and Fissures*. Frankfurt and New York: Campus Verlag.

Cesaire, A. 2000. *Discourse on Colonialism: Translated by Joan Pinkham*. New York: Monthly Review Press.

Chakrabarty, D. 2000. *Provincializing Europe: Postcolonial Thought and Historical Difference*. Princeton, NJ and Oxford: Princeton University Press.

Chen, K-H. 2010. *Asia as Method: Towards Deimperialization*. Durham, NC and London: Duke University Press.

Chibber, V. 2013. *Postcolonial Theory and the Specter of Capital*. London and New York: Verso.

Chinweizu, 1975. *The West and the Rest of Us.* New York: Random House.

Chinweizu, 1987. *Decolonizing the African Mind.* Lagos: Pero Press.

Chinweizu, J. O., & Madubuike, I. 1980. *Toward the Decolonization of Africa Literature.* London and Boston: KPI Limited.

Clapham, C. 1996. *Africa and the International System: The Politics of State Survival.* Cambridge: Cambridge University Press.

Comaroff, J., & Comaroff, J. L. 2012. *Theory from the South or How Euro-America Is Evolving towards Africa.* Boulder, CO and London: Paradigm Publishers.

Connell, R. 2018. 'Meeting at the Edge of Fear: Theory on a World Scale.' In B. Reiter (ed.), *Constructing the Pluriverse: The Geopolitics of Knowledge.* Durham, NC and London: Duke University Press, pp. 19–38.

Cook, J. W., Glickman, L. B., & O'Malley, M. 2008. *The Cultural Turn in U. S. History: Past, Present, and Future.* Chicago, IL: University of Chicago Press.

Cox, O. 1948. *Caste, Class and Race.* New York: Modern Reader.

Cox, O. 1959. *The Foundations of Capitalism.* New York: Philosophical Library.

Cox, O. 1964. *Capitalism as a System.* New York: Monthly Review Press.

Crenshaw, K. 1995. 'Mapping the Margins: Intersectionality, Identity Politics and Violence against Women of Colour.' In K. Crenshaw, N. Gotanda, G. Peller and K. Thomas (eds.), *Critical Theory.* New York: The New Press, pp. 282–313.

Dabashi, H. 2019. *Europe and Its Shadows: Coloniality after Empire.* London: Pluto Press.

Diagne, S. B. 2011. *African Art as Philosophy: Senghor, Bergson and the Idea of Negritude.* London and New York: Seagull Books.

Diop, C. A. 1954. *Nation, Negres at Culture.* Paris: Presence Africaine.

Diop, C. A. 1974a. *The African Origins of Civilization: Myth and Reality.* New York: Lawrence Hill Books.

Diop, C. A. 1974b. *Precolonial Black Africa.* New York: Lawrence Hill Books.

Du Bois, W. E. B. 1935. *Black Reconstruction in America, 1860–1880.* New York: Free Press.

El-Malik, S., & Kamola, I. A. (eds.). 2017. *Politics of African Anticolonial Archive.* London and New York: Rowman & Littlefield International.

Escobar, A. 2018. 'Transition Discourses and the Politics of Relationality: Towards Designs for the Pluriverse.' In B. Reiter (ed.), *Constructing the Pluriverse: The Geopolitics of Knowledge.* Durham, NC and London: Duke University Press, pp. 63–89.

Fanon, F. 1967. *Black Skins, White Masks.* New York: Grove Press.

Fanon, F. 1968. *The Wretched of the Earth.* New York: Grove Press.

Forsdick, C., & Murphy, D. (eds.). 2009. *Postcolonial Thought in the French-Speaking World.* Liverpool: Liverpool University Press.

Getachew, A. 2019. *Worldmaking After Empire: The Rise and Fall of Self-Determination.* Princeton and Oxford: Princeton University Press.

Glissant, E. 1989. *Caribbean Discourse: Selected Essays.* Charlottesville: University Press of Virginia.

Glissant, E. 1997. *Poetics of Relation.* Translated by Betsy Wing. Ann Arbor: the University of Michigan Press.

Guha, R. 1982. 'On Some Aspects of the Historiography of Colonial India.' In R. Guha (ed.), *Subaltern Studies 1: Writings on South Asian History and Society.* Delhi: Oxford University Press, pp. 1–8.

Gunn, P. A. 1986. *The Sacred Hoop: Recovering the Feminine in American Indian Traditions.* Boston, MA: Beacon Press.

Grosfoguel, R. 2007. 'The Epistemic Decolonial Turn: Beyond Political-Economy Paradigms.' *Cultural Studies*, 21(2/3) (March/May), pp. 203–246.

Grosfoguel, R. 2013. 'The Structure of Knowledge in Westernized Universities: Epistemic Racism/Sexism and the Four Genocides/Epistemicides of the Long 16th Century.' *Human Architecture: Journal of the Sociology of Self-Knowledge*, XI(1) (Fall), pp. 73–90.

Grosfoguel, R. 2019. 'What Is Racism? Zone of Being and Zone of Non-Being in the Work of Frantz Fanon and Boaventura de Sousa Santos.' In J. Cupples and R. Ramon (eds.), *Unsettling Eurocentrism in the Westernized University*. London and New York: Routledge, pp. 264–273.

James, C. L. R. 1938. *The Black Jacobins: Toussaint L'Ouverture and the San Domingo Revolution*. New York: Vintage.

Kamola, I. A. 2019. 'A Time for Anticolonial Theory.' *Contemporary Political Theory*, 18(2) (June), pp. 67–74.

Lorde, A. 1984. *Sister Outside: Essays and Speeches*. New York: Cross Press.

Lugones, M. 2003. *Pilgrimages/Peregrinajes: Theorizing Coalitions against Multiple Oppressions*. Lanham, MD: Rowman & Littlefield International Ltd.

Lugones, M. 2007. 'Heterosexualism and the Colonial/Modern Gender System.' *Hypatia*, 22(1), pp. 186–209.

Lugones, M. 2008. 'The Coloniality of Gender.' *Worlds & Knowledge Otherwise* (Spring), pp. 1–17.

Lugones, M. 2010. 'Towards Decolonial Feminism.' *Hypatia*, 25(4) (Fall), pp. 742–759.

Lyotard, J-F. 1984. *The Postmodern Condition: A Report on Knowledge*. Minneapolis: University of Minnesota Press.

Maldonado-Torres, N. 2007. 'On Coloniality of Being: Contributions to the Development of A Concept.' *Cultural Studies*, 21(2–3) (March/May), pp. 240–270.

Maldonado-Torres, N. 2008. *Against War: Views from the Underside of Modernity*. Durham, NC and London: Duke University Press.

Maldonado-Torres, N. 2011. 'Thinking through the Decolonial Turn: Post-Continental Interventions in Theory, Philosophy, and Critique—An Introduction.' *Transmodernity: Journal of Peripheral Cultural Production of Luso-Hispanic World*, 1(2) (Fall), pp. 1–36.

Maldonado-Torres, N. 2017. 'On Coloniality of Human Rights.' *Revista Critica de Ciencias Socials*, 114 (December), pp. 117–136.

Mamdani, M. 1996. *Citizen and Subject: Contemporary Africa and the Legacy of Late Colonialism*. Princeton, NJ: Princeton University Press.

Mamdani, M. 2013. *Define and Rule: Native As Political Identity*. Johannesburg: Wits University Press.

Mazrui, A. A. 1986. *The Africans: A Triple Heritage*. London: BBC Publication.

Mbembe, A. 1999. 'Getting Out of the Ghetto: The Challenge of Internationalization.' *CODESRIA Bulletin*, 3(4), pp. 1–10.

Mbembe, A. 2001. *On the Postcolony*. Berkeley: University of California Press.

Mbembe, A. 2002a. 'On the Power of the False.' *Public Culture*, 14(3), pp. 613–655.

Mbembe, A. 2002b. 'African Modes of Self-Writing.' *Public Culture*, 14(1), pp. 239–273.

Memmi, A. 1974. *The Colonizer and the Colonized*. London: Earthscan.

Mendoza, B. 2016. 'Coloniality of Gender and Power: From Postcoloniality to Decoloniality.' In L. Disch and M. Hawkeworth (eds.), *The Oxford Handbook of Feminist Theory*. Oxford: Oxford University Press, pp. 1–24.

Mignolo, W. D. 1995. *The Darker Side of Renaissance: Literacy, Territory, and Colonization*. Ann Arbor: University of Michigan Press.

Mignolo, W. D. 2000. *Local Histories/Global Designs: Essays on the Coloniality of Power, Subaltern Knowledges and Border Thinking.* Princeton, NJ: Princeton University Press.

Mignolo, W. D. 2002. 'The Zapastistas' Theoretical Revolution: Its Historical, Political, and Epistemological Consequences.' *Review: A Journal of the Fernand Braudel Centre*, 25(3), pp. 245–275.

Mignolo, W. D. 2005. *The Idea of Latin America.* Malden, MA: Blackwell Publishing.

Mignolo, W. D. 2007. 'Introduction: Coloniality of Power and De-Colonial Thinking.' *Cultural Studies*, 21 (2–3) (March/May), pp. 155–167.

Mignolo, W. D. 2008. 'Epistemic Disobedience, Independent Thought and De-Colonial Freedom.' *Theory, Culture and Society*, 26(7–8), pp. 1–23.

Mignolo, W. D. 2011. *The Darker Side of Western Modernity: Global Futures, Decolonial Options.* Durham, NC and London: Duke University Press.

Mignolo, W. D. 2014. 'Further Thoughts on (De) Coloniality.' In S. Broeck and C. Junker (eds.), *Postcoloniality-Decoloniality-Black Critique: Joints and Fissures.* Frankfurt and New York: Campus Verlag, pp. 10–51.

Mikell, G. 1997. *African Feminism: The Politics of Survival in Sub-Saharan Africa.* Philadelphia: University of Pennsylvania Press.

Morana, M., Dussel, E., & Jauregui, C. A. 2008. 'Colonialism and Its Replicants.' In M. Morana, E. Dussel and C. A. Jauregui (eds.), *Coloniality at Large: Latin America and the Postcolonial Debate.* Durham, NC and London: Duke University Press, pp. 1–20.

Nabudere, D. W. 2007. 'Cheikh Anta Diop: The Social Sciences, Humanities, Physical and Natural Sciences and Transdisciplinarity.' *International Journal of African Renaissance Studies-Multi-, Inter- and Transdisciplinarity*, 2(1), pp. 6–34.

Nandy, A. 1983. *The Intimate Enemy: Loss and Recovery of Self under Colonialism.* New Delhi: Oxford University Press.

Ndlovu-Gatsheni, S. J. 2013a. *Coloniality of Power in Postcolonial Africa: Myths of Decolonization.* Dakar: CODESRIA Book Series.

Ndlovu-Gatsheni, S. J. 2013b. *Empire, Global Coloniality and African Subjectivity.* New York and Oxford: Berghahn Books.

Ndlovu-Gatsheni, S. J. 2018. *Epistemic Freedom in Africa: Deprovincialization and Decolonization.* London and New York: Routledge.

Ndlovu-Gatsheni, S. J. 2019. 'The Cognitive Empire and the Challenges of Decolonizing the Mind.' Keynote Address Delivered at the International Conference on Towards A Decolonial Psychology: Theories from the Global South, University of Western Cape, Cape Town, South Africa, 21–22 February.

Neocosmos, M. 2016. *Thinking Freedom in Africa: Towards a Theory of Emancipatory Politics.* Johannesburg: Wits University Press.

Ngugi wa Thiong'o. 1986. *Decolonizing the Mind: The Politics of Language in African Literature.* Oxford: James Currey.

Ngugi wa Thiong'o. 2009a. *Re-Membering Africa.* Nairobi, Kampala, and Dar es Salaam: East African Educational Publishers Ltd.

Ngugi wa Thiong'o. 2009b. *Something Torn and New: An African Renaissance.* New York: Basic Civitas Books.

Nkrumah, K. 1965. *Neo-Colonialism: The Last Stage of Imperialism.* New York: International Publishers.

Nnaekema, O. 1997. *The Politics of (M)Othering: Woman, Identity and Resistance in African Literature.* London and New York: Routledge.

Ogundipe-Leslie, M. 1994. *Re-Creating Ourselves: African Woman and Critical Transformation*. Oxford and Malden, MA: Blackwell Publishers.

Oyewumi, O. 1997. *The Invention of Women: Making an African Sense of Western Gender Discourses*. Minneapolis and London: University of Minnesota Press.

Quijano, A. 2000. 'Coloniality of Power and Social Classification.' *Journal of World Systems*, 6(2) (Summer-Fall), pp. 342–386.

Quijano, A. 2007. 'Coloniality and Modernity/Rationality.' *Cultural Studies*, 21(2–3) (March/May), pp. 168–178.

Quijano, A., & Wallerstein, I. 1992. 'Americanity as a Concept, or the Americas in the Modern World-System.' *International Social Science Journal*, 44, pp. 549–557.

Ranger, T. 1983. 'The Invention of Tradition in Colonial Africa.' In E. Hobsbawn and T. Ranger (eds.), *The Invention of Tradition*. Cambridge: Cambridge University Press.

Reiter, B. (ed.). 2018a. *Constructing the Pluriverse: The Geopolitics of Knowledge*. Durham, NC and London: Duke University Press.

Reiter, B. 2018b. 'Introduction.' In B. Reiter (ed.), *Constructing the Pluriverse: The Geopolitics of Knowledge*. Durham, NC and London: Duke University Press, pp. 1–15.

Robinson, C. J. 1983. *Black Marxism: The Making of the Black Radical Tradition*. Chapel Hill: The University of North Carolina Press.

Rodney. W. 1973. *How Europe Underdeveloped Africa*. Dar-ers-salaam: Bogle L'Ouverture and Tanzania Publishing House.

Santos, B. de S. 2014. *Epistemologies of the South: Justice against Epistemicide*. Boulder, CO and London: Paradigm Publishers.

Santos, B. de S. 2007. 'Beyond Abyssal Thinking: From Global Lines to Ecologies of Knowledges.' *Review: A Journal of the Fernand Braudel Centre*, XXX(1), pp. 45–89.

Spivak, G. C. 1985. 'Can the Subaltern Speak? Speculations on Widow Sacrifice.' *Wedge*, 7/8 (Winter/Spring), pp. 120–130.

Spivak, G. C. 1990. *The Post-Colonial Critic: Interviews, Strategies, Dialogues*. London: Routledge.

Thiam, C. 2014. *Return to the Kingdom of Childhood: Re-Envisioning the Legacy and Philosophical Relevance of Negritude*. Columbus: The Ohio State University Press.

Wallerstein, I. 2004. *Uncertainties of Knowledge*. Philadelphia, PA: Temple University Press.

Wilder, G. 2015. *Freedom Time: Negritude, Decolonization and the Future of the World*. Durham, NC and London: Duke University Press.

Williams, E. 1944. *Capitalism and Slavery*. Chapel Hill: University of North Carolina Press.

Wynter, S. 1991. 'Columbus and the Poetics of the Propter Nos.' *Annals of Scholarship*, 8(2), pp. 251–286.

Wynter, S. 2003. 'Unsettling the Coloniality of Being/Power/Truth/Freedom: Towards the Human, after Man, Its Overrepresentation-An Argument.' *CR: The New Continental Review*, 3(3), pp. 257–337.

Yountae, A. 2017. *The Decolonial Abyss: Mysticism and Cosmopolitics from the Ruins*. New York: Fordham University Press.

Zeleza Email Comments to Francis Nyamnjoh, 19 January 2004.

Zizek, S. 2011. *Living in the End Times*. London and New York: Verso.

3 The Bandung spirit

Introduction

The Bandung spirit of decolonization is an encapsulation of transnational Global South decolonial struggles for liberation and freedom. It is unleashed against multiple racist, imperial, colonial, capitalist, patriarchal, and sexist forms of oppression. At its centre is resistance, its key driver, and the search for alternatives to colonialism, capitalism, and patriarchy. As articulated by Maria Lugones in *Pilgrimages/Peregrinajes: Theorizing Coalition against Multiple Oppression* (2003), resistance has never been straightforward, and at times it is even duplicitous, ambiguous, and even devious because it materializes within the context of strictly guarded, normed, and repressive colonialism and Global coloniality. The Bandung spirit of decolonization is no exception to these ambiguities and ambivalences. However, it is important to note that resistance entails negotiation of life itself within the tensions and nest of multiple oppressions. Thus, revisiting the Bandung spirit of decolonization fundamentally entails thinking of the oppressed people not as 'consumed by oppression, but as resisting or sabotaging a system aimed at moulding, reducing, violating, or erasing the logic of resistance and transformation' (Lugones 2003: 12). Still, on the importance of resistance as a key component of decolonization, Lugones (2003: 11) educates us thus:

> It is in noticing resistance to oppressions in their complex interconnections, including their interlocking to fragment people categorically, that we sense each other as possible companions in resistance, where company goes against the grain of sameness as it goes against the grain of power. Noticing the tensions from within a logic of resistance enables one to acquire a multiple sensing, a multiple perceiving, a multiple sociality.

Lugones is not only a theorist of resistance but also an advocate of coalitions, collaborations, and solidarities of the oppressed. Transnational, if not planetary, solidarity and coalition of colonially oppressed people was key to the Bandung Conference of 1955. Inevitably, however, because of its planetary paradigmatic implications, and indeed 'empire-shaking significance,' the Bandung spirit of decolonization present in what Quynh N. Pham and Robbie Shilliam (2016) termed 'postcolonial orders and decolonial visions' became open to various and excessive 'meanings' and 'sensing(s).' What was even more important was how those who gathered in Bandung in 1955 expressed a deep understanding of the meaning of colonialism in order to inspire correct decolonization measures. The definition was delivered by the host of the Bandung Conference, President Sukarno of Indonesia:

> I beg of you do not think of colonialism in the classical form which we of Indonesia and our brothers in different parts of Asia and Africa, knew. Colonialism has also its modern dress, in the form of economic control, intellectual control, actual physical control by a small but alien community within a nation. It is a skilful and determined enemy, and its appearance in many guises. It does not give up its loot easily.
>
> (Asia-Africa Speaks 1995: 23)

Randolph B. Persaud (2016: 133–141) posited that the anti-colonial and anti-racist struggles that produced the Bandung spirit of decolonization before the convening of the Bandung Conference in 1955 goes as far back as 50 years and noted the formation and meetings of women, such as the 1928 Pan-Pacific Women's Association's Conference in Honolulu, the 1931 All-Asian Women's Conference in Lahore, the 1944 Pan-Arab Feminist Conference in Cairo, the 1949 Conference of the Women of Asia in Beijing, the 1958 Asian-African Conference of Women in Colombo, and the 1961 Afro-Asian Women's Conference in Cairo.

In this chapter, the Bandung spirit of decolonization delves deeper into African and black histories of resistance. The concept of the 'spirit' is deployed to connect the pre-Bandung Conference resistances and struggles, and the post-Banding Conference decolonial initiatives informed by a resilient spirit of resistance. The Haitian Revolution (1791–1804) is mentioned as the precursor to the 'Bandung spirit of decolonization.' This type of historicizing would not make sense if it was not contextualized as a part of the broader unfolding of the technologies of the invention of the Global South and the Global North. Through this historical and decolonial approach, the Bandung spirit of decolonization gains a wider canvas as a name for the long-standing anti-colonial resistances and decolonial struggles, not only against early Global imperial designs and Cold War coloniality but also as a terrain of self-invention in opposition to Northern domination.

Background to resistance and struggles

Even when Africans were in chains under enslavement they never gave up the spirit of resistance. They confronted well-armed colonial invasion forces in what became known as 'primary resistance.' Such resistance movements as the Maji Maji and Mau Mau in Eastern Africa, Ndebele-Shona Uprising and Nama-Herero resistance in Southern Africa, and many others across the rest of Africa underscore the prominence of this spirit. It continued into the post-1945 liberation struggles, including the memorable armed liberation struggles in Guinea Bissau, Mozambique, Angola, Algeria, Namibia, South Africa, and Zimbabwe. Thus, the concept of the 'spirit' encapsulates a melange of resistance and struggles against colonial encounters, colonialism, and coloniality. At the centre of these resistance movements is the Haitian Revolution (1791–1804) and its planetary significance. In the Haitian Revolution, those African human beings who were designated as black and slaves by nature shocked the white world when they rose against enslavement, racism, and domination. The Haitian Revolution and the Bandung Conference sit at a planetary level, defiantly signifying Frantz Fanon's call for the colonized people to turn over a new leaf and produce a new humanism via coalitions, solidarities, resistances, and decolonization.

The Bandung Conference of 1955 occupies a place of pride at the centre of decolonization/decoloniality. Quynh N. Pham and Robbie Shillian (2016) underscored the way in which the Bandung Conference of 1955 occupied the centre of anti- and decolonial world-sensing. Richard Wright (1956: 11–13), who witnessed the unprecedented gathering of 29 nations of Asia and Africa from 18 to 24 April 1955, correctly captured its planetary significance in these words: 'this is the human race speaking.' The concept of the 'spirit' correctly situates it in the long decolonial turn. The Bandung Conference was possible because of the 'spirit' of decolonial turn which has been sweeping the world since the time of the Haitian Revolution (1791–1804). Thus, to fully appreciate the epic significance of the conference as a world-shaping event that galvanized and radicalized a planetary spirit of decolonization and decoloniality, it is important to situate it historically and discursively within the broader context of modernity/coloniality, on the one hand, and decolonization/decoloniality, on the other. The simultaneous invention of both the Global North and the Global South, the former as a centre of the modern world and the latter as the periphery, is part of the planetary technologies of modernity/coloniality. The Bandung spirit of decolonization, then, emerges as a name for an equally planetary liberatory politics of seeking freedom from enslavement, colonial conquest, Eurocentrism, asymmetrical power relations, and economic domination of the Global South by the Global North.

Global imperial designs and the invention of the Global South

Genocides, conquest, law, and cartography played an important role in the making of the modern world. In *The Nomos of the Earth: In the International Law of the Jus Publicum Europaeum* (1950), Carl Schmitt documented how, over a 500-year-long history, Europe actively dominated the making and mapping of the world in its own image and for its own benefit, resulting in the contemporary divisions of the world into 'East' and 'West'; 'South' and 'North'; and 'First,' 'Second,' and 'Third.' This process began in the fifteenth century as part of the unfolding of the 'European game' of making and dominating the modern world. This is why Walter D. Mignolo (2014: 2) posited that 'geopolitical naming and mapping are fictions, and fictions have creators,' but these fictions can only be concretized 'from a position of power that overrules local senses of territoriality.' Below is a brief historical articulation of the invention of the Global South and the Global North—the former as a geography of poverty and the latter as a geography of opulence.

The invention of the Global South is part of the unfolding of colonial matrices of power. The emergence of the Atlantic commercial centre had a part in shaping and ordering the world in accordance with the interests of imperialism and colonialism. At first the world was divided into 'Old World' and 'New World,' and later into 'Eastern' and 'Western' hemispheres (Mignolo 2018: 90–91). Historically speaking, the modern Global imperial designs and technologies of domination of the world by Europe and North America can be traced back to 1415, when the Portuguese invaded the port of Ceuta in North Africa. This invasion, directed by Prince Henry (who is celebrated in imperial historiography as 'the Navigator'), announced Portugal's violent entry into the human trafficking business that laid the foundation for the invention and subsequent underdevelopment of the Global South. The centrality of Ceuta to the development of the Global North (see Rodney 1972, 1975; Frank 1998) is highlighted by Carrie Gibson (2014: 2):

> In Henry's time this port was known for its commerce in wheat and gold. Ceuta sat at a crucial location; mirrored by the rock of Gibraltar in the north, it was the southern part of the 'Pillars of Hercules'—the gateway to the commercial world of the Mediterranean. It was also the exit to the terrifying and mostly unknown waters of the Atlantic. [...] Many people believed that Ceuta was the last link in the long supply chain that connected the Mediterranean with the rumoured riches that lay deep in the unknown African interior.

The next important event in the invention and entrapment of the Global South was Bartholomew Diaz's circumnavigation of the Cape at the southernmost tip of Africa in 1488, which not only exposed the southern part of Africa to mercantile colonization but opened important trade routes to India and the Asian subcontinent. In fact, on 10 October 1487, the Portuguese King Joao II appointed and commissioned Diaz to be in charge of an expedition to find a sea route to India (Nowell 1953: 435). Part of his itinerary was to discover the lands ruled by Prester John, the proverbial opulent King of Ethiopia. Prester John's mystery and fable piqued European imagination. Nowell (1953: 435) observed that:

> Man or myth, Prester John played a great role. From the twelfth century until well after the discovery of America, he was an established part of

> the European pattern of thought. As a potential Christian ally in the rear of the Moslem foe, he figured in the plans for the later crusades and thus had a place in European ideas of world strategy.

In 1481, Diaz also accompanied Diego d'Azambuja in his exploration of the area formerly known as the Gold Coast, which became an important part of the transatlantic slave commerce (Nowell 1953: 433). In his assignment to the East Indies, he was followed by Vasco da Gama, who not only rounded the Cape but managed to reach the East Indies in 1498. Within the same decade, in 1492, Christopher Columbus claimed to have 'discovered' what became known in imperial historiography as the 'New World' (a reference to the Americas). To highlight the close connectedness of the events that brought Africa, the Americas, and Asia into an emerging transatlantic commerce, Diaz and Columbus were, in 1482, companions on a ship to the west coast of Africa to establish a slave fort (Nowell 1953: 433).

The significance of Diaz's 'voyages' and the passage around southern Africa is that it opened a direct sea route and lucrative trade with India, Africa, and Asia, extending Portuguese influence. He also obtained invaluable information that would be used by future 'voyagers,' including Columbus, Vasco da Gama, and Pedro Alvares Cabral. He travelled across nearly 2,000 kilometres of coastline previously unknown to Europeans and found for Europe the south-east and westerly winds that would aid future sailors. On 22 November 1497, Vasco da Gama followed in Diaz's footsteps and rounded the Cape en-route to India. In 1500, both men claimed to have 'discovered' Brazil, but both died on 24 May 1500 in a violent storm near the Cape of Good Hope.

What is important to underscore is that the so-called 'voyages of discovery' were part of the practical unfolding of what James Blaut (1993) termed the 'colonizer's model of the world' and the slow implementation of what Michael Headley (2008) termed the 'Europeanization of the world.' At the centre of the 'colonizer's idea of the world' is the notion of 'emptiness' outside of Europe.

The idea of empty lands (*terra nullius*) was crucial in the invention of the Global South through the schema of colonization. It was backed by religious justification and authorization in the form of the issuing of 'Papal Bulls' by Pope Eugenius IV in 1436 and Pope Nicholas V in 1455, which granted Portugal rights and title to lands outside of Europe and allowed the enslavement of those who were found there (Nowell 1953: 436). In 1493, Alexander VI issued a 'Papal Bull' granting the lands of the Americas to Spain. In 1494, the Treaty of Tordesillas was signed between Spain and Portugal, in which the Pope proclaimed the two hemispheres between the two Iberian imperial powers (Nowell 1953: 437).

The very formation and consolidation of what is today termed European identity is traceable to the period after 1500. But it must be made clear that, initially, 'the Identity formation of Europe-as-Christendom' was 'a negative identity formation that was rooted in insecurity and the alleged threat of Islamic empires' (Terreblanche 2014: 202). Sampie Terreblanche (2014: 202) elaborated that:

> After 1500 the Europeans redefined their identity vis-à-vis black Africans and the indigenous Amerindians. In the new definition the Europeans imagined themselves positively as superior to non-European peoples. In this 'redefinition' of European identity the Europeans developed a superiority complex that has been perpetrated to this day and has served continuously as a legitimation of European and Western empire building, of capitalist exploitation and of the Great Divergence between the West and the Rest.

Taken together, the 'discovery' of the Americas, the European opening of the sea route to the East, and the incursions into African coastal areas and the interior of West Africa laid the foundation for a Euro-North American-centric modernity whose commercial nerve centre was the transatlantic world. Previously the nerve centre of Global commerce had been the Mediterranean and had been dominated by Africans and Muslims (known as Moors). The trans-Saharan trade pre-dated the opening of transatlantic commerce that was underpinned by the emerging capitalist economic system and its Global division of labour.

Cyril L.R. James (1982) highlighted another way in which the Global South was created economically, noting that the eighteenth-century slave-society in San Domingo (later Haiti) connected Europe, Africa, and the Americas as the wealth generated through slavery in the Americas resulted in the rise of the capitalist bourgeoisie in Europe as well as a new civilization underpinned by a capitalist economy (James 1982: 12). He elaborated that the abolition of the slave trade was succeeded by the invention of indentured labour as a new form of enslavement, this time bringing Indians and Chinese into the nexus of evolving capitalist Euro-North American-centric and modernist civilization (James 1982: 13). Building on this background, it becomes clear that the rise of the Global North was predicated on 'a modern racial division of labour' (Lowe 2006: 192–193).

Mignolo (2018: 90–91) is correct in positing that by 1500, radical changes had begun to take place in the history of humankind. A New World emerged in the European consciousness, prompting Renaissance men of letters to set up the foundation of the current world order: the planet was divided into the Old World and the New World, and, by the seventeenth century, into the Western and the Eastern hemispheres. While the Global South was not yet being used in the paradigm of difference, what is clear is that it had a long genealogy before it appeared first as the Third World after 1945 and then as the Global South in our times.

What is beyond dispute is that the invention of both the Global North and the Global South is a tale of successive empires. The first phase is that of

Spanish and Portuguese empire-building supported by the Catholic Church (1500–1630). The second is the age of Dutch colonization of the world and the activities of the Dutch East India Company (1648–1713). The third was dominated by the British from 1688 to1945; this phase included what is known as the period of 'High Imperialism,' running from 1884 to 1914, and the period of inter-imperial warfare from 1914 to 1945. The fourth phase is that of the dominance of the United States of America, characterized by the rise of financial, capitalist, and militarist empires (see Terreblanche 2014: 57–58).

This historical rendition of the invention must not be misread to mean that what is today known as the Global South was simply a victim that never challenged the Global imperial designs. Boaventura de Sousa Santos (2018: 1) depicts the Global South as 'the "anti-imperial South" which suffered injustice, oppression, and destruction caused by capitalism, colonialism and patriarchy.' As will be seen in the following section, the colonized people actively worked, through resistance and diplomacy, to re-make the modern world system. But to gain a deeper understanding of the significance of the Bandung spirit of decolonization, it is vital to understand the discursive terrain within which it emerged and contested. Below is a brief articulation of the key lines of oppression and domination that the Bandung spirit of decolonization had to confront as part of multiple oppressions.

Conceptual and theoretical understanding of the colonizer's model of the world

Conceptually and theoretically, what exists today as the 'Global South' and the 'Global North' are simultaneous inventions introduced by the operationalization of the imperial paradigms of difference and war. At the centre of these paradigms was the imperial 'will to power.' The unfolding Global paradigms of difference and war were processes of not only racial hierarchization of human species and social organization of people in accordance with assumed differential ontologies but also enslavement, mapping, claiming, conquest, and colonization (Mignolo 2000; Quijano 2000; Maldonado-Torres 2007). Out of these processes emerged Europe as the centre of the world and other parts of the world as the periphery (Ndlovu-Gatsheni 2013a, 2013b). At play were the technologies of mapping, naming, defining, ruling, and owning the world.

The work of Ramon Grosfoguel (2007: 216), particularly his distillation and isolation of the interrelated, overlapping, and intertwined hetararchies of power within which the Global South and the Global North formed, is very useful for conceptually and theoretically framing how complex colonial matrices of power produced the Global North and the Global South simultaneously. The unfolding of these matrices resulted in various colonial/capitalist/patriarchal formations and Global technologies of domination and exploitation. The making of 'a particular global class formation' served by 'diverse forms of labour' including 'slavery, semi-serfdom, wage-labour, petty-commodity production,' which is entangled with how 'capital as a source of production of surplus value through the selling of commodities for a profit in the world market' functioned is one of the key formations. The modern colonial/capitalist/patriarchal Global pyramidal power structure is founded on this important matrix. The second formation was the invention of the 'international division of labour of core and periphery where capital organized labour in the periphery around coerced and authoritarian forms.' The making of an 'inter-state system of proto-military organizations controlled by European males and institutionalized in colonial administrations' is the third formation. The introduction of a 'global racial/ethnic hierarchy that privileges European people over non-European people,' together with a 'global gender hierarchy that privileges males over females and European patriarchy over other forms of gender relations,' is the fourth formation.

In the social domain, a 'sexual hierarchy that privileges heterosexuals over homosexuals, lesbians,' and other sexual orientations, and a 'spiritual hierarchy that privileges Christians over non-Christians/non-Western spiritualities institutionalized in the globalization of the Christian (Catholic and later Protestant) church' are also discernible as inventions of modernity/coloniality that concretized the division of the world into south and north. At the epistemic level, there emerged 'an epistemic hierarchy that privileges Western knowledge and cosmology over non-Western knowledge and cosmologies, and institutionalized in the global university system.' The final hetararchy of power emerged in the domain of language. Here, a 'linguistic hierarchy between European languages and non-European languages' was created which enabled colonial languages to displace and marginalize other languages. These are key elements constitutive of the 'European game' of colonialism.

Departing from Africa as the locus of enunciation, Sabelo J. Ndlovu-Gatsheni (2013c, 2015) distilled eight epochs through which the continent's subalternization and peripherization unfolded. These eight epochs relate well to what Nelson Maldonado-Torres (2018) articulated in terms of the terrain within which the decolonial turn unfolded from the vantage point of the Latin American locus of enunciation. The first important epoch ran from the fifteenth to the eighteenth century and was constituted by a *paradigm of discovery and mercantilist order* characterized by the slave trade and mercantilist commerce. This epoch practically laid down the framework for the entrapment of Africa, Latin America, Asia, and other parts of the Global South in the evolving Euro-North American-Atlantic commercial system, which included the selling and buying of black human beings, and, later, the indenturing of those people who were deemed to be 'yellow' (Chinese and Indians) (see Amin 2010). This epoch was decisive in the making of what Chinweizu (1975) termed the 'the west and the rest of us.' Walter Rodney (1972) traced what he termed 'how Europe underdeveloped Africa' from this epoch of discovery and mercantilism. The second epoch is the *Westphalian order* that commenced in 1648 and is credited with laying the foundation for the modern idea of a sovereign nation-state. The Westphalian order cuts across other orders as the notion of nation-state is still ubiquitous across the modern world. This is why Wendy Brown (2010: 21) explained that:

> To speak of a post-Westphalian order is not to imply an era in which nation-state sovereignty is either finished or irrelevant. Rather, the prefix 'post' signifies a formation that is *temporally after but not over* that to which it is affixed. 'Post' indicates a very particular condition of afterness in which what is past is not left behind, but, on the contrary, relentlessly conditions, even dominates a present that nevertheless also breaks in some way with this past.

The third and particularly important epoch is that which commenced with the *1884–1885 Berlin Conference*. This inaugurated what Adekeye Adebajo (2010) depicted as 'the curse of Berlin,' which galvanized the scramble for Africa; heightened the conquest of Africa; and enabled the partitioning, dismemberment, and fragmentation of Africa into various colonies. We are not yet beyond the 'curse of Berlin' as Africans are still trapped within colonially drawn boundaries decided by colonizers in Berlin. This epoch is that of the *age of colonial governmentality*, which involved the implementation of dismembering processes of dispossession and the production of the unique African colonial subjectivity of 'subjects' rather than 'citizens,' and established direct colonial administrations. These direct forms of colonial administrations were known by different names, such as Concessionaire/Company Rule, Assimilation/Association, Lusotropicalism, Indirect/Direct Rule, and Apartheid (Ndlovu-Gatsheni 2013a, 2013b, 2013c).

The *United Nations normative order that commenced in 1945* is the fourth epoch, which witnessed the intensification of African struggles for 'political independence' on the one hand and the active strategizing by the empire to maintain its dominance over Africa on the other. The Global colonial designs included using the United Nations Organization (UNO) as a key new institution of the modern world system through which to invite and accommodate Africa into the lowest echelons of the same modern world system that they set out to change. Reflecting on the post-1945 Global dynamics, John M. Hobson (2012: 185) emphasized the need to decouple Eurocentric institutional racism from scientific racism and argued that 'while IR theory did indeed take on a new guise after 1945 by discarding scientific racism, it nevertheless failed to escape the generic political bias of Western-centrism that had underpinned pre-1945 international theory.' He described what took place after 1945 as 'subliminal Eurocentric institutionalism,' as compared to explicit or conscious Eurocentrism (Hobson 2012: 185). In subliminal Eurocentric institutionalism, the binaries of civilized/barbarian and even whites/blacks are allowed to strategically recede from public discourse and international discourse to the extent that some might become confused and think the post-1945 dispensation was the age of the emergence of the 'postcolonial world' instead of that of the translation of visible direct colonialism into invisible Global coloniality (Grosfoguel 2007; Ndlovu-Gatsheni 2013a, 2013b).

The post-1945 dispensation was entangled not only in the politics of political decolonization but also with what is here termed the process of Cold War *coloniality*, which polarized Africa ideologically and reduced it to a theatre of proxy hot wars (Ndlovu-Gatsheni 2013c, 2015). It is another important epoch that witnessed an Africa entrapped in Global ideological warfare that worked counter to any of the authentic African political and economic formulations and creations. Cold War coloniality invented and financed 'terrorist' movements in Africa, such as Mozambique National Resistance Movement (RENAMO) in Mozambique, United Union for the Total Independence of Angola (UNITA) in Angola, and many others, as part of a strategy to keep Africa entrapped ideologically while disciplining militant nationalists and pan-Africanists, such as Samora Machel, Agostihno Neto, Patrice Lumumba, and Kwame Nkrumah. Military coups and assassinations were also sponsored. Cold War coloniality was as dirty as all other forms (Ndlovu-Gatsheni 2013c, 2015).

The *post-Cold War triumphalism of neoliberal order*, which Francis Fukuyama (1992) wrongly articulated as 'the end of history and the last man,' is another important epoch that revealed the entrapment of Africa in another Euro-North American-centric world order. At the centre of this order was what became known as the Washington Consensus – another important element of Global coloniality that de-structured what remained of African policy space and sovereignty through the introduction of Structural Adjustment Programmes (SAPs).The attack on the United States of America on 11 September 2001 inaugurated another shift in the world order and instantiated the *post-9/11 anti-terrorist dispensation*, under which the paradigm of war gained a new lease on life, and a securitization order emerged. Today, we live under what can best be described as the *current coloniality of markets and new scramble for Africa* as another Global order that is both new and old (Ndlovu-Gatsheni 2013c, 2015).

Both Grosfoguel and Ndlovu-Gatsheni speak to the unfolding of colonialism and coloniality as a constitutive part of the unfolding of Euro-North American-centric modernity. At its centre over the past 500 years has been the invention and re-invention of a superior Global North and an inferior Global South. The terms 'global North/the West' are not used here to refer to a geographical space; rather, as explained by Walter D. Mignolo (2015: xxv):

> What constitutes the West more than geography is a linguistic family, a belief system and an epistemology. It is constituted by six modern European and imperial languages: Italian, Spanish and Portuguese, which were dominant during the Renaissance, and English, French and German, which have been dominant since Enlightenment. [...]. Thus, 'the West' is shorthand for 'Western Civilization.'

On a global scale, what emerged is coloniality as a reference to long-standing patterns of power that began with the unfolding of modernity itself, resulting in what became known as 'voyages of discovery,' which opened up other parts of the world to Europe's rising hegemonic aspirations (Maldonado-Torres 2007). The extermination of the indigenous people of the Americas, the enslavement of lack people from Africa, the indenturing of the Chinese and Indians, the eventual colonization of non-European worlds, the redefinition and re-invention of human cultures and intersubjective relations from a racial perspective, and the theft and appropriations of history and knowledge for colonial purposes form part of the materialization of coloniality (Mignolo 2000; Quijano 2000; Ndlovu-Gatsheni 2013a). Coloniality survived the struggles against juridical colonialism and extended into the postcolony (see Mbembe 2000; Maldonado-Torres 2007; Ndlovu-Gatsheni 2013b). The Bandung spirit of decolonization was and is targeting these inimical processes of dismemberment and dehumanization. Enslavement became candidate number one in the unfolding of African and black resistance.

Haitian Revolution: the foundation of the Bandung spirit of decolonization

Giving historical background to the revolts of enslaved black people and critiquing Karl Marx's articulation of the consciousness of oppression, Cedric J. Robinson, in *Black Marxism: The Making of the Black Radical Tradition* (1983: 121), posited that:

> Marx had not realized fully that the cargoes of labourers also contained African cultures, critical mixes and admixtures of language and thought, of cosmology and metaphysics, of habits, beliefs, and morality. These were the actual terms of their humanity. These cargoes, then, did not consist of intellectual isolates or decultured Blacks-men, women, and children separated from their previous universe. African labour brought the past with it, a past that had produced it and settled on it the first element of consciousness and comprehension.

The African revolts were informed by a history and a reality of enslavement and racism. Earlier on Cyril L. R. James, in *The Black Jacobins* (1938: 11), had highlighted the contradictions and consciousness which produced the conditions for the Haitian Revolution:

> The difficulty was that though one could trap them like animals, transport them in pens, work them alongside an ass or a horse and beat both with the same stick, stable them and starve them, they remained, despite their black skins and curly hair, quite invincibly human beings; with the intelligence and resentments of human beings.

Therefore the significance of the Haitian Revolution (1791–1804) not only drew from this resilient and defiant African humanism but also inevitably and paradigmatically set the tone for resistance and struggles against racism, colonialism, and capitalism. The enslaved, racialized, and colonized people were claiming their humanity and embarking on self-invention after centuries of dismemberment and dehumanization. Physical resistance to Global imperial designs was constitutive of self-invention. Modern South-South solidarity has a long history born out of confrontation and resistance to racism, enslavement, and colonization involving the Diaspora and those in Asia, the Caribbean, and Africa (Cooper 1994). The ideal starting point is the Haitian Revolution, which was one of the earliest well-organized and purposeful resistances in the history of non-European people in general and black people in particular, and which sought to end racism, enslavement, and colonization.

The revolution directly challenged Euro-North American-centric conceptions of black people as slaves by nature, as popularized by early European philosophers such as Aristotle. In a practical sense, the Haitian Revolution demonstrated to the whole world how a people whose very being was denied and who had been reduced to slaves, organized themselves and staged a successful revolution against the Global system of slavery. The decolonial paradigmatic significance of the Haitian Revolution is well captured by the Haitian historian Michel-Rolph Trouillot (1995), in *Silencing the Past: Power and the Production of History*, as challenging the core of the emerging Global system of racism, enslavement, and colonization. The revolution was an epic statement and declaration of the humanity of black people in the midst of an emerging and violent anti-black Euro-North American-centric world.

Because of its decolonial paradigmatic significance, the Haitian Revolution became one of the Global events that had seemed 'unthinkable' to those who had convinced themselves that black enslaved people were not human beings and were natural slaves with no capacity to rebel. The revolution challenged 'the iron bonds of the philosophical milieu in which it was born' (Trouillot 1995: 74). Trouillot made it clear that:

> The Haitian Revolution did challenge the ontological and political assumptions of the most radical writers of the Enlightenment. *The events that shook up Saint-Domingue from 1791 to 1804 constituted a sequence for which not even the extreme political left in France or in England had a conceptual frame of reference.* They were 'unthinkable' facts in the framework of Western thought.
>
> (Trouillot 1995: 82, emphasis in the original)

Any acceptance of the fact that enslaved black people were up-in-arms against the system of slavery amounted in Western thought to an acknowledgement of the humanity of black people. The slave masters were not prepared for this challenge. Europeans and plantation owners in general were not prepared to concede that they were being faced with a people claiming their denied humanity. On a Global scale, the Haitian Revolution, as noted by Trouillot, was a major test:

> The Haitian Revolution was the ultimate test to the universalist pretensions of both the French and the American revolutions. And they both failed. *In 1791, there is no public debate on the record, in France, in England, or in the United States on the right of black slaves to achieve self-determination, and the right to do so by way of the armed resistance.*
>
> (1995: 88, emphasis in the original)

The difficult philosophical and intellectual problem for Western thought included how to think about and conceptualize black revolution in a world in which black people were not considered to be rational and human in the first place. This is why 'international recognition of Haitian independence was even more difficult to gain than military victory over the forces of Napoleon' (Trouillot 1995: 95). The most important but silenced significance of the Haitian Revolution is that it led to the collapse of the entire system of slavery and constituted a major chapter in the history of the resistance of black people. It was truly an anti-systemic revolution that must occupy a central position in the history of anti-systemic resistance, marked by the definitive entry of the enslaved and colonized into modern history as human beings opposed to all forms of domination. As such, the Haitian Revolution formed an important base from which to articulate resistance and black solidarity-building as part of self-invention within a context of racism, imperialism, colonialism, and racial capitalism. The pan-Africanist initiatives and struggles emerging in the African Diaspora and embraced by continental Africans became another planetary terrain of resistance and contestations of physical colonialism and discursive Global coloniality.

Bandung spirit of decolonization and pan-Africanism

In her recent book, *Worldmaking after Empire: The Rise and Fall of Self-Determination* (2019), Adom Getachew identified anti-colonial nationalists as 'worldmakers' and 'nation-builders.' She elaborated that their resistance and struggles for decolonization constituted three core tasks: (1) the transformation of the principle of self-determination into a human right, (2) the push for a New International Economic Order (NIEO), and the invention of a transnational pan-African federation as a guarantor of the hard-won political independence and protection from neo-colonialism (Getachew 2019: 2–3).

Getachew (2019: 5) posited that 'To understand this history of anticolonial worldmaking, we need to grasp the worlds of Pan-Africanism.' This was a quest for unity and freedom predicated on black internationalism, which transcended imperial boundaries and resulted in the formation of strong political collaborations across the Atlantic. For the black people who had been dismembered into two (the continental and diasporic Africans), the idea of black solidarity and one united Africa stemmed from members of the Diaspora and was readily embraced by those who remained on the continent. William E. Du Bois observed that 'Here various groups of Africans, quite separate in origin, became so united in experience and so exposed to the impact of a new culture, that they began to think of Africa as one idea and one land' (Du Bois 1963: 13). The key objective above attainment of political independence was to change the international order into 'a domination-free' world of equality on a Global scale.

Black solidarity crystallized within the series of Pan-African Congresses, which were organized by Du Bois. These formed one of the vehicles through which black consciousness and black solidarity on a Global scale emerged and crystallized into a decolonial project. The first Pan-African Congress of 1900 took place when Africa was experiencing conquest and colonization. Henry Sylvester-Williams from the West Indies was so touched by the experience of the colonization and brutalization of Africans by imperial powers that he convened the Congress to map out strategies to save the black race from abuse and dehumanization. The Congress brought together 30 delegates from Britain and the West Indies. It was at the 1900 Congress that the word 'pan-African' was used for the first time (Du Bois 1963).

The next Congress was organized by Du Bois in 1919 in the course of the Paris Peace Conference aimed at ending the First World War (1914–1918). It was attended by 57 delegates from 15 countries, nine of which were African. The conference produced the Mandates Commission that appealed to Western powers to protect indigenous people and demanded that land be given to them; the regulation of capital; the abolishment of slavery, corporal punishment, and forced labour; the right to education; and rights for indigenous people in Africa to participate in government affairs (Du Bois 1963). The third Congress took place in August and September 1921, and its venues were London, Brussels, and Paris. It called for the equality of races and appealed to the League of Nations for intervention (Du Bois 1963).

The most important Pan-African Congress was the one held in Manchester in 1945, which was organized by, among others, Du Bois, Marcus Garvey's widow Amy Jacques Garvey, Jamaican Dr Harold Moody, T. Ras Makonnen from Guyana, George Padmore from the West Indies, Kwame Nkrumah from Ghana, Peter Abrahams from South Africa, and Jomo Kenyatta from Kenya; it was attended by over 200 delegates and observers (Du Bois 1963, 1965). The Congress called for the independence of African people, the end of racial discrimination and forced labour, and a granting of the universal franchise. The Congress Declaration to the Colonial People called for a United Front in the struggle against colonialism. In addition, a memorandum signed by 36 organizations from the Americas, Africa, and Britain was presented to the UNO, calling for adequate representation of coloured people in the organization (Sherwood 1966). According to Shepperson and St. Clare Drake (1986), the conference laid the foundation for independence movements in British Africa.

The key achievement of the pan-African bloc at the United Nations was pushing the General Assembly to adopt Resolution 1514: Declaration on the Granting of Independence to Colonial Countries and Peoples in 1960 (Getachew 2019: 14). This resolution changed the principle of self-determination to a human right and resulted in colonialism's being declared a human right violation and indeed a crime against humanity. However, like all political formations and knowledges emerging from the battlefields of history, pan-Africanism was never a singular movement. Rita Abrahamsen (2019: 1) posited that pan-Africanists were divided into what she termed 'internationalists,' 'sovereigntsists,' and 'nativists,' with resultant diverse visions 'a world of continental unity and transnational solidarity; a world of national sovereignty; and a world of racially defined units.' After 1945, the Bandung spirit of decolonization confronted planetary Cold War coloniality.

Bandung spirit of decolonization in confrontation with Cold War coloniality

George Padmore, in *Pan-Africanism or Communism? The Coming Struggle for Africa* (1956), clearly explained that the decolonial political awakening of Africa and the rest of the Global South was not inspired by communism; he further staked out an autonomous trajectory of decolonization and pan-Africanism within a world that was polarized into communists and capitalists. If anything, decolonization and pan-Africanism were intended to deliver 'Africa for Africans,' in the words of Marcus Garvey. This does not mean that there were no communists and Marxists among the leading anti-colonial nationalists and pan-Africanists. The majority of these people were self-declared Marxists, but they deployed this viewpoint within the remit of decolonization and pan-Africanism. Indeed the Bandung Conference took place in the midst of the Cold War in 1955, but African and Asian leaders continued to push for decolonization rather than communism or capitalism as a vision of liberation. Richard Wright, in his book *The Color Curtain* (1956: 12), underscored the meaning of the Bandung Conference in the following words:

> The despised, the insulted, the hurt, the dispossessed—in short, the underdogs of the human race were meeting. Here were class and racial and religious consciousness on a global scale. Who had thought of organizing such a meeting? And what had these nations in common? Nothing, it seemed to me, but what their past relationship to the Western world had made them feel. This meeting of the rejected was itself a kind of judgment upon the Western world.

But it was the host, President Ahmed Sukarno of Indonesia, who highlighted the importance and purpose of the Bandung Conference in his opening speech:

> This is the first intercontinental conference of colored people in the history of mankind. [...]. Sisters and Brothers, how terrifically dynamic is our time! I recall that, several years ago, I had occasion to make a public analysis of colonialism, and I drew attention to what I called the 'life line of imperialism.' This line runs from Strait of Gibraltar, through the Mediterranean, the Suez Canal, the Red Sea, the Indian Ocean, the South China Sea, the Sea of Japan. For most of that enormous distance, the territories of both sides of the life line were colonies, the peoples were unfree, their futures mortgaged to an alien system. Along that life line, that main artery of imperialism, there was pumped the life-blood of colonialism.
>
> (Quoted in Wright 1956: 136–137)

What is paradigmatic about the Bandung Conference is that it tried to 'unite [not] the workers of the world but the world of people of color' (Mignolo 2014: 27). Even though anti-colonial liberation movements were caught up in 'Cold War coloniality' to the extent of being divided between those who claimed the socialist ideological position and those who adhered to liberal nationalism, they had common roots in resisting colonialism. It would seem that beginning with the Bandung Conference, the anti-colonial movements in Africa and Asia were clear about the Cold War coloniality's snares, and hence they declared that they were for not capitalism or communism but decolonization. It was in the 1950s and 1960s that Aime Cesaire's *Discourse on Colonialism* (1950 [2000]) and Frantz Fanon's *Black Skins, White Masks* (1952 [2008]) and *The Wretched of the Earth* (1968 [2004]) laid down a deeper understanding of the blackness as a predicament in a white world and explained the humanistic aspect of decolonization.

Taken together, the works of Cesaire and Fanon were a radical call for the emergence of a 'new human' which paradigmatically shifted from the established logics and political designs of the Cold War (see Fanon 1968 [2004]). Nelson Maldonado-Torres (2017: 122–123) correctly captured the significance of the interventions of Cesaire and Fanon as marking a shift from the Christian discourse of the chain of being, otherwise known as the 'humanist turn,' to the 'decolonial turn,' which was predicated not only on questioning Euromodernity and challenging Eurocentrism but also on rejecting the imposed inferiority of black colonized peoples and advocating for decolonization as much more than simple attainment of political independence, more along the lines of an avenue for the invention of new humanism (see Maldonado-Torres 2017: 124).

In the decolonial spirit of freeing themselves from the snares of Cold War coloniality, the Asian and African nationalists imbued with the Bandung spirit formed the Non-Aligned Movement (NAM) in 1961 and the Group of 77. These two formations comprised Third World countries and they formed the fulcrum of South-South solidarities. What is clear is that anti-enslavement, anti-imperialism, anti-colonialism, and anti-apartheid all entailed building transnational solidarities between those who have been dehumanized and peripheralized by the Euro-North American-centric world system. After the attainment of 'political independence' those countries that had been subalternized fought to change the Northern-dominated world system. Kevin Gray and Barry K. Gills (2016: 588) noted that:

> While the Bandung and the NAM embodied the political dimensions of an emergent SSC [South-South Cooperation], the Group of 77, named after the number of countries present at the founding of the United Nations Conference on Trade and Development (UNCTAD), called for the establishment of an NIEO.

The 1960s and 1970s were dominated by the Bandung sprit of trying to avoid not only neo-colonialism's interference in the domestic affairs of the 'independent' states but also Cold War coloniality. This involved a push for non-alignment in a world of alignments and East-West divisions. In the economic domain, the spirit of Bandung translated into the struggle for an NIEO that emphasized structural change so as to create a new Global relationship of equality. Resource nationalism entailed guarding the sovereignty of natural resources for the benefit of citizens; this was to be achieved through the nationalization of the economy (Gray and Gills 2016: 558). The overarching decolonization philosophy was for uneven development and underdevelopment to be eradicated, and the vestiges of colonialism, inequality, and poverty in the Global South to be banished, the Global North had to structurally alter its extractive-oriented colonial economies. This spirit is well captured by Gray and Gills (2016: 557):

> Development is a concept that attempts to encompass a vast complexity of processes of social transformation. It conveys meanings of great promise and hope to billions of human beings concerning human betterment, and refers to a long-term historical project of the liberation of peoples and nations from vestiges of colonialism, poverty, oppression and underdevelopment. South–South cooperation (SSC) has been a key organizing concept and a set of practices in pursuit of these historical changes through a vision of mutual benefit and solidarity among the disadvantaged of the world system.

The idea of South-South solidarity also entailed the poor, creating alliances and solidarities of mutual assistance while consistently fighting for structural transformation of the world system, its Global orders, and the world economy. The goal of de-structuring and re-structuring of the economic order was pushed forward through UNCTAD. UNCTAD became a space within which to advocate for the 'adjustment of the international patent system to the developmental needs of the global South' (Gray and Gills 2016: 558).

The late 1970s and 1980s signalled the retreat of South-South initiatives aimed at changing the world economic order. The period witnessed the rise of neoliberalism and the hegemony of the Washington Consensus. New ideas of adjusting not the world economic order but the economies of the powerful countries through what became known as SAPs kicked in. UNCTAD was 'eclipsed by the General Agreement on Tariffs and Trade (GATT), and its successor, the World Trade Organization (WTO)' (Gray and Gills 2016: 588). The emphasis shifted from demands for structural changes to the architecture of the world economy to the issues of technology transfers. However, in Africa, for instance, the spirit of NIEO endured as African leaders adopted the *African Declaration on Cooperation, Development and Economic Independence* in 1973, which articulated Africa's strategy for gradual disengagement from the world economy through an escalation of national and continental self-reliance.

This was followed by *The Revised Framework of the Principles for the Implementation of New International Economic Order in Africa* in 1976. This was produced by the United Nations Economic Commission for Africa (UNECA) and became the intellectual and theoretical foundation for the drafting of the *Monrovia Strategy for the Economic Development of Africa* of 1979. The Monrovia Declaration emphasized the collective self-reliance and economic integration of African economies, investment in science and technology as the backbone of Africa's development process, and a commitment to ensuring Africa's self-reliance in terms of food production and the achievement of modern African economies by the year 2000 (Baah 2003).

The Bandung and NIEO spirits also influenced Africa, in particular, to continue fighting for autonomous development through the formulation of the following economic plans: the *Lagos Plan of Action (1980–2000)*, the *African Priority for Economic Recovery (1986–1990)*, the *African Alternative Framework to Structural Adjustment Programmes for Socio-Economic Recovery and Transformation*, the *African Charter for Popular Participation for Development (1990)*, and the *United Nations New Agenda for the Development of Africa in the 1990s* (Baah 2003). The Nigerian economist Adebayo Adedeji (2002: 4) argued that these initiatives were disciplined by powerful institutions like the World Bank (WB) and International Monetary Fund (IMF) through what he termed the 'Development Merchant System' (DMS), a goal of which was to keep Africa in particular and the Global South in general tied to asymmetrical economic power relations in order to facilitate continued exploitation and underdevelopment.

Within the African context, the Bandung spirit remained embodied in state nationalism. It is yet to expand into what Mireille Fanon Mendès

France called 'a Bandung of the peoples' or what Samir Amin (2008) termed the 'internationalism of the peoples' expressed by the 'Bamako Appeal' of 2006. Its three commitments were: the (i) construction of an internationalism that unites the people of the South and the North who have been ravaged by the dictatorship of financial markets and the uncontrolled Global expansion of transnational corporations; (ii) construction of a solidarity between the people of Asia, Africa, Europe, and the Americas confronted with the challenges of development in the twenty-first century; and (iii) construction of a political, economic, and cultural consensus that is an alternative to neoliberal and militarized globalization, and the hegemony of the United States and its allies (Amin 2008).

What emerges poignantly from the above analysis is that the Bandung spirit of decolonization embodied the progressive nationalism of the twentieth century which anchored NIEO as well as the strategy of 'dewesternization' (see Mignolo 2011) which is related to but different from decoloniality. Dewesternization is a term which refers to the rise of China under Deng Xiaoping and Russia under Vladimir Putin, on the one hand, and the formation of BRICS (Brazil, Russia, India, China, and South Africa), on the other – all of them appropriating 'capitalism to enact divergent politics,' which makes multipolarity possible after 500 years of unipolar Westernization (see Mignolo 2018: 194). It was the Argentinean semiotician and decolonial theorist Walter D. Mignolo (2011) who initially sought to articulate the Bandung Conference of 1955 as the original departure point of decoloniality. Nelson Maldonado-Torres (2019: 2) notes that, more recently, Mignolo connected the Bandung spirit with the idea of dewesternization rather than decoloniality (see Mignolo and Walsh 2018). He posited that dewesternization was the outcome of the Bandung Conference of 1955 and that 'Dewesternization on the contrary activates non-western memories, languages, politics, religion, sensibilities and overall praxis of living that refuse to be submitted to neoliberal westernization' (Mignolo and Walsh 2018: 128). Somehow concurring with Mignolo, Gray and Gills (2016: 588) argued that such formations as BRICS emerged in the context of a 'significant global shift in production and manufacturing from global North to global South, altering the economic geography of the world.' It is in this context that Alice H. Amsden (2001) asserted the 'decline of the West' and the 'rise of the rest.'

What needs to be underscored is that what is presented here as the 'Bandung Spirit of Decolonization' not only pre-dates and post-dates the Bandung Conference of 1955 but also embodies multiple initiatives and a family of thoughts. These threw into the public domain such concepts and initiatives as 'Ethiopianism,' 'Garveyism,' 'Negritude,' 'pan-Africanism,' 'black consciousness movements,' 'dewesternization,' 'delinking,' 'non-alignment,' 'decolonization,' 'decoloniality,' and many others – with others gesturing towards a counter-hegemonic horizon and still others gesturing towards another possible world (Amin 1990; Irele 2010; Ndlovu-Gatsheni 2018). What Maldonado-Torres (2018) mapped out as the 'decolonial turn' is a multifaceted discursive formation embodying multiple initiatives and a family of thoughts (see also Maldonado-Torres 2011). Such leading lights of decolonization of the economy of Africa as Thomas Sankara and such militant anti-colonial revolutionaries as Amilcar Cabral were inspired by both Marxism and the Bandung spirit of decolonization (see Cabral 1973, 1979).

For example, the launch of the BRICS' New Development Bank, announced in July 2014, and the establishment of a Contingency Reserve Arrangement (CRA) indicated the BRICS project's gesture towards a counter to Western economic hegemony. While launching these initiatives, BRICS has also not given up on explicitly pushing for the reform of Global multilateral governance institutions. The Global North is not simply watching these developments unfold. It is engaged in what Mignolo (2011: 36) has termed 'rewesternization':

> Rewesternization touches all the levels of the colonial matrix of power. In the sphere of economy, the task is to 'save capitalism,' to re-imagine the 'future capitalism.' In the sphere of authority, the United States is trying to maintain its leadership in international relations. In the sphere of knowledge, the United States is promoting what the country has done best—science and technology—now clearly oriented towards the corporations, which means knowledge to revamp the economy. [...]. In the sphere of subjectivity, the financial crisis made evident how important it is for the future of capitalism to have 'consumers.'

BRICS is pushing an agenda that is not anti-North but seems to be adopting and adapting to what is useful from the Global North for use in the development of the Global South. Its investment thrust is on infrastructure, energy, and communications – those areas of development that were neglected by donors from the Global North. What is apparent is that the elites from the Global South working through BRICS are not challenging the dominant structures of Global capitalism but, rather, are trying to domesticate and reproduce a working peripheral capitalism for their own benefit in the Global South. This seems to be a different strategy from the strategy of the 1960s and 1970s that imagined a new economic order. In the 1960s and 1970s many (ex-)colonized peoples and states were enchanted by Marxism, and they strongly believed that proletarian revolutions were best positioned to deliver socialism as an alternative to capitalism. This time BRICS is emphasizing 'economic growth, industrialization and financial capacity by many countries across the global South' as part of a move 'on the path to an eventual restructuring of global power relations and the reform of global governance institutions and of the norms and rules of the global economy' (Gray and Gills 2016: 559).

Conclusion

The Bandung spirit of decolonization is one broad encapsulation of a melange of resistances, struggles, solidarities, and initiatives aimed at enabling Africa to turn over a new leaf. Thus, if we say the 'Bandung spirit of decolonization' pre-dates and post-dates the Bandung Conference of 1955, we mean that its logics have a longer genealogy, which goes as far back as the Haitian Revolution of 1791–1804. The Bandung Conference of 1955 was made possible by a long confluence and convergence of multiple initiatives and a family of thought that cut across the lives of those who experienced such dehumanizing and inimical processes as the slave trade, colonialism, dispossession, exploitation, and underdevelopment. It was these people of Asia and Africa who met at Bandung without Europeans or North Americans. Europe and North America were the authors and inventors of the asymmetrically organized modern world, consisting of a centre and periphery, and hence were not yet considered comrades in the decolonial reordering of the world.

The Bandung spirit of decolonization gestured towards a harmonious pluriversal world with everyone at the centre and no peripheries. Europe and North America's adherence to a paradigm of difference automatically excluded them from the Bandung Conference. This was meant to create planetary neighbourliness that Europe and North America had continually destroyed and rejected. While Europe and North America were de-worlding, the 'Bandung spirit of decolonization' was for re-worlding (re-membering) what had been dismembered. Indeed before 1500, that is, before the invention of prison walls called continents and states, the world was limitless without being chaotic. Today, the 'Bandung spirit of decolonization' has successfully unmasked coloniality and is galvanizing the project of construction of the pluriverse (see Mignolo 2018). This pluriverse can only be the result of 'a Bandung of the peoples'/'an international of the peoples.'

References

Abrahamsen, R. 2019. 'Internationalists, Sovereigntists, Nativists: Contending Visions of World Order in Pan-Africanism.' *Review of International Studies*, doi:10.1017/S0260210519000305, pp. 1–19.

Adebajo, A. 2010. *The Curse of Berlin: Africa after the Cold War*. Scottsville: University of KwaZulu-Natal Press.

Adedeji, A. 2002. 'From the Lagos Plan of Action to the New Partnership for African Development and from the Final Act of Lagos to the Constitutive Act: Wither Africa?' (Unpublished Keynote Address delivered at the African Forum for Envisioning Africa, Nairobi, Kenya, 26–29 April).

Amin, S. 1990. *Delinking: Towards a Polycentric World*. London and New York: Zed Books.

Amin, S. 2008. *The World We Wish to See: Revolutionary Objectives in the Twenty-First Century*. New York: Monthly Review Press.

Amin, S. 2010. *Global History: A View from the Global South.* London: Pambazuka Press.

Amsden, A. H. 2001. *The Rise of 'the Rest': Challenges to the West from Late-Industrializing Countries.* Oxford: Oxford University Press.

Baah, A. 2003. 'History of African Development Initiatives.' Paper presented at the African Labour Research Network, Johannesburg, South Africa.

Blaut, J. M. 1993. *The Coloniser's Model of the World: Geographical Diffusionism and Eurocentric History.* New York: The Guilford Press.

Brown, W. 2010. *Walled States, Waning Sovereignty.* New York: Zone Books.

Cabral, A. 1973. *Return to the Source: Selected Speeches by Amilcar Cabral.* New York: Monthly Review Press.

Cabral, A. 1979. *Unity and Struggle: Speeches and Writings by Amilcar Cabral.* New York: Monthly Review Press.

Cesaire, A. 1955/1972 [2000]. *Discourse on Colonialism.* Translated by James Pinkham. New York: Monthly Review Press.

Chinweizu, I. 1975. *The West and the Rest of Us: White Predators, Black Slaves, and the African Elite.* New York: Random House.

Connell, R. 2007. *Southern Theory: The Global Dynamics of Knowledge in Social Science.* Cambridge, MA: Polity Press.

Cooper, F. 1994. 'Conflict and Connection: Rethinking Colonial African History.' *The American Historical Review*, 99(5), pp. 1516–1545.

Du Bois, W. E. B. 1963. 'The Pan-African Movement.' In George Padmore (ed.), *Colonial and Coloured Unity: History of Pan-African Congress.* London: Hammersmith Bookshop, pp. 13–27.

Du Bois, W. E. B. 1965. *The World and Africa.* New York: International Publishers.

Fanon, F. 1968 [2004]. *The Wretched of the Earth.* Translated by Richard Wilcox. New York: Grove Press.

Fanon, F. 1952 [2008]. *Black Skins, White Masks.* Translated by Richard Wilcox. New York: Grove Press.

Frank, A. G. 1998. *RE-ORIENT: Global Economy in the Asian Age.* Berkeley and Los Angeles: University of California Press.

Fukuyama, F. 1992. *The End of History and the Last Man.* New York: Avon Books.

Getachew, A. 2019. *Worldmaking after Empire: The Rise and Fall of Self-Determination.* Princeton, NJ and Oxford: Princeton University Press.

Gibson, C. 2014. *Empire's Crossroads: A History of the Caribbean from Columbus to the Present.* Basingstoke and Oxford: Macmillan.

Gray, K., & Gills, B. K. 2016. 'South-South Cooperation and the Rise of the Global South.' *Third World Quarterly*, 37(4), pp. 557–574.

Grosfoguel, R. 2007. 'The Epistemic Decolonial Turn: Beyond Political-Economy' Paradigms. *Cultural Studies*, 21(2–3), pp. 211–223.

Headley, J. M. 2008. *The Europeanization of the World: On the Origins of Human Rights and Democracy.* Princeton, NJ and Oxford: Princeton University Press.

Hobson, J. M. 2012. *The Eurocentric Conception of World Politics: Western Theory, 1760–2010.* Cambridge: Cambridge University Press.

Irele, A. 2010. *The Negritude Moment: Explorations in Francophone African and Caribbean Literature and Thought.* Trenton, NJ: Africa World Press.

James, C. L. R. 1938 [1963]. *The Black Jacobins: Toussaint L'Ouverture and the San Domingo Revolution.* New York: Random House.

James, C. L. R. 1982. *The Black Jacobins: Toussaint L'Ouverture and the San Domingo Revolution.* New York: Vintage Press.

Lowe, L. 2006. 'The Intimacies of Four Continents.' In Ann Laura Stoler (ed.), *Haunted by Empire: Geographies of Intimacy in North American History.* Durham, NC and London: Duke University Press, pp. 191–211.

Lugones, M. 2003. *Pilgrimages/Peregrinajes: Theorizing Coalition against Multiple Oppressions.* Lanham, MD: Rowman & Littlefield Publishers, Inc.

Maldonado-Torres, N. 2007. 'On Coloniality of Being: Contributions to the Development of a Concept.' *Cultural Studies*, 21(2–3), pp. 240–270.

Maldonado-Torres, N. 2011. 'Thinking through the Decolonial Turn: Post-Continental Interventions in Theory, Philosophy and Critique—An Introduction.' *Transmodernity: Journal of Peripheral Cultural Production of the Luso-Hispanic World*, 1(2), pp. 1–15.

Maldonado-Torres, N. 2017. 'On the Coloniality of Human Rights.' *Revista Critica de Ciencias Socials*, 144 (Decembro), 117–136.

Maldonado-Torres, N. 2018. 'The Decolonial Turn.' In Juan Poblete (ed.), *New Approaches to Latin American Studies: Culture and Power.* New York and London: Routledge, pp. 111–127.

Maldonado-Torres, N. 2019. 'Frantz Fanon, Decoloniality, and the Spirit of Bandung [in Korean translation].' *Journal of Global World Literature*, 13(9), pp. 236–252.

Mbembe, A. 2000. *On the Postcolony.* Berkeley: University of California Press.

Mignolo, W. D. 2000. *Local Histories/Global Designs: Coloniality, Subaltern Knowledges, and Border Thinking.* Princeton, NJ: Princeton University Press.

Mignolo, W. D. 2011. *The Darker Side of Western Modernity: Global Futures, Decolonial Options.* Durham, NC and London: Duke University Press.

Mignolo, W. D. 2014a. 'Further Thoughts on (De)Coloniality.' In S. Broeck and C. Junker (eds.), *Postcoloniality-Decoloniality-Black Critique.* Frankfurt and New York: Campus Verlag, pp. 21–51.

Mignolo, W. D. 2014b. 'The North of the South and the West of the East: A Provocation to the Question.' Available: www.ibraaz.org/essays/108 (accessed 21/12/2019).

Mignolo, W. D. 2015. 'Foreword: Yes, We Can.' In H. Dabashi (ed.), *Can Non-Europeans Think*? London and New York: Zed Books, pp. viii–vlii.

Mignolo, W. D. 2018. 'On Pluriversality and Multipolar World Order: Decoloniality after Decolonization; Dewesternization after the Cold War.' In Bernd Reiter (ed.), *Constructing the Pluriverse: The Geopolitics of Knowledge.* Durham, NC and London: Duke University Press, pp. 90–116.

Mignolo, W. D., & Walsh, C. E. 2018. *On Decoloniality: Concepts, Analytics, Praxis.* Durham, NC and London: Duke University Press.

Ndlovu-Gatsheni, S. J. 2013a. *Empire, Global Coloniality and African Subjectivity.* Oxford and New York: Berghahn Books.

Ndlovu-Gatsheni, S. J. 2013b. *Coloniality of Power in Postcolonial Africa: Myths of Decolonization.* Dakar: CODESRIA Books.

Ndlovu-Gatsheni, S. J. 2013c. 'The Entrapment of Africa within the Global Matrices of Power: Eurocentricism, Coloniality, and Deimperialization in the Twenty-First Century.' *Journal of Developing Societies*, 29(4), pp. 331–353.

Ndlovu-Gatsheni, S. J. 2015. 'Genealogies of Coloniality and Implications for Africa's Development.' *Africa Development*, XL(3), pp. 13–40.

Ndlovu-Gatsheni, S. J. 2018. *Epistemic Freedom in Africa: Deprovincialization and Decolonization.* New York and London: Routledge.

Nkrumah, K. 1965. *Neo-Colonialism: The Last Stage of Imperialism.* London: Thomas Nelson and Sons Ltd.

Nowell, C. E. 1953. 'The Historical Prester John.' *Speculum: A Journal of Mediaeval Studies,* XXVIII(3), pp. 435–445.

Padmore, G. 1956 [1971]. *Pan-Africanism or Communism? The Coming Struggle for Africa.* New York: Doubleday.

Persaud, R. B. 2016. 'The Racial Dynamic in International Relations: Some Thoughts on the Pan-African Antecedents of Bandung.' In Q, N. Pham and R. Shillian (eds.), *Meanings of Bandung: Postcolonial Orders and Decolonial Visions.* London and New York: Rowman & Little Field International, pp. 133–142.

Pham, Q. N., & Shillian, R. (eds.). 2016. *Meanings of Bandung: Postcolonial Orders and Decolonial Visions.* London and New York: Rowman & Little Field International.

Quijano, A. 2000. 'The Coloniality of Power and Social Classification.' *Journal of World Systems,* 6(2) (Summer-Fall), pp. 533–579.

Robinson, C. J. 1983. *Black Marxism: The Making of the Black Radical Tradition.* London: Zed Books.

Rodney, W. 1972. *How Europe Underdeveloped Africa.* London and Dar es Salaam: Bogle-L'Ouverture Publications.

Rodney, W. 1975. 'Aspects of the International Class Struggle in Africa the Caribbean and the Americas.' In Horace Campbell (ed.), *Pan-Africanism: Struggle against Neo-Colonialism and Imperialism: Documents of the Sixth Pan-Africa Congress.* Toronto: Afro-Carib Publications, pp. 18–41.

Santos, B. de S. 2014. *Epistemologies of the South: Justice against Epistemicide.* Boulder, CO and London: Paradigm Publishers.

Santos, B. de S. 2018. *The End of the Cognitive Empire: The Coming of Age of Epistemologies of the South.* Durham, NC and London: Duke University Press.

Schmitt, C. 1950 [2003]. *The Nomos of the Earth: In the International Law of the Jus Publicum Europaeum.* Translated by G. L. Ulmen. New York: Telos Press Publishing.

Shepperson, G., & Drake, S. C. 1986. 'The Fifth Pan-African Conference, 1945 and the All-African People's Congress, 1958.' *A Journal of African and Afro-American Studies,* 8(5), 35–66.

Sherwood, M. 1966. 'There Is No New Deal for Blackman in San Francisco': African Attempts to Influence the Founding Conference of the United Nations, April–July 1945.' *The International Journal of African Historical Studies,* 29(1), pp. 71–94.

Terreblanche, S. 2014. *Western Empires, Christianity, and the Inequalities between the West and the Rest, 1500–2010.* Johannesburg: Penguin.

Trouillot, M.-R. 1995. *Silencing the Past: Power and the Production of History.* Boston, MA: Beacon Press.

Wright, R. 1956. *The Color Curtain: A Report on the Bandung Conference.* New York: World Publishing.

4 The problem of blackness

Introduction

The subject of identity exists as a conceptual migraine. It is a powerful idea which always becomes a fact through processes of social engineering, construction, and reconstruction. Thus, the problem of blackness initially emerged as an invention within the politics governing what it means to be a human being. It is an existential question. It is a problem created by racism. Blackness is best understood as a problematic state of being. When it mutated into an identity, it became part of the assertion of humanity by those denied it as well as a decolonial declaration: 'I am a human being.' This declaration only makes sense and only becomes necessary within the context of an anti-black, white-dominated modern world where being black is invented as a sign of sub-humanness.

This chapter maps the state of knowledge in the field of identity, with a focus on race, and grapples with the complex genealogies of the politics of the invention of non-beings and their symbolization by blackness on a world scale. Such complex and brutal global technologies of dismemberment as Hellenocentrism, Eurocentrism, genocides, epistemicides, linguicides as well as infantilization, inferiorization, dehumanization, feminization, conquest, dispossession, peasantization, and proleterianization are examined. The chapter proceeds to document the equally complex politics of turning over a new leaf for Africa via the initiative of 're-memberment,' constitutive of what Nelson Maldonado-Torres (2008a) termed the 'Third Humanist Revolution.' This 'revolution' 'has existed alongside the Renaissance and the Enlightenment, always pointing to their constitutive exclusions and aiming to provide a more consistent narrative of the affirmation of the value of the entire human species' (Maldonado-Torres 2008a: 115). Turning over of a new leaf in the domain of complex identity politics means recapturing the agency and African genius of self-definition.

Mapping the minefield of identity (race)

In 2016, the celebrated novelist Toni Morrison delivered a series of important and illuminating lectures at Harvard University in the USA. The overarching theme of these lectures was in general identity and in particular the subject of race, which has haunted the modern world since its birth in 1492. Morrison's lectures were published under the title *The Origins of Others* (2017). She covered the six overlapping issues of slavery, being, 'becoming a stranger,' 'configurations of Blackness,' 'narrating the other,' and 'the foreigner's home.' Her key thesis is that

> The necessity of rendering the slave a foreign species appears to be a desperate attempt to confirm one's own self as normal. The urgency of distinguishing between those who belong to the human race and those who are decidedly non-human is so powerful the spotlight turns away and shines not on the object of degradation but on its creator.
>
> (Morrison quoted in a foreword by Coates 2017: xiii)

Morrison nailed it here. She elaborated that 'Race has been a constant arbiter of difference, as have wealth, class, and gender—each of which is about power and the necessity of control' (Morrison 2017: 3). With specific reference to the subject of 'Blackness,' she (2017: 55) also posited that:

> The definitions of 'black' and descriptions of what blackness means are so varied and loaded with slippery science and invention that it may be interesting, if not definitively clarifying, to examine the term's configurations and the literary uses to which they are put as well as the activity they inspire—both violent and constructive.

Earlier on, Lewis R. Gordon, in *Bad Faith and Antiblack Racism* (1999), had also delved into the contentious subject of racism and the dehumanizing condition of blackness. He stated that the very 'study of racism is dirty business' because 'It unveils things about ourselves that we prefer not to know' (Gordon 1999: ix). With specific reference to anti-black racism, Gordon (1999: 1), like Achille Mbembe (2017), posited that it 'may embody the extreme poles of the possibility of a universal human kind' since 'it wrenches human beings into the most extreme visual metaphors of difference.' Gordon (1999: 2) defined racism as 'the self deceiving choice to believe either that one's race is the only race qualified to be considered human or that one's race is superior to others.' More importantly he (1999: 8) introduced the powerful concept of 'bad faith,' which he defined as 'the effort to hide from responsibility for ourselves as freedom,' which involves seeking to 'flee a displeasing truth for a pleasing falsehood.' The very history of the social classification of the human population and racial hierarchization is saturated with and sedimented by 'bad faith.' Thus, Gordon (1999) made a correct intervention by examining how Europeans used 'bad faith' in their construction of some people as black and therefore fundamentally inferior and sub-human. Unmasking 'bad faith' offers a constant possibility of human coexistence and freedom.

In the same year (2016) that Morrison delivered her lectures at Harvard University, Kwame Anthony Appiah, a leading African philosopher, delivered the Annual Reith Lectures under the overarching title *Mistaken Identities: Creed, Country, Colour, Culture*. The lectures were later published under the title *The Lies that Bind: Rethinking Identity: Creed, Country, Colour, Class, Culture* (2018), in which Appiah grappled with some of the most tormenting identitarian questions: who am I? How did I become who I am? To whom am I connected or disconnected? Who do you think you are? What do you think you are? He set out to make sense of such vectors of identity and filiations of self as gender, religion, race, nationality, class, and culture – which he contended were, on the one hand, 'multiple systems of classification human beings employ' and, on the other, largely 'lies that bind' humans (Appiah 2018: xiv). Appiah's (xvi) thesis is that:

> There is no dispensing with identities, but we need to understand them better if we can hope to reconfigure them, and free ourselves from mistakes about them that are often a couple of hundred years old. Much of what is dangerous about them has to do with the way identities—religion, nation, race, class, and culture—divide us and set us against one another. They can be the enemies of human solidarity, the sources of war, horsemen of a score of apocalypses from apartheid to genocide. Yet these errors are also central to the way identities unite us today. We need to reform them because, at their best, they make it possible for groups, large and small, to do things together. They are lies that bind.

In his edited volume *Nations, Identities, Culture* (1997: 3), Valentin Y. Mudimbe demonstrates in a rather Eurocentric way the recentness of some of the strong identities and the historical events that animated them:

> One could hypothesize that the French Revolution initiated a representation of the *political society* as essentially *national*, and thus the promotion of the concept of *nationality*. Next, the October Revolution in Russia articulated a new conception of the political society as essentially a *class society*, thus the promotion of the concept of *class*. Finally, the recent implosion of the Soviet bloc was paralleled by a representation of the political society as *civil society*.
>
> (Emphasis is in the original text)

Mudimbe is well aware that the filiations (which he termed the 'three paradigms') of nation, class, and civil society pre-dated the nineteenth century, and he argued that 'they became indispensable then for the description and management of the state and its secularised society' (Mudimbe 1997: 3). Achille Mbembe's *Critique of Black Reason* (2017) directly addresses the complex subject of blackness from the vantage point of the epistemology and sociology of black identity as well as the concerns with human future. His entry point is the issue of racism as 'the delirium produced by modernity' (Mbembe 2017: 2). Mbembe identified 'three critical moments in the biography of the vertiginous assemblage that is Blackness and race,' including (1) the Atlantic slave trade (fifteenth through nineteenth centuries); (2) the birth of black writings demanding 'the status of full subjects in the world of the living' in the eighteenth century; and (3) 'the globalization of markets, the privatization of the world under the aegis of neoliberalism,' together with the proliferation of electronic and digital technologies (Mbembe 2017: 3).

Mbembe agrees with Morrison that 'Blackness' is a product and a sign of dehumanization under the conditions of modernity and its transnationalization through imperialism and colonialism. What is worrying in Mbembe's (2017: 27) analysis is his somehow disdainful understanding of what he terms 'black reason,' to the extent of defining it as consisting of 'a collection of voices, pronouncements, discourses, forms of knowledge, commentary, and nonsense, whose object is things or people "of African origin"' and underplaying the fact that these are thoughts, writings, and texts produced in the battlefield of history, written in tears and blood, and indeed artefacts of epic decolonial struggles (see Robinson 1983; el-Malik and Kamola 2017; Dabashi 2019).

From the broader problem of blackness emerged the equally problematic question of Africanness. Edward Wilmot Blyden's *Christianity, Islam and the Negro Race* (1888), Kwame Nkrumah's *Consciencism: Philosophy and Ideology for Decolonization and Development with Particular Reference to the African Revolution* (1964), Ali A. Mazrui's *The Africans: A Triple Heritage* (1986), Mudimbe's twin volumes *The Invention of Africa: Gnosis, Philosophy and the Order of Knowledge* (1988) and *The Idea of Africa* (1994), and Charles Ngwena's *What is Africanness? Contesting Nativism in Race, Culture and Sexualities* (2018) are a good sample of the literature on the vexing questions of the idea of Africa and the definitions of Africanness as subtexts of the broader problem of blackness on a world scale. What emerges from this body of knowledge is Africa as an idea imposed by external forces of imperialism and colonialism, Africa as an African idea born out of resistance, Africa as a product of the tyranny of modern cartography, Africa as a 'triple heritage,' and many other articulations (see Zeleza 2006). Emma Hunter, in *Citizenship, Belonging, and Political Community in Africa: Dialogues Between Past and Present* (2016), and Toyin Falola and Aribidesi Usman, in *Movements, Borders, and Identity in Africa* (2009), demonstrate empirically that at the centre of the struggles and debates about the problem of blackness and the meaning of Africanness are the key existential issues of being human, citizenship, belonging, rights, dignity, privileges, movement, and indeed life itself.

For Kehinde Andrews in *Back to Black: Black Radicalism in the 21st Century* (2018: 284), 'Blackness is essential as a concept because it can be nothing other than political.' Thus, claiming Blackness is part of the commitment to revolutionary politics. Andrews (2018: 284) elaborated that 'Black is not negative. It is taking on the words of the oppressor. It is not to be racialised.' Rather:

> Embracing Blackness means uniting around not only our oppression but also our connection via Africa. It means taking on the responsibility for all those in the global African nation. Blackness is a choice, a commitment to the 'dead and unborn' to engage in a politics of true liberation. Black is crucially different to African in this regard. Black is politics, Africa is place.
>
> (Andrews 2018: 285)

Within the broader strategic identity of Blackness exist other issues of class, gender, and sexuality. This is why Andrews (2018: 286) posited that 'You do not escape the oppression that comes from being Black because you are a woman or queer.' What is important to understand is the complex processes of dismemberment which gave rise to Blackness and the politics of black radicalism which connects the present struggles of Rhodes Must Fall in South Africa and Black Lives Matter in the USA to the long history of black freedom movements.

Dismemberment and the colonial death project

What can be rendered as 'Blackism' on a world scale captures the ontological split created by the imperial racist paradigm of difference. At the centre of contemporary debates on blackness are two opposing imperatives: namely the 'dismemberment' fuelled by the 'will to power' and the 're-membering' informed by resistance and liberatory politics. What further complicates the divide between the 'dismemberment' and the 're-membering' is a resilient but invented ontological split that gave birth to blackness on a world scale on the one side and whiteness on a world scale on the other. As understood by the Portuguese sociologist and decolonial theorist Boaventura de Sousa Santos (2007), what divides the invented world of blacks and whites is an 'abyssal thinking' mediated by race (the colour line). The long-term consequences of this invented ontological split have come back to haunt the contemporary modern world with virulence, challenging the logics of an imagined postraciality that was said to have emerged with the election of Barack Obama in 2008 as the first black president of the USA (Goldberg 2015).

This racist configuration of the world is the fuel and justification for the 'dismemberment.' Racism is anti-human. It is opposed to the existence of a genuine 'postcolonial' world. It works against struggles aimed at pushing for the 'will to live' and making of new and genuine postracial humanism. Invisible racism continues to underpin a modern world that is comfortable with the production and reproduction of coloniality long after the dismantling of direct colonialism. Consequently, the invented ontological split created by racism continues to sustain whitism on a world scale in a hegemonic position and blackism on a world scale in a subaltern state of dehumanization. The invention of blackism in particular threw all those who were designated as non-white into a problematic 'liminal state of being' characterized by a perpetual feeling of being incomplete or a never-ending state of 'becoming' human (Ndlovu-Gatsheni 2013a, 2013b). Philosophically speaking, liminal identity constitutes a long, unending transitional state of being – located between dismemberment (separation/fragmentation/denial of humanity) and re-membering (reaggregation/wholeness/unity/re-gaining of denied humanity). Liminality is therefore a state of ontological limbo framed by what William E. B. Du Bois (1903) termed the 'colour line.'

The leading philosopher of black existentialism, Lewis R. Gordon (2009), building on the work of Du Bois, articulated blackism on a world scale as that of existing as a problem to be eliminated or solved rather than as a self-defining human being with a voice to be heard. What is understood as 'postcolonial' politics is characterized by various initiatives aimed at 'casting light at last onto subjugated peoples, knowledges, histories and ways of living' in such a way that it 'unsettles the toxic pond' of racism, ring-fenced by visible and invisible Eurocentrism (Hoppers and Richards 2012: 8). The invention of blackism on a world scale led to the 'museumization' of all those designated as black.

Blackism on a world scale is understood at two broad levels in this chapter. The first level is that of 'dismemberment,' that is, the process of ontological splitting that pushes all those designated as black out of the human family (Maldonado-Torres 2007; Ndlovu-Gatsheni 2015). This ontological splitting of humanity lies at the foundation of the Euro-North American-centric modern world. Race worked and continues to work as an organizing principle. The fossilization, unfolding, and expansion of Euro-North American-centric modernity took the form of what Valentin Y. Mudimbe (1994: xii) described as the submission of the world to European memory through exploration, surveying, 'discovering,' mapping, conquest, colonization, naming, dispossession, and claims of ownership of everything in the modern world. On one end was a self-defining Cartesian subjectivity, claimed and monopolized by the emerging European male bourgeois. Mobilizing and deploying unfounded claims of scientific racism, the early European philosophers and scientists justified naturalizing and routinizing the Cartesian self-definition of European subjectivity. At the other end was invented blackness as a sign and symbol of incomplete and disabled humanity (Ndlovu-Gatsheni 2013a, 2013b).

Blackism on a world scale emerged at a time when continents were being invented not only through cartography but through the spreading of the exploitative and inhuman capitalist economic system across the human globe and the nascent unfolding of a global colonial division of labour. How the invention of blackism on a world scale was inextricably intertwined with the unfolding of the capitalist economic system is articulated by C. L. R James (1982), who argued that the eighteenth century slave-society in San

Domingo (later Haiti) connected Europe, Africa, and the Americas as the wealth generated through slavery in the Americas resulted in the rise of the capitalist bourgeoisie in Europe as well as a new civilization underpinned by a capitalist world economy. The abolition of the slave trade was succeeded by the invention of indentured labour as a new form of enslavement, this time bringing Indians and the Chinese into the nexus of evolving capitalist Euro-North American centric and modernist civilization. Building on this background, it becomes clear that blackism on a world scale, materially speaking, articulates the global emergence not only of 'a modern racial division of labour' but also of a new world social order underpinned by racial hierarchization and the social classification of human species in accordance with race as an organizing principle (Lowe 2006: 192–193).

Enrique Dussel, in *Politics of Liberation: A Critical World History* (2011), identified six interrelated discursive and instrumental technologies of dismemberment. These are Hellenocentrism, Westernization, Eurocentrism, Secularism, Periodization, and Colonialism (Dussel 2011: xv–xviii). Hellenocentrism is not only based in an invented myth of the foundation of Europe but also the progenitor of what James Blaut (1993) termed 'the colonizer's model of the world.' Its declaration, according to Dussel (2011: xv), is simply that 'All start in Greece.' Hellenocentrism is a central leitmotif of usurpation, if not outright the beginning of what the anthropologist Jack Goody (1996) described as a 'theft of history' by Europe. Hellenocentrism gave birth to Eurocentrism and Westernization as part of the consolidation of the projection of Europe as the centre of the world.

Taken together, Hellenocentrism, Eurocentrism, and Westernization amounted to what David Marriott (2012) termed 'inventions of existence,' with Europe playing the role of a 'discoverer' of other human species – almost claiming the place of the 'Creator'/God. Such historians as John M. Headley have been intellectually blinded by the unfounded claims of Hellenocentrism, Westernization, and Eurocentrism, to the extent of writing a book revealingly entitled *The Europeanization of the World* (2008). This book valorizes Europe as the progenitor of the values of humanism, democracy, and human rights. The consequence of this enchantment by Hellenocentrism, Westernization, and Eurocentrism is clearly exemplified by Headley's unproblematic acceptance of the imperial and colonial 'paradigm of discovery' as laying the basis for common humanity rather than coloniality.

Headley's defence of Westernization and its so-called unique gifts reveals his obliviousness to coloniality – particularly how the unfolding of a Euro-North American-centric modernity unleashed mercantilism, enslavement of black people, and colonialism, and how it was predicated on racial hierarchization of the human species for the purposes of the exclusion of some from the common human race. Decolonially speaking, human rights are not derived from the European Renaissance, natural law, or Protestant Reformation. Rather they are products of resistances and struggles of those who were written out of the human ecumene. The Haitian Revolution, rather than the Renaissance and Protestant Reformation, or even the French and American Revolutions, constitutes a better base for human rights because at the centre of the struggle is those whose humanity was denied, proclaiming their humanity to the world. So to argue, as Headley does, that no other civilization in human history has bequeathed so sustained a tradition of universalizing aspirations as Western civilization is to ignore two issues. The first is that modern Western civilization has been predicated on a paradigm of difference that systematically denied the humanity of non-European people across the globe (Ndlovu-Gatsheni 2016). The second is that modern Western civilization has been predicated on a paradigm of war and a fetishized notion of politics as the 'will to power' rather than the 'will to live' (Dussel 2008). These dehumanizing constitutive elements of Western civilization and its method of spreading across the world through conquest, enslavement, colonizing, exploiting, and racially hierachizing the human species led Aime Cesaire (2000: 31–32) to describe it as a decadent, sick and deceitful, and indefensible civilization.

The very act of stealing history and denying others their humanity is the highest form of barbarism. Eurocentric secularism became predicated on imperial reason and what Lewis R. Gordon (1999) articulated as 'bad faith.' Bad faith refers to the politics of endlessly proclaiming tenets of humanity at the level of rhetoric while practically killing humanity itself everywhere. Bad faith is claiming humanity for a particular race and denying it from all other human species. Bad faith reveals itself in attempts to mobilize secularism and Eurocentric science to justify coloniality of being. It is to try to use secularism and science to steal the place of God. Eurocentrism is itself a form of arrogance founded on ignorance (arrogance of ignorance). It is founded on another problematic concept that Dussel (2011: xvi) terms 'periodization,' in which human history is cut into a linear chronology of 'Ancient, Middle and Modern Ages.' In this periodization, all other civilizations are dismembered and pushed into the category 'Ancient,' and Europe claims the category 'Modern.' This is part of the broader technology of dismemberment, called 'theft of history' through the 'colonization of time itself.' Colonization, in its theoretical, intellectual, political, social, cultural, and economic constitutive character, has mutated and metamorphosed into a global coloniality underpinned by invented asymmetrical power relations, hegemonic knowledge, and particular articulations of human ontology based on race.

What has emerged from all this is the foundational dismemberment of black people, taking the form of a denial of their very humanity. For example, Christopher Columbus's question of whether the natives of Latin America had 'souls' sparked the historic Valladolid Debates (1550–1551), in which Bartolome de La Casas and Gines De Sepulveda argued the ontological question of the humanity of the natives. This debate became illustrative of the genesis of the 'colonial death project' that eventually engulfed Asia, Africa, and the rest of the colonized world (Castro 2007). Julia Suarez-Krabbe (2016: 3) defined the 'death project' as a reference 'to the exercise of violence in coloniality, which targets the actual processes of life and the conditions for existence: in short, polarity.' At the centre of the death project is what Achille Mbembe (2003: 11) termed 'necropolitics' and what Maldonado-Torres (2008b: 4) understood as the 'ethics of war.' Taken together and in combination these two strategies of the 'death project' distinguished those who 'may live' from those 'who must die.' Outright denial or questioning of the humanity of non-European people was a deliberate effort to enable the 'death project' of coloniality. When it became increasingly difficult to outright deny the humanity of non-Europeans, there was a shift to the imperial/colonial logic of the racial hierarchization and social classification of the human species in accordance with assumed and invented differential ontological densities. In this scheme of things, those people with black pigmentation were pushed to the lowest echelons of the invented pyramid of the human species.

Ramon Grosfoguel (2013), building on the expansive work of the Argentinean philosopher, historian, and theologian Enrique Dussel, identified what he termed the 'four genocides/epistemicides of the long 16th century,' which are foundational to the politics of dismemberment and the modern colonial death project. These include the conquest of Al-Andalus, the enslavement of Africans in the Americas, the killing in Europe of millions of women accused of being witches, and the extermination of natives of Latin America (Grosfoguel 2013: 74). The conquest of Al-Andalus in 1492 targeted Muslims and Jews, and was propelled by the logic of 'purity of blood' as a form of dismemberment. At this time colour was not yet used as a criteria of exclusion. Purity of blood and religion were the key technologies of dismemberment. Here lies the origination of the fundamentalist ideas of 'one identity, one political authority, and one religion' (Suárez-Krabbe 2016: 54).

The next groups to experience dismemberment, this time taking the form of physical extermination (genocide/ethnocide), were the indigenous peoples of the Americas, Caribbean, Asia, and Africa as well as the Roma/'Gypsies.' The black people of Africa experienced not only genocides but, more specifically, enslavement, with what became known as the 'transatlantic slave trade' naturalizing 'the colonial criteria of inferiority, linking racism and capitalism' (Suárez-Krabbe 2016: 56). Du Bois traces the genealogy of the terms 'Negro' and 'black' as racially inferiorizing categories to this time of the enslavement of black people and their shipment as cargo across the Atlantic Ocean to the Americas. He argued that:

> The word 'Negro' was used for the first time in world history to tie colour to race and blackness to slavery and degradation. The white race was pictured as 'pure' and superior; and the black race as dirty, stupid, and inevitably inferior; the yellow race as sharing, in deception and cowardice, much of this colour inferiority. Mixture of races was considered the prime cause of degradation and failure of civilization.
>
> (Du Bois 1965: 20)

It is important here to understand the European conception of being and its shifting meanings and articulations. Maldonado-Torres (2017: 119) provided an impressive summary of the 'great chain of being,' ranging from Pico's 'Oration' to the 'Universal Declaration of Human Rights.' In between were such interventions as 'meditations,' 'treatise,' 'discourse,' and 'essay,' all aimed at defining and explaining being human (inaugurating the humanist turn). African people were always dismissed as not human. One of the ironies of the shifting European discourses of the human is that when they eventually partially and sceptically acknowledged the native people of America's humanity, still maintaining that they were inferior, they did so at the expense of the black people who were being shipped from Africa to the Americas. Sylvia Wynter (2003: 297) correctly captured what the enslavement of black people created: 'a model for the invention of a by-nature difference between "natural masters" and "natural slaves."' When the abolition of the slave trade came, it was replaced by indentured labour that brought Chinese people and Indians into the nexus of a new form of enslavement. The historian Moon-Ho Jung (cited in Lowe 2006: 202) correctly observed that the indentured labour of Chinese people and Indians constituted 'a transitional figure, mid-way between slavery and free labour, used both to define and to obscure the boundary between enslavement and freedom.'

With specific reference to Africa, Ngugi wa Thiongo (2009a: 5) argued that the 'dismemberment' of Africa unfolded in two stages. The first stage is traceable to the enslavement of black people and their shipment as 'cargo' across the Atlantic to the Americas and the Caribbean. The second form took place at the Berlin Conference of 1884–1885, taking the literal form of the fragmenting and reconstitution of 'Africa into British, French, Portuguese, German, Belgian, and Spanish Africa' (Ngugi wa Thiong'o 2009a: 5). Ngugi wa Thiong'o further argues that those black people who were physically removed from the continent experienced 'an additional dismemberment' in the form of separation 'not only from his[/her] continent and his[/her] labour but also from his[/her] very sovereign being' (Ngugi wa Thiong'o 2009a: 6). Those who remained on the continent experienced the 'scramble' for and 'partition' of Africa, and were thus subjected to further 'dismemberment' in the form of dispossession of land: 'The land is taken away from its owner, and the owner is turned into a worker on the same land, thus losing control of his natural and human resources' (Ngugi wa Thiong'o 2009a: 6).

The school, the church, and the university play an active role in the colonial and even 'postcolonial' process of 'dismemberment.' This is so because 'Cultural subjugation was a necessary condition for economic and political mastery' (Ngugi wa Thiong'o 1997: 9). Colonial education is identified by Ngugi wa Thiong'o as the most important force for 'dismemberment' and alienation because it invades and takes control of the mental universe in order to produce a distorted consciousness among the colonized (Ngugi wa

Thiong'o 2012: 28). Highlighting the alienating consequences of the colonial process in general, Ngugi wa Thiong'o posited that:

> The colonial process dislocates the traveller's mind from the place he or she already knows to a foreign starting point even with the body still remaining in his or her homeland. It is a continuous alienation from the base, a continuous process of looking at oneself from the outside of self or with the lenses of a stranger. One may end up identifying with the foreign base as the starting point toward self, that is from another self towards one-self, rather than the local being the starting point, from self to other selves.
>
> (Ngugi wa Thiong'o 2012: 39)

In summary, one can identify six forms of 'dismemberment.' The first is what I have termed 'foundational dismemberment,' involving the questioning of the very humanity of black people as well as the invention of blackness (Ndlovu-Gatsheni 2015; Ndlovu-Gatsheni and Zondi 2016: 5). The second is enslavement is that which resulted not only in the reduction of black African people into a commodity but also in the fragmentation of African personhood into continental and Diasporic people The third is the scramble and partition of Africa that took place in Berlin, resulting in not only the fragmentation of the continent into various colonies but also the invention of contending ethnicities enclosed within colonially crafted boundaries or forms of colonial encirclement. The fourth is the theft/usurpation/erasure/silencing of African history so as to deny its existence and hereby establish the Hegelian notion of a people without a history and a continent of darkness and emptiness. The fifth is the production and reproduction of dismemberment by the 'postcolonial' state under the leadership of a colonially produced black bourgeoisie who are trapped in neo-colonialism/coloniality.

The final form is the continuation of the perpetration of patriarchy in order to dismember women from power, knowledge, and being itself. The gender line of exclusion, oppression, and dehumanization is often treated tangentially as though it is not an important part of dismemberment. In *Liminal Subjects: Weaving (Our) Liberation* (2018) Sara C. Motta directly delves into and articulates the complexities and depths of the wounding enacted by patriarchal capitalist coloniality. This is how she explained the dehumanization of Black, indigenous, and Mestiza women:

> She becomes subject to both negation as a rational and knowing subject and thus invisible, at the same time she is hyper-visible as the sexualized temptress who is legitimately raped in order to domesticate her, and ensure the assimilation of the colonized through reproduction of mestizo child.
>
> (Motta 2018: 6)

Angela Davis (1972) also explained how black women were denied the identity of 'woman' in these revealing words: she is 'simultaneously annulled from the category of woman, released from the myth of femininity' and 'violently coerced into taking up the gendering function from which she has been barred' (quoted in Motta 2018: 6). These interventions resonate with those of Maria Lugones, discussed in Chapter 2 of this book.

What clearly emerges is that in the social classification, racial hierarchization, and engendering of human population, black women, indigenous women, and Mestiza women undergo animalization. This became possible after colonized indigenous people's worlds had been destroyed. Oyewumi Oyeronke convincingly argued in *The Invention of Women: Making an African Sense of Western Gender Discourses* (1997) that in pre-colonial societies like that of the Yoruba in Nigeria gender was not the organizing principle of society. What exacerbates the gender line is that once it had been invented, it became naturalized and routinized, to the extent that even African governments have continued to reproduce it under the guises of restoration of African tradition and indigenous ideologies of authenticity. The consequences are that such inimical cultures and practices patriarchy, misogyny, and hyper-masculinity – which are not conducive for women's freedom and flourishing are embraced.

At the centre of each of these forms of 'dismemberment' are clear technologies of the colonial 'death project': namely genocides (physical killing of colonized peoples and black peoples in general, even after the so-called end of enslavement and colonialism: for example, the rising number of cases of white police shooting black Americans); epistemicides (killing and appropriations of the knowledges of the colonized); and linguicides (killing of the languages and cultures of the colonized) (Ndlovu-Gatsheni 2015). Achille Mbembe provides us with another technology of the colonial 'death project' known as 'conversion.' He argues that:

> [T]he act of conversion is also involved in the destruction of worlds. To convert the other is to incite him or her to give up what she or he believed. Theoretically, the passage from one belief system to another ought to entail the submission of the convert to the institution and the authority in charge of proclaiming the new belief. [...]. A test or ordeal of defamiliarization and disorientation, conversion distances the convert from family, relatives, language, customs, even from geographical environment and social contacts—that is, from various forms of inscription in a genealogy and an imaginary. This distancing is supposed to allow the neophyte to situate himself or herself within an absolutely different horizon—a horizon that paganism, in its horror, can no longer attain or recuperate.
>
> (Mbembe 2001: 228–229)

Since Euro-North American-centric modernity unfolded as a combination of enslavement, genocides, conquest, colonization, epistemicides conversion, and linguicides, the major challenge facing 'ex-colonized' people is how to 'recuperate.' This difficult and complex process of recuperation is called 're-membering.'

Re-membering/re-humanization

What is also clear is that from the very beginning of the construction of the modern Euro-North American-centric world system and its global orders, imperial technologies of dismemberment always locked horns with resistant forces of re-membering. Therefore, the concept of blackism on a world scale is used in the latter sense in this chapter: that of 're-membering.' Re-membering encapsulates the consistent and complex contestations, resistances, and struggles against dismemberment that took the form of not only initiatives aimed at counter-self-creation, self-definition, recovery, and restoration of denied humanity but also the systematic self-re-writing of black people back into human history. These struggles and initiatives ranged from Garveyism to Ethiopianism, Negritude, African Personality, Pan-Africanism, African Nationalism, African Humanism, African Socialism, the Black Consciousness Movement, the Harlem Renaissance, and the African Renaissance.

The two terms, 'dismemberment' and 're-membering,' are borrowed from the leading African novelist and intellectual Ngugi wa Thiong'o (2009a, 2009b). He understood 'dismemberment' as 'An act of absolute social engineering, the continent's dismemberment was simultaneously the foundation, fuel, and consequence of Europe's capitalist modernity' (Ngugi wa Thiong'o 2009b: 5). For him (2009b: 35) 're-membering' is 'the quest for wholeness, a quest that has underlain African struggles since the Atlantic slave trade.' Thus, at the centre of 'dismemberment' and 're-membering' is the politics of modern humanism, accurately articulated by Lisa Lowe (2006: 206) in these revealing words:

> In this sense modern humanism is a formalism that translates the world through an economy of affirmation and forgetting within a regime of desiring freedom. The affirmation of the desire for freedom is so inhabited by the forgetting of its conditions of possibility, that every narrative articulation of freedom is haunted by its burial, by violence of forgetting. What we know as 'race' or 'gender' are the traces of this modern humanist forgetting.

Because dismemberment was implemented through usurpation and theft of history, re-membering involves recovery of history. Indeed without 'dismemberment' there would be no need for 're-membering.' Archie Mafeje (2011: 31–32) captured this point very well when he argued that 'we would not proclaim Africanity; if it had not been denied or degraded; and we would not insist on Afrocentrism, if it had not been for Eurocentric negations.' Following Mafeje's logic, one can safely argue that such re-membering initiatives, ideologies, and movements as Garveyism, Ethiopianism, Negritude,

African Personality, African Socialism, African Humanism, the African Renaissance, and many others emerged within a context of realities of 'dismemberment' and existed as props developed by the dismembered over time to help in the 're-membering' process. For example, Leopold Sedar Senghor explained the circumstances that led him and Cesaire to launch the Negritude Movement:

> In what circumstances did Aime Cesaire and I launch the word negritude between 1933 and 1935? At that time, along with several other black students we were plunged into panic-stricken despair. The horizon was blocked. No reform was in sight and the colonizers were justifying our political and economic dependence by the theory of the *tabula rasa* [...]. In order to establish an effective revolution, our revolution, we had first to divest ourselves of our borrowed attire—that of assimilation—and assert our being, that is to say our negritude.
>
> (Senghor quoted in Ba 1973: 12)

It is clear from Senghor's words that the Negritude Movement was part of the broader search for identity within a context of dismemberment. Therefore, Wole Soyinka's widely quoted critique of Negritude from the perspective that a tiger does not articulate its 'tigritude' was misplaced as it ignored the context of dislocation and alienation. Negritude is one of the earliest re-membering initiatives. Cheikh Thiam (2014) correctly understood it as part of an early expression of an 'Afri-centred' conception of the human that was consistently critical of the Western universalization of human that excluded those with black pigmentation. Negritude was propelled by what Cesaire termed the 'tormenting questions, who am I? Who are we? What are we in this world?' (Cesaire quoted in Thiam 2014: 2). The best articulation of the logic behind re-membering initiatives came from the leading Nigerian novelist and intellectual Chinua Achebe:

> You have all heard of the African personality; of African democracy, of the African way to socialism, of negritude, and so on. They are all props we have fashioned at different times to help us get on our feet again. Once we are up we shall not need any of them anymore.
>
> (Achebe quoted in Moore-Gilbert 1997: 179)

Historically speaking, one can legitimately posit that the Haitian Revolution (1791–1804) occupies a place of pride at the centre of black people's 're-membering' struggles, aimed at transcending the 'colonial,' and can legitimately be credited for setting the stage for the 'postcolonial.' In the first place, it defied the Eurocentric, colonial and imperial, and even Western philosophical idea of denial of the humanity of black people. It turned upside down the racist myths of a people who were naturally slaves and unable to develop any notions of fighting for freedom simply because they were not rational human beings. The enslaved black people revolting on a large scale in the Haitian Revolution was 'unthinkable' for those who had convinced themselves that black people were naturally slaves and had no capacity to rebel. The second significance of the Haitian Revolution is that it was part of the unfolding modern history of slavery, racism, and colonization, and the revolt of the enslaved challenged 'the iron bonds of the philosophical milieu in which it was born' (Trouillot 1995: 74). On the paradigmatic importance of this event in human history, Trouillot argued that:

> The Haitian Revolution did challenge the ontological and political assumptions of the most radical writers of the Enlightenment. *The events that shook up Saint-Domingue from 1791 to 1804 constituted a sequence for which not even the extreme political left in France or in England had a conceptual frame of reference.* They were 'unthinkable' facts in the framework of Western thought.
>
> (Trouillot 1995: 82 emphasis in the original)

Any acceptance of the fact that enslaved black people were up-in-arms against the system of slavery amounted in Western thought to an acknowledgement of the humanity of black people. Europeans in general and speculative plantation owners in particular were not prepared to concede that they were faced with a people claiming their denied humanity. This is why Trouillot (1995: 88) argued that:

> The Haitian Revolution was the ultimate test to the universalist pretensions of both the French and the American revolutions. And they both failed. *In 1791, there is no public debate on the record, in France, in England, or in the United States on the right of black slaves to achieve self-determination, and the right to do so by way of the armed resistance.*
>
> (Emphasis is in the original)

The Haitian Revolution indeed posed a difficult philosophical and intellectual problem for Western thought: how to think about and conceptualize black revolution in a world in which black people were not considered to be rational or even humans in the first place. This is why even 'international recognition of Haitian independence was even more difficult to gain than military victory over the forces of Napoleon' (Trouillot 1995: 95). The most important but silenced significance of the Haitian Revolution is that it led to the collapse of the entire system of slavery and constituted a major chapter in the history of the 're-membering' of black people. It was truly an anti-systemic revolution that continues to occupy a place of pride in the anti-systemic revolution marked by the definitive entry of the enslaved and the colonized into modern history as human beings opposed to all forms of 'dismemberment.'

The Haitian Revolution forms an important base from which to articulate what Ngugi wa Thiong'o (2009a) underscores as the importance of 're-membering visions.' What preceded the Haitian Revolution were numerous re-membering initiatives, including Ethiopianism and Garveyism. Ngugi wa Thiong'o (2009a: 35) noted that at the centre of Ethiopianism and Garveyism lay 'the quest for wholeness, a quest that has underlain African struggles since the Atlantic slave trade.' He elaborated:

> Though Ethiopianism and the like preceded these struggles, Garveyism and Pan-Africanism are the grandest secular visions for reconnecting the dismembered. Garveyism, with its Caribbean roots, unfolded on the terrain of America, but its vision—embodied in the title of Garvey's organization, the Universal Negro Improvement Association—was focused on the continent and its diaspora. 'Africa for Africans, those at home and abroad' was the chorus of Garvey's speeches and plans. The name was meant to 'embrace the purpose of all black humanity': to be free and equal members of the community of nations and peoples. For behind the rhetoric of blackness was also the universalist-humanist vision of using the Universal Negro Improvement Association to inspire African peoples with pride in self and with the determination of going ahead in the creation of those ideals that will lift them to the unprejudiced company of races and nations. There is no desire for hate or malice, but every wish to see all mankind linked into a common fraternity of progress and achievement that will wipe the odour of prejudice, and elevate the human race to the height of real godly love and satisfaction.
>
> (Ngugi wa Thiong'o 2009a: 36)

From the time of the Haitian Revolution to the age of Marcus Garvey and, later, the pan-Africanist movements, those human beings who have been designated as black have continued to fight for freedom and the recovery of their denied humanity. Pan-Africanism emerged as one broad re-membering initiative, from the time of William Sylvester, who planned and hosted the first Pan-African Congress in 1900, to William E. B. Du Bois's series on Pan-Africanism to Kwame Nkrumah's struggle to unify Africa into a Pan-African Nation. In the USA, black people launched the civil rights movements as part of the re-membering initiatives. These initiatives have taken both intellectual and political forms. At their centre has germinated the African idea as opposed to the idea of Africa – 'the African idea as the quest for freedom on a Pan-African scale extended from the diaspora to the continent and back again' (Ngugi wa Thiong'o 2009a: 75). The African idea captures the efforts of Africans defining themselves as opposed to the idea of Africa invoked by Valentin Y. Mudimbe (1994), which spoke of an external definition of Africa and Africans.

The period from the 1950s to the late 1960s was dominated by struggles for political decolonization and the emergence of 'postcolonial' states. Re-membering took the form of:

> Country after country in Africa reclaimed their independence, announcing themselves as players on the modern stage—and, in the process, reshaping that stage, or at least the colour of it. Each country may have emerged as a nation-state, territorially speaking, but beneath their national colours all of their people saw themselves as Africans. The journey of the African idea, beginning in Haiti and championed by Pan-African congresses, reached its climax in the independence of Angola, Guinea Bissau, and Mozambique and the liberation of South Africa in the 1980s and 1990s.
>
> (Ngugi wa Thiong'o 2009a: 77)

The major challenge to re-membering initiatives continues to be active global imperial designs (Mignolo 2000; Ndlovu-Gatsheni 2013a, 2013b). As noted by Grosfoguel (2007), political decolonization amounted to what he termed 'the most powerful myths of the twentieth century' because the withdrawal of direct colonial administrations and juridical apartheid did not 'amount to the decolonization of the world.' Grosfoguel elaborated that:

> This led to the myth of a 'postcolonial' world. The heterogeneous and multiple global structures put in place over a period of 450 years did not evaporate with the juridical-political decolonization of the periphery over the past 50 years. We continue to live under the same 'colonial power matrix.' With juridical-political decolonization we moved from a period of 'global colonialism' to the current period of 'global coloniality.'
>
> (Grosfoguel 2007: 219)

Accommodation of the newly 'independent states' into the United Nations Organization (UNO) mainly symbolized accommodation into an existing and un-decolonized Euro-North American-centric world system and un-deimperialized global order. Attempts by anti-colonial nationalists, pan-Africanists, and other leaders from the Global South to fight from within the structures of the UNO were limited. This was not what re-membering entailed. The so-called newly 'independent states' occupied the lowest echelons in an asymmetrical world system. The New World Economic Order (NWO) demanded by those who fought against colonialism did not materialize. As noted by Kwame Nkrumah (1965), neo-colonialism as a form of coloniality emerged, and the so-called independent states became entrapped in global coloniality.

At the internal level, the African leaders that had spearheaded the anti-colonial struggle displayed deep-seated 'pitfalls of national consciousness,' to borrow a term from Frantz Fanon (1968), and the consequences were what Basil Davidson (1992) calls the 'black man's burden' of reproducing what was invented by colonialism and imposing it on Africa. To be more specific, African nationalist leaders imposed the Westphalian template of nation-building on Africa. The consequences of this are well captured by Liisa Laakso and Adebayo O. Olukoshi:

> However, at the heart of the modern nation-state project was the idea, flawed from the outset, of tight correspondence between the nation and the state whereby each sovereign state was seen as a nation-state of people who shared common language or culture [...]. This notion of the nation-state stood in direct contradiction to the reality that most states were, in fact, multi-cultural, multi-lingual, and multi-religious and that not all ethnic groups (however defined) were sufficiently large or powerful or even willing to achieve a state of their own. [...]. At independence, most African governments set themselves the task of undertaking a vigorous process of nation-building with the aim of welding their multi-ethnic, multi-lingual, multi-cultural, and multi-religious countries into 'one-nation.' [...]. The nation-building project was, therefore, state-driven from the outset, often relying on a top-down approach that carried far-reaching centralising implications. In time, the unity project increasingly took the form of a unitary project which sometimes rested on a narrow ethnic base around which a system of patronage networks was then built linking other groups and their elites. Another key element of the nation-building project was the assumption that the diversity of ethnic identities was inherently negative and obstructive and that it was a requirement of successful nation-building that different identities be eradicated, submerged under or subordinated to the identity of the group(s) that dominated state power.
>
> (Laakso and Olukoshi 1996: 11–13)

The nation-building project as a re-membering initiative continues to show limits. Colonial mentalities continue to haunt African leadership and the population alike, hence the current push for the completion of the unfinished business of decolonization. The African Renaissance, as reformulated by President Thabo Mbeki of South Africa as a re-membering of Africa, witnessed the conversion of the Organization of African Unity (OAU), formed in 1963, to the African Union; the adoption of the New Partnership for Africa's Development (NEPAD); the launch of the African Peer Review Mechanism (APRM); and the opening of the Pan-African Parliament (PAP) in South Africa (Ndlovu-Gatsheni 2013a). All these initiatives were premised on the pan-African agenda, and they require vigorous translation of African nationalism into pan-Africanism.

Conclusion

The key task is how to translate Blackism into a force of liberation beyond present discourses of victimhood. Black radicalism, as defined by Andrews (2018), aims at overthrowing the existing social order. While re-membering continues to elude Africa and the Africans, there is no reason to surrender to global coloniality and its reproduction of toxic politics of dismemberment. What is clear is that a genuinely 'postcolonial' African identity which is pan-African in orientation and consciousness is yet to be born. What is promising is the continuation of decolonial struggles by youth and students across the Global South, represented by such formations as Black Lives Matter, the Rhodes Must Fall movements, and others fighting to complete incomplete decolonization/decoloniality.

At the continental level, even almost 60 years after celebrations of 'political decolonization,' the African Union has not given up on the ideas and spirit of Kwame Nkrumah, and is still pushing for the rebuilding and achieving of a prosperous, united, self-defining, and peaceful Africa by 2063. This means that even though coloniality continues to actively foreclose any possibilities of a postracial and postcolonial world order in which new humanism will be allowed to flourish, African people in particular and people from the Global South in general are not giving up the fight for decolonization/decoloniality. What emerged clearly after the exhaustion of Marxism and the failure of neo-liberalism is that new humanism can only be achieved within a decolonized, de-patriarchized, de-imperialized, detribalized, de-corporatized, and genuinely democratized world. Such an envisaged postcolonial and postracial world has to be pluriversal in character rather than universal.

This is the demand of such movements as Black Lives Matter in the USA, where coloniality continues to devalue the lives of those designated as black, and the Rhodes Must Fall and Fees Must Fall movements in South Africa – a country where intersections of race and racial capitalism continue to generate deep inequalities, exclusions and alienations, domination and oppressions, exploitation, and dehumanization, but also one that Richard Pithouse (2016: 120) correctly characterized in these revealing words: 'South Africa is a colonial creation that has not fully escaped the iron cage in which it was born.' In this context, the turning over of a new leaf by Africa entails the advancement of the 'African idea of Africa' as opposed to the general 'idea of Africa' defined by global imperial designs. Because the contested definition of being African is a subset of the broader problem of blackness on a world scale, turning over a new leaf entails a deepening of pan-Africanism and the promotion of transatlantic coalitions and indeed solidarities with the rest of the Global South. When Nkrumah posited that Africa was born in him, he was taking charge of the definition of Africa and Africanness. It is on the shoulders of this giant that Africa must stand and claim its place under the sun.

References

Andrews, K. 2018. *Back to Black: Black Radicalism for the 21st Century*. London: Zed Books.

Appiah, K. A. 2018. *The Lies that Bind; Rethinking Identity: Creed, Country, Colour, Class, Culture*. New York and London: Liverlight Publishing Corporation.

Ba, S. W. 1973. *The Concept of Negritude in the Poetry of Leopold Sedar Senghor*. Princeton, NJ: Princeton University Press.

Blaut, J. M. 1993. *The Colonizer's Model of the World: Geographical Diffusion and Eurocentric History*. New York and London: The Guilford Press.

Blyden, E. W. 1888 [1967]. *Christianity, Islam and the Negro Race*. London and New York: Edinburgh University Press.

Castro, D. 2007. *Another Face of Empire: Bartolome de La Casas, Indigenous Rights and Ecclesiastical Imperialism*. Durham, NC and London: Duke University Press.

Cesaire, A. 2000. *Discourse on Colonialism*. Translated by Joan Pinkham. New York: Monthly Review Press.

Coates, T. N. 2017. 'Foreword.' In T. Morrison (ed.), *The Origin of Others*. Cambridge, MA and London: Harvard University Press, pp. i–xvii.

Dabashi, H. 2019. *Europe and Its Shadows: Coloniality after Empire*. London: Pluto Press.

Davidson, B. 1992. *The Black Man's Burden*. London: James Currey.

Davis, A. 1972. 'Reflections on the Black Women's Role in the Community of Slaves.' *The Massachusetts Review*, 13, pp. 13–26.

Du Bois, W. E. B. 1903. *The Souls of Black Folk*. New York: Dover Publications, INC.

Du Bois, W. E. B. 1965. *The World and Africa: An Inquiry into the Part Which Africa Has Played in World History*. New York: International Publishers.

Dussel, E. 2008. *Twenty Theses on Politics*. Translated by George Ciccariello-Maher. Durham, NC and London: Duke University Press.

Dussel, E. 2011. *Politics of Liberation: A Critical World History*. Translated by Thia Cooper. London: SCM Press.

El-Malik, S. S., & Kamola, I. A. (eds.). 2017. *Politics of African Anticolonial Archive*. London and New York: Rowman and Littlefield International.

Falola, T., & Usman, A. (eds.). 2009. *Movements, Borders, and Identities in Africa*. New York: University of Rochester Press.

Fanon, F. 1968. *The Wretched of the Earth*. New York: Grove Press.

Hunter, E. (ed.). 2016. *Citizenship, Belonging, and Political Community in Africa: Dialogues between Past and Present*. Athens: Ohio University Press.

Goldberg, D. T. 2015. *Are We All Postracial Yet? Debating Race*. Cambridge: Polity.

Goody, J. 1996. *The Theft of History*. Cambridge: Cambridge University Press.

Gordon, L. R. 1999. *Bad Faith and Anti-Black Racism*. New York: Humanity Books.

Gordon, L. R. 2009. *Existentia Africana: Understanding Africana Existential Thought*. New York: Routledge.

Grosfoguel, R. 2007. 'The Epistemic Decolonial Turn: Beyond Political-Economy Paradigms.' *Cultural Studies*, 21(2/3) (March), pp. 211–336.

Grosfoguel, R. 2013. 'The Structure of Knowledge in Westernized Universities: Epistemic Racism/Sexism and the Four Genocides/Epistemicides of the Long 16th Century.' *Human Architecture: Journal of the Sociology of Self Knowledge*, XI(1) (Fall), pp. 73–90.

Headley, J. M. 2008. *The Europeanization of the World: On the Origins of Human Rights and Democracy*. Princeton, NJ and Oxford: Princeton University Press.

Hoppers, C. O., & Richards, H. 2012. *Rethinking Thinking: Modernity's 'Other' and the Transformation of the University*. Pretoria: UNISA Press.

James, C. L. R. 1982. *The Black Jacobins: Toussaint L'Ouverture and the San Domingo Revolution*. New York: Vintage Press.

Laakso, L., & Olukoshi, A. O. 1996. 'The Crisis of the Post-Colonial Nation-State Project in Africa.' In A. O. Olukoshi and L. Laakso (eds.), *Challenges to the Nation-State in Africa*. Uppsala: Nordic Africa Institute, pp. 7–39.

Lowe, L. 2006. 'The Intimacies of Four Continents.' In Ann Laura Stoler (ed.), *Haunted By Empire: Geographies of Intimacy in North American History*. Durham, NC and London: Duke University Press, pp. 191–211.

Mafeje, A. 2011. 'Africanity: A Combative Ontology.' In R. Devisch and F. B. Nyamnjoh (eds.), *The Postcolonial Turn: Re-Imagining Anthropology and Africa*. Bamenda and Leiden: Langaa and African Studies Centre, pp. 31–44.

Maldonado-Torres, N. 2007. 'On Coloniality of Being: Contributions to the Development of a Concept.' *Cultural Studies*, 21(2/3) (March/May), pp. 240–270.

Maldonado-Torres, N. 2008a. 'Lewis Gordon: Philosopher of the Human.' *CLR James Journal*, 14(1), pp. 103–137.

Maldonado-Torres, N. 2008b. *Against War: Views from the Underside of Modernity*. Durham, NC and London: Duke University Press.

Maldonado-Torres, N. 2017. 'On the Coloniality of Human Rights.' *Restiva Critica De Ciencias Sociais*, 114, Decembro, pp. 117–136.

Marriott, D. 2012. 'Inventions of Existence: Sylvia Wynter, Frantz Fanon, Sociogeny and the 'the Damned.' *CR: The New Centennial Review*, 11(3), pp. 45–90.

Mazrui, A. A. 1986. *The Africans: A Triple Heritage*. London: BBC Publications.

Mbembe, A. 2001. *On the Postcolony*. Berkeley: University of California Press.

Mbembe, A. 2003. 'Necropolitics.' *Public Culture*, 15(1), pp. 11–40.

Mbembe, A. 2006. 'What Is Postcolonial Thinking?' Available: www.eurozone.com/articles/2008-01-09-membe-en.html (accessed 15 October 2016).

Mignolo, W. D. 2000. *Local Histories/Global Designs: Coloniality, Subaltern Knowledges, and Border Thinking*. Princeton, NJ: Princeton University Press.

Moore-Gilbert, B. 1997. *Postcolonial Theory: Contexts, Practices, Politics*. London: Verso.

Morrison, T. 2017. *The Origin of Others*. Cambridge, MA and London: Harvard University Press.

Motta, S. C. 2018. *Liminal Subjects: Weaving (Our) Liberation*. London and New York: Rowman & Littlefield International Ltd.

Mudimbe, V. Y. 1988. *The Invention of Africa: Gnosis, Philosophy and the Order of Knowledge*. Bloomington and Indianapolis: Indiana University Press.

Mudimbe, V. Y. 1994. *The Idea of Africa*. Bloomington and Indianapolis: Indiana University Press.

Mudimbe, V. Y. 1997. 'Introduction.' In V. Y. Mudimbe (ed.), *Nations, Identities, Cultures*. Durham, NC and London: Duke University Press, pp. 1–6.

Ndlovu-Gatsheni, S. J. 2013a. *Empire, Global Coloniality and African Subjectivity*. Oxford and New York: Berghahn Books.

Ndlovu-Gatsheni, S. J. 2013b. *Coloniality of Power in Postcolonial Africa: Myths of Decolonization*. Dakar: CODESRIA Books.

Ndlovu-Gatsheni, S. J. 2015. 'Decoloniality in Africa: A Continuing Search for a New World Order.' *Australasian Review of African Studies*, 36(2) (December), pp. 22–50.

Ndlovu-Gatsheni, S. J. 2016. *The Decolonial Mandela: Peace, Justice and the Politics of Life*. Oxford and New York: Berghahn Books.

Ndlovu-Gatsheni, S. J., & Zondi, S. 2016. 'Introduction: The Coloniality of Knowledge: Between Troubled Histories and Uncertain Futures.' In Sabelo J. Ndlovu-Gatsheni and Siphamandla Zondi (eds.), *Decolonizing the University, Knowledge Systems and Disciplines in Africa*. Durham, NC: Carolina Academic Press, pp. 3–24.

Ngugi wa Thiong'o. 1997. *Writers in Politics: A Re-engagement with Issues of Literature and Society*. Oxford: James Currey.

Ngugi wa Thiong'o, 2009a. *Something Torn and New: An African Renaissance*. New York: Basic Civitas Books.

Ngugi wa Thiong'o, 2009b. *Re-membering Africa*. Nairobi: East African Educational Publishers Ltd.

Ngugi wa Thiong'o. 2012. *Globalectics: Theory and The Politics of Knowing*. New York: Columbia University Press.

Ngwena, C. 2018. *What Is Africanness? Contesting Nativism in Race, Culture and Sexualities*. Pretoria: Pretoria University Law Press.

Nkrumah, K. 1964 [1970]. *Concienscism: Philosophy and Ideology for Decolonization and Development with Particular Reference to the African Revolution*. New York: Monthly Review Press.

Nkrumah, K. 1965. *Neo-Colonialism: The Last Stage of Imperialism*. London: PANAF.

Oyewumi, O. 1997. *The Invention of Women: Making African Sense of Western Gender Discourses*. Minneapolis and London: University of Minnesota Press.

Pithouse, R. 2016. 'Frantz Fanon: Philosophy, Praxis, and the Occult Zone.' *Journal of French and Francophone Philosophy*, XXIV(1), pp. 116–138.

Robinson, C. J. 1983. *Black Marxism: The Making of the Black Radical Tradition*. New York: University of North Carolina Press.

Santos, B. de S. 2007. 'Beyond Abyssal Thinking: From Global Lines to Ecologies of Knowledge.' *Review*, XXX(1), pp. 45–89.

Suarez-Krabbe, J. 2016. *Race, Rights and Rebels: Alternatives to Human Rights and Development from the Global South*. London: Rowman & Littlefield International Ltd.

Thiam, C. 2014. *Return to the Kingdom of Childhood: Re-Envisioning the Legacy and Philosophical Relevance of Negritude*. Columbus: The Ohio State University Press.

Trouillot, M. R. 1995. *Silencing the Past: Power and the Production of History*. Boston, MA: Beacon Press.

Wynter, S. 2003. 'Unsettling the Coloniality of Being/Power/Truth/Freedom: Towards the Human, after Man, Its Overrepresentation—An Argument.' *New Centennial Review*, 3(3), pp. 257–337.

Zeleza, P. T. 2006. 'The Inventions of African Identities and Languages: The Discursive and Developmental Implications.' In O. F. Arasanyin and M. A. Pemberton (eds.), *Selected Proceedings of the 36th Annual Conference on African Linguistics*. Somerville, MA: Cascadilla Proceedings Project, pp. 15–26.

5 African political economy

Introduction

There is nothing called 'economy' which is not 'political.' This is why Marxists preferred the concept of the 'political economy.' However, decolonial theorists like Ramon Grosfoguel (2007) went even farther, proposing a decolonization of 'political economy' itself based on the argument that the concept still retained Eurocentric dualistic, hereby atomizing thinking and privileging economism instead of opening up to the realities of 'hetararchies' of power (see also Kontopoulos 1993). At the centre of this is knowledge which creates, gives meaning, and frames what is known as politics, economy, and society. The key thesis of this chapter is that what appears on the surface as the problem of political economy and as development challenges in Africa are rooted in the epistemic domain. This means that even the apparent strong grip of global coloniality on what has been termed African economies is enabled by the 'hetararchies' of racist/colonial/imperial/capitalist/patriarchal/sexist/modern asymmetrical power structures and configuration which are underpinned by Eurocentric epistemology (Grosfoguel 2007).

As stated in the first chapter of this book, knowledge frames reality. What exists as or is known as 'economy' is an epistemic creation. Thus, what appears in Africa as an 'economic crisis' or a 'development impasse' is a reflection of an epistemic crisis. Scholarly enquiry will need to delve into four areas: (1) the epistemic question, especially how knowledge and economy/development intersect; (2) the normative question, particularly the shaping of contemporary world views and world sensing; (3) the discursive question, notably the history of empire, colonialism, and decolonization; and finally, (4) the existential question of exclusion, injustices, inequalities, and poverty (see Ndlovu-Gatsheni 2019). The predicament of Africa is fundamentally an epistemic one: that of trying to use Eurocentric epistemology in its struggles for decolonization and thus failing to liberate itself from classical economic and conventional thinking. This point emerged poignantly in Amin (1990: 58): 'The genuine implementation of the principle of autocentric development implies very different reasoning that has the nerve to challenge the criteria of economic rationality observed by conventional economics.'

The concept of 'colonial matrices of power' offered by Latin American decolonial theorists such as Anibal Quijano (2007) is very useful in making sense of a historical and contemporary transnational, and indeed global pyramidal, power structure which enables 'development' in the Global North and 'maldevelopment' in the Global South (see also Rodney 1972; Amin 1990). Walter Mignolo and Cathrine E. Walsh (2018: 142) posited that 'The colonial matrix of power (the CMP) is a complex structure of management and control composed of domains, levels, and flows,' and as 'a theoretical concept' it 'helps to make visible what is invisible to the naked (or rather nontheoretical) eye.' They further explained that the concept of a 'colonial matrix of power' emerged in the 1970s 'out of theoretical-political struggles in South America' and 'bears the impulse of liberation theology' (Mignolo and Walsh 2018: 142). It was motivated by the limits of both modernization and dependency theories. The colonial matrix of power speaks to control of sex, labour, authority, subjectivity/intersubjectivity, and resources (human and natural) (Quijano 2000). Mignolo and Walsh (2018: 114) elaborated on this concept:

> In the colonial matrix of power, the creators of illusions (modernity), using human bodies (labour) energies as well as energy from biosphere (water, land, and oxygen) and the cosmos (sunlight and moonlight) are human bodies inside the colonial matrix of power but believing, or making believe, that there is an instance outside the colonial matrix from which it can be observed.

Interestingly, Samir Amin, an African Marxist decolonial thinker (2019: 41), offered the concept of five monopolies, control of technology, global financial flows (through the banks, insurance cartels, and pension funds of the centre), access to the planet's natural resources, media and communications, and weapons of mass destruction, as constitutive of the capitalist world system. This seems to resonate with the concept of the 'colonial matrix of power,' as introduced by Quijano. Amin (2019: 41) elaborated that

> Taken together, these five monopolies define the framework within which the law of global value expresses itself. The law of value is hardly the expression of a 'pure' economic rationality that can be detached from its social and political frame, rather, it is the condensed expression of the totality of these circumstances.

In addition to the concept of the 'colonial matrix of power,' Ngugi wa Thiong'o's (2016) conception of the four 'journeys of capital,' namely the slave trade, the slave plantation system, colonialism, and global debt slavery, enables an expansive and deep historicization as well as a decolonial explanation of how Africa increasingly became entrapped in global coloniality. Entrapment as a concept speaks to two predicaments for Africa.

At one level, it highlights the reality of Africa's having been captured by the spiderweb of global 'hetararchies of power' and expresses its invidious position within the global coloniality/global political economy/global imaginary, characterized by the ambivalence of being simultaneously at the 'centre' and at the 'periphery' of the modern world capitalist system. At another level, it underscores the discursive entanglement of Africa in the global colonial/imperial/capitalist matrices of power that sustains the asymmetrical global architecture and configuration of power, whereby even an anti-systemic resistance and an extra-structural agency are deeply shaped by the metaphysical/cognitive empire, long after the dismantlement of the direct physical empire.

The leading Africanist historian Frederick Cooper (2014: 9) posed the long-standing question, 'How did the relationship of Africa to Europe come to be so asymmetrical?' This chapter offers a response as it lays bare the core problems within the African political economy. The first part of the chapter introduces the concept of 'entrapment.' The second discusses the conceptual/theoretical terrain of the unfolding of entrapment and brings Ngugi wa Thiong'o's four journeys of capital into dialogue with the work of Karl Marx, particularly his distillation of the four foundational events in the 'rosy dawn of capitalism'; Aime Cesaire's five ways in which modernity/coloniality worked to destroy existing civilizations, cultures, and economies outside Europe; Ramon Grosfoguel's nine hetararchies of power; and Ali A. Mazrui's six forms of entrapment of Africa in the evolving modern world capitalist system. Even though Mazrui preferred to be labelled a liberal scholar on the issue of how Africa was entrapped into global coloniality, his explanation was in sync with such radical Afro-Marxists as Walter Rodney and Amin as well as with the Latin American decolonial theorists.

The third section articulates the eight epochs of entrapment of Africa from the time of the 'slave trade' to the present 'coloniality of markets.' The chapter does not in any way present a continent and a people who were and are mere victims in the making of the modern world system and its global orders. While the chapter highlights the structural straitjacket of coloniality within which African people have been launching resistance, it also explains such initiatives as the demand for a New International Economic Order (NIEO), revealing how its weaknesses were mainly epistemic as it failed to delink with classical and conventional economic thought while it grappled with the racially hierarchized modern international system and global order. The last section of the chapter examines two interrelated examples of the continuation of decolonial struggles in Africa: namely the African Union-driven launch and ratification of the African Continental Free Trade Area (AfCFTA) and the African protests over the French monetary imperialism that has been in place in 'Francophone Africa' since the dawn of political independence. The current protests over CFA (colonial currency) are not a lone struggle of one particular radical African leader, as in the 1950s/1960s, with Sekou Toure of Guinea and Sylvanus Olympio of Togo, and in the 1970s, with Thomas Sankara of Burkina Faso; this time there is popular pan-African resistance by youth and students. Let us begin with the epistemological question before proceeding to the historical issues.

Critique of economic theory and economic thought

In Chapter 1 of this book, it is made clear that the universe is an epistemic creation. The modern world is an epistemic creation. The modern world system is an epistemic creation, and its shifting global orders are epistemic creations. By the same logic what exists as economy, society, and politics are all epistemic creations. What is termed 'development' is also an epistemic creation. Perhaps it was such an understanding of the world that prompted the Indian psychologist Ashis Nandy (1983: 3) to posit that 'Perhaps that which begins in the minds of men must also end in the minds of men' and the leading African intellectual and novelist Ngugi wa Thiong'o (1997: 8–9) to argue that 'Mind control through culture was the key! Cultural subjugation was a necessary condition for economic and political mastery.'

Therefore, politics and functions of knowledge constitute the central question of our time. This should, in fact, be the central question for all proponents of decolonization and deimperialization in the imperialist metropolitan centres as well as in the dominated countries of the Global South. It is at the core of the quests for liberation and freedom. Samir Amin, who studied economics in Paris to the doctorate level, immediately rebelled against the discipline. In his first major publication building on his doctoral studies, entitled *Accumulation on a World Scale: A Critique of the Theory of Underdevelopment* (1974: 5), he posited that 'The only possible science is the science of society, for social reality is one: it is never "economic" or "political" or "ideological."' He elaborated that 'The conceptual equipment of this "pure" economic theory is situated at the level of abstraction that makes it useless for analysing the working of the mechanisms—even the economic mechanisms—of any society whatsoever.'

In *Imperialism and Unequal Development* (1977: 35), Amin offered an extended critique of 'micro-economics' at two levels, that is, as a quantitative technique (for the measurement of individual profitability and a description of behaviour without explanation) and as a theory which abandons common-sense accounting and becomes 'ideological trickery.' In a fundamental sense Amin (1974: 5) challenged the idea of pure economic science with laws which are 'true whatever the economic and social system may be.' In his *Maldevelopment: Anatomy of a Global Failure* (2011: 15), Amin proposed 'political analysis' as a better science of society and development, arguing that

> for discussion of the options in the framework of macro-economic schema provides no more commonplace and foreseeable findings. We must aim higher and integrate in the discussion all the economic,

> political, social and cultural facets of the problem and at the same time fit them into local framework that takes account of interaction on a world scale.

The critique of economics is important because it is offered in Eurocentric epistemology as the disciplinary anchor for understanding development and defined as a science of human relations with things. In *Rethinking Thinking: Modernity's 'Other' and the Transformation of the University* (2012: 24), Cathrine Odora Hoppers and Howard Richards, like Amin, posited a key epistemic critique: 'Thinking is calculating. Calculating is economics. Economics is development. Sell yourself, sell yourself, they utter night and day, buzzing with their mercantile message from ear to ear like bees seeking not honey in flowers but salt in wounds.'

In the same vein Maria Lugones (2008: 8) explained the cognitive needs of capitalism in these revealing words:

> The cognitive needs of capitalism include measurement, quantification, externalization (or objectification) of what is knowable with respect to the knower so as to control the relations among people and nature and among them with respect to it, in particular the property in means of production. This way of knowing was imposed on the whole capitalist world as the only valid rationality and as emblematic of modernity.

Seeking a deeper understanding of the 'economic paradigm,' Hoppers and Richards (2012: 65–66) delved into what they termed the 'constitutive rules of the economic game;' this led them to understand the foundational writings of Adam Smith as the origins of economics as a discipline. They discovered and concluded that 'economics articulated the rules of a cultural structure' and is not 'a science of universal cross-cultural validity.' Gilbert Rist, in *The History of Development: From Western Origins to Global Faith: Fifth Edition* (2019: 277), also highlighted how exhausted the 'economic paradigm' is and argued that the 'whole of economic "science"' must be called into question. He boldly stated that:

> Economic 'science' has nothing scientific. It is no more than a battle of opinions, which fluctuates according to the conjuncture in ways that enable the strongest to impose their will. [...]. Ultimately, the belief in 'development' rests upon the credence given to economics. Neither can be shaken off unless the other is shaken off too.
>
> (Rist 2019: 277)

Perhaps, the proliferation of 'schools of economics,' such as the Chicago School of Economics, the Austrian School of Economics, the London School of Economics (LSE), and others, confirms Rist's thesis that 'economics' is a 'battle of opinions' and Amin's notion of 'ideological trickery.'

Deploying the decolonial epistemic perspective founded on a thorough historicization of the operations of modernity, colonialism, capitalism, and patriarchy, and taking into account scholarly interventions of a heterodox of critical thinkers, including Karl Marx, Walter Rodney, Ngugi wa Thiong'o, Ali A Mazrui, Aime Cesaire, Ramon Grosfoguel, Mahmood Mamdani, and many others, this chapter delves deeper into the dynamics and processes of the emergence, unfolding, and fossilization of the modernist/colonial/capitalist system. With specific reference to Africa and other geo-political constructions that experienced enslavement and colonialism, the intention is to unpack how Africa became entangled in the world capitalist mode of production. It was Ngugi wa Thiong'o (2016: 31) who clearly articulated the ways in which it has been a victim of a series of global colonialities:

> Each moment in the journey of capital has Africa as a captive. Under the slave trade, the African body becomes a commodity. Under the ensuing slave plantation system, Africa supplies unpaid labour that works the sugar and cotton fields. Under colonialism, Africa supplies raw materials—gold, diamonds, copper, uranium, coffee and cocoa—without having control over the prices. Under the new global situation of debts, debt servicing and conditionality, Africa is weighed down by debt slavery. Just as Africa became a net exporter of the labour it most needed for its own development and the net exporter of minerals and raw materials it most needed for its own development, today, under debt slavery, Africa becomes the net exporter of the very capital it most needs. [...]. In relation to Africa, slavery is the continuous theme in the journey of capital: the plantation dissolving into colonial rule dissolving into debt slavery.

What is understood as the African political economy in this case becomes a catalogue of invasions and economic extroversions, with capital as its projectile, if not its arsenal. Political economy as a human science revealed how macro-histories consisting of the unfolding of the modern world system and its global orders impinged upon local African economies in various ways (see Cooper 2014: xi). At the centre of African political economy (the very convergence of politics and economy) is the rampaging journey of capital and the world division of labour. This re-making of the modern world system and its global orders explains the perennial question of how Africa has come to occupy a subaltern position in the modern world system and global order since the fifteenth century. Today, at the centre of political economy analysis is the discourse of poverty and the necessity to reduce it.

The colonial matrix of power and the fate of Africa

The spiderweb of coloniality is called the colonial matrix of power. Mignolo and Walsh (2018: 97) defined this as 'a complex structure of management and control,' and a 'theoretical concept that helps make visible what is invisible to the naked (or rather the nontheoretical) eye.' As a theoretical concept, the colonial matrix of power acts as a way out of the exhausted 'economic paradigm' of economics, beginning by revealing that coloniality is constitutive of modernity (there is no modernity without coloniality). This means that the positive rhetoric of modernity is always hiding the negative aspects of global coloniality (Mignolo 2018: 98). The colonial matrix of power unfolded in terms of control of economy, authority, subjectivity, and knowledge (Mignolo 2007: 155). These were initially framed by theo-politics, then by ego-politics (philosophy) and racist science; today mainstream media sustains these matrices as it disseminates the rhetoric of modernity and its salvationist pretensions.

What is described in conventional economic thought as the political economy of Africa is fundamentally a tale of how the continent and its people were dragged into the evolving and unfolding global coloniality through such processes as enslavement, mercantilism, and colonialism. This is the tale of the entrapment of Africa, which captures the paradoxical situation of the continent – that of 'simultaneous involvement and marginalization' in the modern world system, modern global order, modern knowledge economy, and modern world economy (Austen 1987). Entrapment highlights how a colonized people exist as a human species that has been dragged kicking and screaming into the nexus of the modern world system, modern global order, modern knowledge economy, modern world economy, and forcible conversion to Christianity. What emerged from this is an invidious position not just of being pushed to the periphery but also of being insiders who have been pushed outside of the very human oecumene/family (Ndlovu-Gatsheni 2017).

The unfolding of modern history some 500 years ago unleashed colonialities of space (cartography and settlement), time (cutting it into linear pre-modern and modern conceptions), human species/being (social classification and racial hierarchization), nature (turning it into a natural resource), knowledge (theft of history, epistemicides, and linguicides), and power/authority (asymmetrical configurations and legal codification of difference). Human history itself acquired a new definition and meaning. In the analysis of Eduard Galeano (1997: 2–3), it became understood through the imperial categories of competition, rivalry, and survival of the fittest. This re-definition of history announced the arrival of Euro-North American hegemonic aspirations predicated not only on the paradigms of difference and war but on the legitimation of enslaving, pillaging, colonizing, and entrapping human beings in the grand imperial designs of the emerging Euro-North American-centric world system, world order, and world capitalist economy.

In this modernist/capitalist/imperial-oriented definition of human history, unequal development, underdevelopment, inequalities, and poverty were explained as a sign of being inherently primitive or having failed to effectively compete. Paget Henry (2000: 4) wrote about how human history assumed the character of 'a Faustian/imperial struggle to subdue all nature and history. This was an insurrectionary rapture with the established cosmic order of things that inaugurated a new era in the relations between the European ego and the world.' This radical shift, according to Henry (2000: 4) (described as the globalization of 'the European project of existence'), 'weakened the powers of the gods, relocated Europeans at the centre of this new world,' and re-invented the rest of the non-European world 'into one of its subordinate peripheries.'

The question of centre-periphery which dominated dependency theory in the 1970s, is one of the concerns that have given birth to decoloniality in the 21st century mainly because the issue of 'peripherization' as technology of coloniality is still very important. This technology of coloniality works by ensuring that the peripherized remains inside the orbit of modernity/coloniality to service capitalist/colonial/patriarchal logics but is always pushed to the margins of power and influence (an insider pushed to the outside but at the same time not allowed to operate outside). At the political level, entrapment entailed succumbing to the political logics and asymmetries of coloniality of power (Cox 1948; Fanon 1968; Ekeh 1983; Robinson 1983; Quijano 2000). Entrapment in coloniality of power began with physical conquest and dragging the colonized into the nexus of modern racial global asymmetrical power relations. This continues to disadvantage Africa and the rest of the Global South today.

At the epistemological level, entrapment entailed epistemicides, linguicides, cultural imperialism, appropriations, and 'theft of history' (Goody (1996), resulting in the coloniality of knowledge. At the intersubjective level, it involved tweaking ontology itself, resulting in what became known as the coloniality of being (Wynter 2003; Maldonado-Torres 2007). This form of entrapment materialized through the social classification of the human species in accordance with the assumed differential ontological densities and racial hierarchization of humanity. At the material level, a world capitalist economy that survives on exploitation of natural and human resources has been fishing in Africa, and the Global South in general, for cheap labour, cheap raw materials, and open markets.

Modern subjects of the periphery are born entrapped in global coloniality. Mahmood Mamdani (1996) delved into the colonial technologies of the reproduction of 'citizens' and 'subjects' – technologies and processes that also determined the consciousness of the colonized and forms/formats/grammars of resistance. He posited that to 'come to grips with the specific nature of power through which the population of subjects excluded from civil society was actually ruled' entails understanding 'how the subject population was incorporated into—and not excluded from—the arena of colonial power' (Mamdani 1996: 15). His key thesis is that 'every movement against decentralized despotism bore the institutional imprint of the mode of rule,' and 'Every movement of resistance was shaped by the very structure of power against which it rebelled' (Mamdani 1996: 24). This is what I mean by 'discursive entrapment.'

Africa in a global colonial/capitalist system

In a book entitled *Secure the Base: Making Africa Visible in the Globe* (2016: 31), Ngugi wa Thiong'o articulated how Africa has been kept captive by capital from the time of the slave trade to the current age of debt slavery. Before Ngugi wa Thiong'o, Karl Marx set the tone regarding the entrapment of the Global South in colonial/racial capitalism when he categorically stated that the 'rosy' dawn of the era of capitalism was predicated on four specific events and processes. The first was 'the discovery of gold and silver in America.' The second was 'the uprooting, enslavement and entombment in the mines of aboriginal population.' The third was 'the beginning of the conquest and looting of the East Indies.' The last was 'the turning of Africa into a warren for the commercialized hunting of black skins' (Marx quoted in Tucker 1978: 476–477).

No one captured the processes of disruption, dispossession, and entrapment as eloquently as Aime Cesaire (2000). In poetic language, Cesaire articulated four modes of disruptions and entrapment. The first related to the destruction of the essence of colonized societies by trampling over their cultures, undermining their institutions, confiscating their land, smashing their religions, destroying their 'magnificent artistic creations,' and wiping out their 'extraordinary possibilities'(Cesaire 2000: 43). What was imposed after these dehumanizing processes was economic extractivism, ontological extractivism, and epistemological extractivism (Grosfoguel 2016).

The second mode entailed the tearing and severing of the colonized 'from their gods, their land, their habits, their life—from life, from the dance, from wisdom' (Cesaire 2000: 43). This process amounted to alienation as a form of entrapment. The third colonial intervention entailed instilling fear in the colonized, 'who have been taught to have an inferiority complex, to tremble, kneel, despair, and behave like flunkeys.' The last colonial device described by Cesaire (2000: 43) was extractivism, dispossession, and disruptions of

> natural economies that have been disrupted—harmonious and viable economies adapted to the indigenous population—about food crops destroyed, malnutrition permanently introduced, agricultural development oriented solely towards the benefit of the metropolitan countries; about the looting of products, looting of raw materials.

Ali A. Mazrui (1986) added his voice to this important issue by identifying six forms of entrapment. The forcible incorporation of Africa into the world capitalist economy began, according to Mazrui (1986: 12), with the enslavement of black people, 'which dragged African labour itself into the emerging international capitalist system.' This constitutes the first layer of entrapment and the first journey of capital, according to Ngugi wa Thiong'o (2016). The slave labour from Africa contributed immensely to creating the transatlantic economic nerve centre and the rise of Europe and North America into the most developed nations of the world. The second entrapment took the form of denial of entry and exclusion of Africa from the developing and new nation-state sovereignty system that emerged in 1648, making the continent available for partitioning in 1884–1885. The Westphalian meeting was significant because it constituted part of European conferences to order the world in accordance with their interests and fears. Mazrui (1986: 12) noted that Africa was only incorporated into the world system of nation-states after 1945, with the rise of the United Nations sovereign state global order. As will be demonstrated later, even the post-1945 incorporation of Africa into the world system entailed entrapment in the lowest echelons of asymmetrical global power relations. This means that if 'denial of entry' was a problem in 1648, after 1945, 'recognition' became problematic too because it adhered to the principles that maintained the hegemony of Europe and North America. Reflecting on the post-Second World War dispensation, Amin (2019: 38) posited that:

> The Second World War inaugurated a new phase in the world system. The take off of the post-war period (1945–1975) was based on three social projects of the age, projects that stabilised and complemented each other. These social projects were (i) in the West, the welfare state project of national social democracy based on the productive interdependent national system; (ii) the "Bandung project' of bourgeois national construction on the system's periphery (development ideology);'and (iii) the Soviet-style of capitalism without capitalists,' existing in relative autonomy from the dominant world system.

While in Chapter 2 of this book, the 'Bandung spirit of decolonization' is venerated, Amin depicted the 'Bandung project' as nothing more than a bourgeois national construction taking place in the periphery but still driven by the mainstream ideology of developmentalism. So, according to Amin's analysis, the 'Bandung project' was still part of entrapment, not decolonization and decoloniality. Perhaps this is why so far, it has reincarnated itself in the form of 'dewesternization.'

Going back to Mazrui (1986: 13): he identified the linguistic entrapment of Africa as another major challenge. His thinking on this subject is similar to what Ngugi wa Thiong'o (1986: 5) characterized as 'linguistic encirclement,' which created a continent and a people who defined 'themselves in terms of the languages of Europe: English-speaking, French-speaking, or Portuguese-speaking African countries.' There are six modern imperial languages that have been imposed on Africa in particular and the Global South in general: Italian, Spanish, Portuguese, English, French, and German. At a fourth level, according to Mazrui (1986: 12), Africa was incorporated into a heavily skewed Western-centric 'international law' that constituted another enduring form of entrapment. The fifth layer he describes is that of the incorporation of Africa into 'the modern technological age,' which resulted in Africa being 'swallowed by the global system of dissemination of information.' This analysis by Mazrui on technology and information communication system resonates with Amin's (2019: 41) analysis of five monopolies. Finally, to Mazrui (1986: 12), Africa has been dragged into and entrapped in a Western-centric moral order predicated on Christianity as a hegemonic world religion as well as liberalism as a civic ideology. Building on this analysis, Mazrui (1986: 13) concluded that 'what Africa knows about itself, what different parts of Africa know about each other, have been profoundly influenced by the West.'

In Chapter 3 of this book, Ramon Grosfoguel's (2007) ideas were used to theoretically frame the complex processes involved in the invention of the global south and the global north, and here, the same conceptual and theoretical interventions are deployed to understand the economic entrapment of Africa within the evolving and hegemonic modern world capitalist economy. The making of 'a particular global class formation' serviced by 'diverse forms of labour,' including 'slavery, semi-serfdom, wage-labour, petty-commodity production,' and entangled with the functioning practice of how 'capital as a source of production of surplus value through the selling of commodities for a profit in the world market,' constituted a strong base for capitalism (Grosfoguel 2007: 216). It laid a solid basis for the invention of an uneven 'international division of labour of core and periphery where capital organized labour in the periphery' through the coercion and deployment of other authoritarian means, which is another important layer of coloniality of power. To further consolidate itself, a confluence of political and economic considerations, interests, and fears enabled the formulation of the 'inter-state system of proto-military organizations controlled by European males and institutionalized in colonial administrations' (Grosfoguel 2007: 216). At the base of all this was a 'global racial/ethnic hierarchy that privileges European people over non-European people,' together with a 'global gender hierarchy that privileges males over female and European patriarchy over other forms of gender relations' (Grosfoguel 2007: 216).

A 'sexual hierarchy that privileges heterosexuals over homosexuals and lesbians,' and a 'spiritual hierarchy that privileges Christians over non-Christians/non-Western spiritualities institutionalized in the globalization of the Christian (Catholic and later Protestant) church' reinforced the fossilization of Eurocentrism (Grosfoguel 2007: 216). Since epistemology has always framed ontology, at the epistemic and linguistic domains, Europe developed 'an epistemic hierarchy that privileges Western knowledge and cosmology over non-Western knowledge and cosmologies, and institutionalized in the global university system,' and a 'linguistic hierarchy between European languages and non-European languages that privileges communication and knowledge/theoretical production in the former and subalternized the latter as sole producers of folklore or culture but not knowledge/theory.'

In Chapter 3, dealing with the question of the Bandung spirit of decolonization, insights from Sabelo J. Ndlovu-Gatsheni (2015) were utilized to examine how the global South was invented and marginalized. But just like the conceptual and theoretical insights of Grosfoguel, Ndlovu-Gatsheni's interventions are useful in framing the economic extroversion of Africa. The age of 'discovery and mercantilist order,' which saw the slave trade as the nerve centre of mercantilist commerce, practically laid the framework for the entrapment of Africa, Latin America, Asia, and other parts of the Global South in the evolving Euro-North American-Atlantic commercial system that included the selling and buying of black human beings and, later, the indenturing of those people who were deemed to be 'yellow' and 'brown' (Chinese people and Indians) in the modern racialization discourse of imperialism and capitalism.

It was at this very beginning that ontological extractivism and economic extroversion intersected resulting in the reduction of black people of Africa to commodities for sale (slaves) and later to propertyless people who survived through sale of labour. As represented by the journeys and activities of Christopher Columbus and James Cook, the so-called 'discoveries' entailed epistemological extractivism as the explorers collected materials ranging from minerals, flowers, and animals to the decapitated heads of human beings for display in Europe. Thus, the paradigm of discovery and its mercantilist activities began the practice of filling European museums with materials looted from other parts of the world. A paradigmatic case is that of Sarah Batman, an African woman who was captured and displayed alive in museums in Europe. She was reduced to a guinea pig for European experiments, as informed by their pseudo-scientific racial thinking. Her genitals were exposed to the European public gaze. All this constituted the political economy of mercantile looting.

Historically speaking, and with Africa as a focal point, the discovery paradigm and mercantilist order began to envelop Africa in 1415 when Portugal invaded the port of Ceuta in North Africa (Newitt 2010). Ceuta formed a bridgehead for further Portuguese imperial expansion, which challenged the Muslim dominance in North Africa and the broader Mediterranean region that had been in place since the seventh century. The strategic importance of Ceuta as a bustling centre of trade, which attracted even 'Henry the Navigator' and became an entry point in the mercantile invasion of Africa, is highlighted by Carrie Gibson (2014: 2):

> Ceuta sat at a crucial location; mirrored by the rock of Gibraltar in the north, it was the Southern part of the 'Pillars of Hercules'—the gateway to the commercial world of the Mediterranean. It was also the exit to the terrifying and mostly unknown waters of the Atlantic. [...]. Many

> people believed that Ceuta was the last link in the long supply chain that connected the Mediterranean with the rumoured riches that lay deep in the unknown African interior.

What cascaded from the discovery paradigm and the mercantilist order of the fifteenth century was a commercial shift from the Mediterranean-centred to the Atlantic-centred economy, linking western Africa, the eastern coasts of North Africa and South America, as well as the Atlantic coastline of Europe and North Africa (Newitt 2010: 1). At the same time that the Spanish Atlantic sphere was being extended to the Pacific, the Philippines, and China, the Portuguese were creating the Indian Ocean sphere, which in the process of extending to the East Indies. Eventually four continents, Europe, Africa, Asia, and the Americas, were linked through economic activities, the migration of people, and the selling of human beings as slaves (Newitt 2010: 1).

The mercantile order was also characterized by banditry and warfare as European individuals and powers competed to loot the resources of Africa. The leading external imperial powers were, first, Portugal, Spain, and Holland; they were later joined by Britain, France, and others. The Arabs were also very active in what became known as the slave trade as were explorers, merchants, hunters, and missionaries of different European nationalities. Walter Rodney (1972: 140) emphasized that what were generally described as explorers were in fact the early scramblers for Africa: 'Make no mistake about it; gentlemen like Carl Peters, Livingstone, Stanley, Harry Johnston, De Brazza, General Gordon and their masters in Europe were literally scrambling for Africa. They barely avoided a major military conflagration.'

Another distinctive feature of the mercantile order was the dominance of merchant companies such as the Dutch East India Company, formed in 1602; the British Company of Royal Adventurers Trading in Africa, formed in 1660; the French West Indies Company/Senegal Company, formed in 1664; the British Royal Africa Company, formed in 1672; and others. These chartered companies were granted extensive powers that included enslaving, conquest, and colonization. Christopher Kinsey (2006: 38) provided the best description:

> The sixteenth century saw the creation of a new type of commercial entity, the mercantile company. Chartered by the state to engage in long-distance trade and establish colonies, the mercantile company drove European imperialism for the next 350 years. They were unusual institutions in that they distorted the distinction between economics and politics, non-state and state, property rights and sovereignty, and public and private. As a consequence of these distortions, they presented their rulers with complex dilemmas.

The expansion to the Indian Ocean commenced with two voyages of discovery: the first by Bartholomew Diaz in 1488 and the second by Vasco da

Gama in 1498, who successfully circumnavigated the southern tip of the African continent until he reached the East Indies. To get a clear grasp of the unfolding of the paradigm of discovery and the creation of a mercantilist order, one needs to understand the sequence of historical events. Even though Kwame Nimako and Glenn Willemsen (2011: 14) characterized the age of mercantilism as the 'age of banditry,' the merchants were inspired by ideology and philosophy of primitive accumulation. A 'paradigm of discovery' framed it, and the accumulation of bullion was its *modus operandi*. According to Terreblanche (2014: 220):

> Mercantilism was based on the idea, or ideology, that wealth, especially in the form of precious metals, was finite and that it was essential for a particular European country to experience as large as possible an influx of wealth and precious metals to the detriment of other European and non-European countries. The logical consequence of this mercantilist philosophy was that both war and trade—or whatever other methods of looting—could and should be implemented rigorously to ensure that a particular country could be on the winning side of what was essentially a zero-sum game.

Terreblanche (2014: 8) correctly emphasized that the unequal development, underdevelopment, or even non-development of the part of the world that experienced European domination has to be explained by taking into account 'the severity of the exploitation, repression and destruction directed at colonized peoples by Western empires, Western capitalism, Western industrialization, Western war-making and Western propaganda.'

Spain, Portugal, the Netherlands, Britain, France, Belgium, Italy, and the USA have been active at the forefront of modern empire-building from 1500 up to today. Spain and Portugal (Iberian nations) supported by the Catholic Church were active during the first phase of empire-building from 1500 to 1630 (Terreblanche 2014). They fanned out into the Americas, Asia, and Africa during the mercantilist phase and were also actively involved in the enslavement of black people. The age of Spanish and Portuguese empire-building coincided with internal transformations in Europe, taking the form of a disintegration of feudal theocratic/divine monarchs and the emergence of capitalism, driven by the emerging bourgeois class. What distinguished the period of Spanish and Portuguese empire-building is what is termed mercantilism:

> The guiding principle for European empire building was that trade should always be in surplus to provide a stream of bullion for the mother country. [...]. The obsession with precious metals was closely linked to another unique characteristic of Spanish imperialism, i.e. the culture of conquest. Driven by this culture the Spaniards conquered the whole of Latin America (excluding Brazil) and parts of North America—now part of the United States—without developing their huge new land

> mass. [...]. At the end of the eighteenth century Spain had the largest, most powerful and longest surviving empire in the Americas. In its territorial extent, it was the true modern rival of the Roman Empire.
> (Terreblanche 2014: 202)

Portuguese expansion displayed a combination of religious zealotry, insatiable commercial appetite, geo-political grandstanding, and hegemonic aspirations to defeat the Muslims and take over their commercial spheres of influence. Fortified trade bases in Asia and Africa signified this Portuguese empire-building. Chinese people and Muslims in Asia had strong militaries that hindered Portuguese conquest (Terreblanche 2014: 198). Portugal dominated and controlled the Asia trade zone; in Africa 'For a period of over 400 years Portugal was a big player in the slave trade;' and in Brazil the Portuguese empire 'became important in the seventeenth century after gold was discovered there' (Terreblanche 2014: 198–199). Grosfoguel and Cervantes-Rodriguez (2002: xii) emphasized that:

> The capitalist world-system was formed by the Spanish/Portuguese expansion to the Americas in the long sixteenth century [...]. The first modernity (from 1492 to 1650) built the foundations of the racist/colonial culture and global capitalist system that we are living today. [...]. The Spanish and Portuguese expansion to the Americas was crucial for the construction of the racial categories that would later be generalized to the rest of the world. [...]. The myth of the 'superiority' of the 'civilized' Westerners/Europeans over the 'uncivilized' non-Europeans, based on racial narratives on 'superior/inferior' peoples and cosmovisions was constructed in this period.

However, the intra-European wars, such as the Eighty Years' War between Spain and Holland, and the Thirty Years' War (1618–1648), affected the empire-building adventures of the Spanish and the Portuguese. The next phase of empire-building was led by the Netherlands (1648–1713). As a modern nation-state with imperial aspirations, the Netherlands emerged from the Thirty Years' War to be created by the Westphalian Treaty of 1648. It took advantage of the fact that Germany had emerged damaged from the war and that Britain and France were engrossed in what Terreblanche (2014: 75) termed 'the mercantilist struggle for hegemony in the seventeenth century.' The Dutch Republic replaced Portugal and Spain in inter-continental trade and began to expand into an empire:

> In Asia the Dutch conquered the Portuguese and established profitable trading and looting posts. On the Atlantic, the Dutch plundered the Spanish silver fleets and in Europe they plundered the Genoese caravans transporting precious metals overland from Seville to Antwer.
> (Terreblanche 2014: 214)

By 1650 Amsterdam had become the centre of the world, having emerged from the 'mercantilist wars of the seventeenth century' 'remarkably successful' (Terreblanche 2014: 216). At the centre of its empire-building was the Dutch East India Company (VOC), which formed in 1602 as a chartered company. Terreblanche (2014: 218) argued that 'The VOC can be regarded as one of the first MNCs. It was a real "octopus," with tentacles in international trade, piracy, the slave trade and colonialism.' VOC conquered the world for the Dutch until it collapsed in 1799 as a result of bankruptcy. The next empire-building process was British-led (1775–1945). The looting of the resources of the Global South produced the Industrial Revolution. This gave Britain an edge over others. Just like the Dutch, the British formed the British East India Company, which survived for almost 300 years (1600–1874). Thus, to Nimako and Willemsen (2011: 20):

> If the period between 1492 and the Peace of Westphalia (1648), including the Thirty Years' War (1618–48), can be characterized as the age of banditry in relation to chattel slavery, the period between the Peace of Westphalia and the outbreak of the French Revolution in 1789 can be characterized as the age of sovereignty.

What the 'age of sovereignty' tried to put to rest was the paradigm of war that dominated during the mercantile period. The key wars include *Reconquista*, which aimed at defeating the Muslims (Moors) and was a long war, lasting for centuries until the fall of Grenada in 1492; this was followed by the conquest of the Americas, the Eighty Years' War (1568–1648), the Thirty Years' War (1618–1648), the Nine Years' War (1689–1692), and the Spanish War of Succession (1701–1714) (Terreblanche 2014: 104).

The 'Westphalian order' that began with the Treaty of Westphalia of 1648 is credited in European history for laying the foundation for the modern idea of the sovereign nation-state system. It cuts across other orders as the notion of the nation-state is still ubiquitous throughout the modern world. This is why Wendy Brown explained that:

> To speak of a post-Westphalian order is not to imply an era in which nation-state sovereignty is either finished or irrelevant. Rather, the prefix 'post' signifies a formation that is *temporally after but not over* that to which it is affixed. 'Post' indicates a very particular condition of afterness in which what is past is not left behind, but, on the contrary, relentlessly conditions, even dominates a present that nevertheless also breaks in some way with this past.
>
> (Brown 2010: 21)

The people of Africa were not considered worthy of the national sovereignty that was introduced at Westphalia. This made them vulnerable to conquest and colonization. The decision to only restore national sovereignty to emerging European states and to exclude Africa portended the scramble and partitioning of Africa in the nineteenth century. To Nimako and Willemsen (2011: 20), 'For the "outside world," the importance of the Peace of Westphalia lay not in the reciprocal recognition of the sovereignty of the signatories, but rather in the non-recognition of the sovereignty of others.'

If Europeans considered African sovereignty in the same way that they did their own, the 1884–1885 Berlin Conference would not have happened. Adekeye Adebajo (2010) depicted this as 'the curse of Berlin' because it legitimized and galvanized the scramble for Africa; heightened the conquest of Africa; and enabled the partitioning, dismemberment, and fragmentation of the continent into various colonies. Today Africa finds itself trapped within colonially drawn boundaries decided by the colonizers in Berlin. The 'Berlin consensus' portended the physical empire and its colonial governmentality.

The Berlin Conference enabled what became known as 'effective colonization' and the 'age of colonial governmentality,' which involved the practical implementation of dismembering processes of dispossession and the production of a unique African colonial subjectivity of rightless people devoid of the privileges of citizens and the establishment of direct colonial administrations. These direct forms of colonial administrations were known by different names, such as Concessionaire/Company Rule, Assimilation/Association, Lusotropicalism, Indirect/Direct Rule, Trusteeship, Protectorates, and Apartheid (Ndlovu-Gatsheni 2013, 2015). For Mahmood Mamdani (2013), the DNA of colonial governmentality was the practice of 'defining' the colonized for the purposes of 'ruling' over them.

At the economic level, colonial governmentality produced what Samir Amin (1976: 317–333) termed the 'three macro-regions' of colonial economic formations and inventions. The first was the '*economie de traite*' that was implemented in West Africa. This involved changing the production direction from food crops to cash crops for export. This shift was imposed on peasants without dispossessing them of land. Agricultural production concentrated on four export crops: cocoa, oil palm, cotton, and groundnuts (Bernstein 2005: 68). What colonialism created in West Africa became known as peasant trade colonies, which were predicated on peasant commodity production. This meant that peasants were entrapped in the colonial cash economy. Food security suffered in the process. In countries like Ghana, the situation was worsened when imposed peasant commodity production was accompanied by land expropriations for mining purposes. This complicates the typology offered by Amin (1976).

The second colonial economic invention involved the 'labour reserve' colonies. According to Amin (1976: 317–333), these stretched from east Africa through parts of central Africa and became dominant in southern Africa. Labour reserves were created through large-scale land dispossessions in countries like South Africa, Kenya, Zimbabwe, and many others. Two logics informed this colonial scheme. The first was that white settlers themselves came, settled, and inaugurated large-scale commercial capitalist farming, which meant they had to dispossess the indigenous people of their land.

The second logic was to create a pool of cheap labour for the farms and plantations (Bernstein 2005: 69). The dispossessed indigenous people were then concentrated in what became known as 'native reserves' or 'Bantustans' in South Africa, specifically. The 'native reserve' and 'Bantustans' were a form of entrapment for peasants. They had to survive on subsistence agriculture in crowded areas while also supplying cheap labour to the white-owned farms and plantations. In the southern African region, such colonies as Angola and Mozambique became characterized by both 'labour reserve' economies and peasant commodity production (Bernstein 2005: 69).

The third colonial economic invention, according to Amin (1976), was the 'concessionary companies,' a well-known example of which is King Leopold II of Belgium's Congo Free State rubber plantations. Even in areas dominated by concessionary companies, like the Congo, the discovery of minerals in Katanga meant that a mining industry was competing for cheap labour with the plantations. In all the colonies, the introduction of an array of colonial taxes pushed more and more indigenous people into the nexus of the colonial capitalist monetary commodity economy (Bernstein 2005: 70). This analysis offered insight into how indigenous people became entrapped in colonial economies. However, Africans did not just succumb to the spiderweb of coloniality. They devised many initiatives aimed at escaping coloniality.

African struggles for economic decolonization

Adom Getachew (2019) distilled three key African initiatives of resisting global and local colonial racial economics of domination and exploitation. Because economy and politics were intertwined, even the three initiatives were simultaneously economic and political in orientation. The first initiative was to fight to transform the 'principle' of self-determination into a 'human right.' The second was to try and create sustainable transnational 'federations' to counter neo-colonialism. The third was to demand an NIEO to de-hierarchize the racially hierarchical international order and hereby enable Africa to develop. At the national level, such African leaders as Kwame Nkrumah and Julius Nyerere also developed national economic plans aimed at setting afoot an autonomous development path. Nkrumah's economic thought was informed by Marx's and Lenin's notions of scientific socialism, whereas Nyerere pushed the agenda of African socialism.

While the African leaders, in collaboration and solidarity with other leaders from the Global South, successfully pushed the United Nations General Assembly to accept self-determination as a human right in 1960, they were not equally successful in changing the Euro-North American-centric modern world system into a domination-free structure of power. In the previous chapters of this book, I mentioned that what symbolized the successful struggle to make self-determination a human right was United National General Assembly Resolution 1514: Declaration on the Granting of Independence to Colonial Countries and Peoples of 1960. As put by Getachew (2019: 14):

> Resolution 1514 offered a complete repudiation of foreign rule and rejected any prerequisites for attainment of independence. Soon after its passage, the resolution formed the basis for a new committee with broad powers to investigate colonial rule and hear petitions from colonial subjects, making colonial rule subject to international scrutiny and to the demands for self-determination.

Getachew (2019: 2) correctly defined decolonization itself as a 'project of reordering the world that sought to create a domination-free and egalitarian international order.' To her, anti-colonial nationalism was aimed at 'worldmaking.' She elaborated that such leaders as Nkrumah, Nyerere, and others 'reinvented self-determination reaching beyond its association with the nation to insist that achievement of this ideal required juridical, political, and economic institutions in the international realm that would secure non-domination' (Getachew 2019: 2). This is an important intervention because it makes it clear why African leaders developed three initiatives for the institutionalization of a right to self-determination at the United Nations as an essential pre-requisite for other forms of decolonization of power, economy, and systems.

National self-determination without an NIEO was deemed to be useless by such visionaries as Nkrumah because it could be easily overturned by the forces of neo-colonialism. Thus, decolonization was underpinned by various strategies of re-making the world. According to Getachew (2019: 23), 'Anticolonial worldmaking offered a number of strategies to mitigate, circumvent, and undo the hierarchies that facilitated domination.' Through the deployment of the right to self-determination, colonized people and their leaders escalated the decolonization struggle to demand the sovereign equality of nations. Through the constitution of 'regional federations' (regional, political, and economic integration), the colonized peoples and their leaders 'sought to evade the economic dependence inherent in the global economy' (Getachew 2019: 24). The NIEO was meant to confront colonially created economic hierarchies at the world systemic level.

The creation of the Organization of African Unity (OAU) in 1963, which became the African Union in 2002, is a watered down and weak product of the struggles for regional federations, aimed at countering forces of neo-colonialism. In a radical fashion, the leading pan-Africanist Nkrumah even fought to add a clause to the national constitution of Ghana which conferred on Ghanaian parliament the 'power to provide for the surrender of the whole or any part of the sovereignty of Ghana' in favour of the USA (see Getachew 2019: 108). As early as 1958, the Ghana-Guinea-Mali Union was launched as a build up to continental union. Like all aspects of the decolonization struggles, the push for continental union was characterized by differences between what Rita Abrahamsen (2019) termed 'internationalists, sovereigntsists, and nativists.' While those aligned with Nkrumah wanted immediate declaration of the political union of Africa as an indispensable condition for the economic integration and indeed survival of African self-determination in a neo-colonial world, others, like Nnamdi Azikiwe of Nigeria, Haile Selassie of Ethiopia, and Nyerere of Tanzania, preferred a gradualist approach to the political and economic union of Africa. Still, many of the leaders of Francophone Africa were taking instructions from France, which was hell-bent on maintaining neo-colonial relations with its former colonies through the *Francafrique* colonial strategy.

The demand for an NIEO sought to recast the rules of the international economy in favour of the newly created African states. At the centre of the demand were specific ideas based on equality of nations and peoples, interdependence, common interest, and cooperation between all states (Cox 1948). The decolonial logic of the proponents of the NIEO was that the 'present system makes harmonious development impossible' (Rist 2019: 148). Despite the efforts of anti-colonial nationalists to realize the dream of an NIEO, this never materialized. What needs explanation here is why the initiatives to turn over a new economic leaf became difficult, if not impossible to bear fruits.

There are a number of explanations:

i Beginning with the Bandung Conference, which was discussed in Chapter 3 of this book, the epistemic question becomes very useful in making sense of how anti-colonial nationalists, pan-Africanists, and indeed other advocates for 'Third World liberation' all remained imprisoned in conventional and classical economic thought and bourgeois ideas of progress, to the extent that their push for economic decolonization was underpinned by bourgeois 'technical' models of development imbued with problematic nationalist modernist thinking.

ii The African national projects were always undercut by a 'combination of their internal fragility and imperialist aggression' to the extent that internally the African nationalists failed to mobilize popular support as the base for new development thought predicated on endogenous knowledge (Amin 2011: 77).

iii Even the demands for an NIEO became informed by knowledge from mainstream economics – notions of economic growth, expansion of trade, and increased sourcing of 'aid' from industrialized countries.

iv Gilbert Rist (2019: 148), like Samir Amin and Frantz Fanon, is very critical of the national bourgeois in charge of African states and their commitment to development, to the extent that he thinks their criticism of the international economic order was based on selfish class interest of seeking a compradorial relation with global colonial capitalists. In this way the national bourgeoisie played a role in perpetuating maldevelopment and dependence. There was clear lack of theoretical imagination and innovation by most of the African nationalist leaders beyond fighting for inclusion – hence commitment to ideas of 'international community,' 'mutual interests,' and 'partnerships' characterised their politics at the global engagement level.

v In bourgeois-driven development initiatives, the question of culture as the anchor for development was ignored. It only featured in *The 1975 Dag Hammarskjold Report* entitled *What Now* (1975), where it posited that development was not simply an economic process but a broader and complex societal change that has to arise endogenously from society, and dismissed notions of a universal formula for development (see Rist 2019: 155).

vi With the failure of Africa's development years (1955–1975), the imperial 'development merchant system' gained a new lease on life, and began to intervene directly on African economies including prescribing such programmes as the *Structural Adjustment Programme* and imposing conditionalities which resulted in 'recolonization' and 're-compradorization' (Amin 2011: 83).

The British historian Robert Gildea, in *Empires of the Mind: The Colonial Past and the Politics of the Present* (2019), introduced the concept of 'imperialism of decolonization' to explain the initiatives and efforts taken by empires to make sure they retained strategic and economic control over the colonies. The strategies included the neo-colonialist, French strategy of *Francafrique*; the European Union (EU) strategy of *Eurafrica*; the British strategy of the Commonwealth; the Washington Consensus and its Structural Adjustment programmes (neoliberalism); and many others, such as the strategic use of aid to create debt slavery. However, the empire is not always as strong as it projects its power over others. Some important factors have weakened the empire in the current age. The global financial crisis that began in 2008 and the emergence of anti-capitalist and anti-globalization forces has weakened Europe and North America to the extent that they are still on a recovery trajectory.

The danger is that once the powers of the Global North experience internal crisis, especially of an economic nature, they will increase their interference in the developments in the Global South, including through military invasions of those countries endowed with strategic resources, especially oil, like Iraq, Libya, and Venezuela. The internal fracture inside Europe has also resulted in Brexit. Narrow nationalism and xenophobia triggered by migrations of people from the Global South into the Global North and symbolized by the election of Donald Trump in the USA have proven and exposed the limits of neoliberalism. In concurrence with these developments are the resurgence and insurgence of decolonization/decoloniality struggles throughout the world.

Conclusion: resurgent and insurgent decolonization

Samir Amin, in his posthumously published book *Only People Make Their Own History: Writings on Capitalism, Imperialism, and Revolution* (2019: 197), emphasized that throughout the entire history of capitalist development, the 'North-South conflict between centres and peripheries' has been a central factor. He (2019: 197) further posited that the

> South has been slowly awakening, clearly apparent during the twentieth century, from the revolutions undertaken in the name of socialism, first the Russian semi-periphery, then in the peripheries of China, Vietnam, and Cuba, to the liberation movements in Asia and Africa and the advances in Latin America.

Amin (2019: 197) posited that 'The liberation struggles of peoples in the South—increasingly victorious—have been and still are closely linked with the challenge of capitalism. This conjunction is inevitable.' Such initiatives as the building of regional economic communities and South-South solidarities tend to embrace capitalist logics that are hoping only to leverage on their numbers to gain more benefits from the existing system. The key lesson concerns the futility of trying to fight by participating in the institutions created to serve the Eurocentric international system and its global orders. Such a strategy pre-occupied anti-colonial nationalists in the twentieth century and did not deliver genuine decolonization.

The resurgent and insurgent decolonization efforts of the twenty-first century need to take their lessons from Africa's long history of contact and entrapment in global coloniality and its intensification of unfinished decolonization struggles. Second, the knowledge which carried the African people to the present crisis cannot be the same knowledge that propels the resurgent and insurgent decolonization of the twenty-first century. As defined by Ngugi wa Thiong'o (1993) decolonization has to result in the movement of the centre towards decoloniality, which emphasizes delinking from colonial matrices of power and entrapment. What has to radically change are the logics of capital as well as 'assumptions, presuppositions, praxis of living' introduced by global coloniality (Mignolo 2018: 105). The third lesson is to take advantage of the fact that the Eurocentric knowledge which has always underpinned the colonial matrices of power has been exhausted. This fundamentally means that Europe and North America have lost the high ground of offering solutions to the world. The capitalist economic system is experiencing a terminal crisis. The modern world system is haunted by a systemic crisis. There is a planetary epistemic crisis. These are indeed fertile conditions for change in general and decolonial turn in particular – turning over a new leaf seems to be inevitable.

What is promising about the resurgent and insurgent decolonization of the twenty-first century is that they are mainly driven by youth, students, and decolonially conscious intellectuals and activists. The Rhodes Must Fall Movement which broke out in South Africa in 2015 was spearheaded by students, and it influenced other youth, including those inside the empires. The Black Lives Matter movements in the USA are also composed of students and youth, and are supported by social movements and progressive intellectuals. What is even more promising is that such formations are emerging within institutions of higher learning, where the decolonization of knowledge is very urgent. The youth in Francophone Africa have also risen against CFA colonial currency, and together with their leaders, they are confronting what has come to be known as French 'monetary imperialism' in Francophone Africa (Sylla 2019). Kemi Seba of Senegal became the face of the fighters against monetary imperialism when he publicly burnt a 5,000 CFA note in public in Dakar, Senegal. Previously, the struggle against French neo-colonialism and monetary tutelage was spearheaded by isolated leaders like Sekou Tore of Guinea, Sylvanus Olympio of Togo, and Thomas Sankara of Burkina Faso. Now that the masses are contributing to the pressure, the possibility of success is better than it was in the 1960s and 1970s.

The other current and ongoing initiative is one pushed by the African Union (AU) to implement the long-standing African Continental Free Trade Area (AfCFTA) so as to leverage the African numbers as well as intra-trade among African states. Despite the fact that this initiative is crafted in a pan-African discourse of recreating Africa as a strong economic power, the knowledge driving it is not decoupled from classical economic thought and neoliberal economic thoughts and its definition of people as a market. For example, the initiative is praised for its potential to create the world's largest trade, with 'a combined consumer and business spending of $6.7 trillion in 2030' (Signe and van de Ven 2019: 1). However, it is linked with the protests against CFA in Francophone Africa because its main idea is to drop the French colonial currency and adopt a pan-African currency being introduced by leaders of the Economic Community of West African States (ECOWAS), known as 'ECO.' Despite debates on technical questions, the key question which remains ignored involves the decolonization of knowledge in order to make sure that there is indeed new thought about the development of Africa. This chapter opened with a critique of economic theory and economic thought to underscore the importance and urgency of shifting from Eurocentric epistemology, which is underpinned by what Amin termed 'ideological trickery.'

References

Abrahamsen, R. 2019. 'Internationalists, Sovereigntists, Nativists: Contending Visions of World Order in Pan-Africanism.' *Review of International Studies*, doi: 1017/S026010519000305, pp. 1–19.

Adebajo, A. 2010. *The Curse of Berlin: Africa: After the Cold War*. Scottsville, KY: University of KwaZulu-Natal Press.

Amin, S. 1974. *Accumulation on a World Scale: A Critique of the Theory of Underdevelopment.* London: The Harvester Press Ltd.
Amin, S. 1976. *Unequal Development: An Essay on the Social Formations of Peripheral Capitalism.* Hassocks: Harvester.
Amin, S. 1977. *Imperialism and Unequal Development.* London: The Harvest Press Ltd.
Amin, A. 1990. *Delinking: Towards A Polycentric World.* London: Zed Books.
Amin, S. 2011. *Maldevelopment: Anatomy of a Global Failure.* Second Edition. Cape Town/Dakar/Nairobi/Oxford: Pambazuka Press.
Amin, S. 2019. *Only People Make Their Own History: Writings on Capitalism, Imperialism, and Revolution.* New York: Monthly Review Press.
Austen, R. 1987. *African Economic History.* London: James Currey.
Bernstein, H. 2005. 'Rural Land and Land Conflicts in Sub-Saharan Africa.' In S. Moyo and P. Yeros (eds.), *Reclaiming the Land: The Resurgence of Rural Movements in Africa, Asia and Latin America.* London and New York: Zed Books, pp. 67–101.
Brown, W. 2010. *Walled States, Waning Sovereignty.* New York: Zone Books.
Cesaire, A. 2000. *Discourse on Colonialism.* New York: Monthly Review Press.
Cooper, F. 2014. *Africa in the World: Capitalism, Empire, Nation-State.* Cambridge and London: Harvard University Press.
Cox, C. 1948. *Caste, Class and Race: A Study in Social Dynamics.* New York: Monthly Review Press.
Cox, A. 1979. 'Ideologies and the New International Order: Reflections on Some Recent Literature.' *International Organization*, 33(2), pp. 275–308.
Ekeh, P. 1983. *Colonialism and Social Structure: University of Ibadan Inaugural Lecture, 1980.* Ibadan: University of Ibadan Press.
Fanon, F. 1968. *The Wretched of the Earth.* New York: Grove Press.
Galeano, E. 1997. *Open Veins of Latin America: Five Centuries of the Pillage of a Continent.* New York: Monthly Review Press.
Getachew, A. 2019. *Worldmaking after Empire: The Rise and Fall of Self-Determination.* Princeton, NJ: Princeton University Press.
Gibson, C. 2014. *Empire's Crossroads: A History of the Caribbean from Columbus to the Present Day.* London: Macmillan.
Gildea, R. 2019. *Empires of the Mind: The Colonial Past and the Politics of the Present.* Cambridge: Cambridge University Press.
Goody, J. 1996. *The Theft of History.* Cambridge: Cambridge University Press.
Grosfoguel, R. 2007. 'The Epistemic Decolonial Turn: Beyond Political-Economy Paradigms.' *Cultural Studies*, 21(2/3) (March/May), pp. 211–223.
Grosfoguel, R. 2016. 'Del 'Extractivismo Economico' al 'Extractvismo Epistemico' y al 'Extractivism Ontologico': Una Forma Desstructiva De Conocer, Ser y Estar en el Mundo.' *Tabula Rasa*: Bogota-Colombia, 24, pp. 123–143.
Grosfoguel, R., & Cervantes-Rodriguez, A. M. 2002. 'Introduction: Unthinking Twentieth-Century Eurocentric Mythologies: Universalist Knowledge, Decolonization, and Developmentalism.' In R. Grosfoguel and A. M. Cervantes-Rodriguez (eds.), *The Modern/Colonial/Capitalist World-System in the Twentieth Century: Global Processes, Antisystemic Movements, and the Geopolitics of Knowledge.* London, Westport and Connecticut: Praeger, pp. ix–xxix.
Henry, P. 2000. *Caliban's Reason: Introducing Afro-Caribbean Philosophy.* New York and London: Routledge.

Hoppers, C. O. and Richards, H. 2012. *Rethinking Thinking: Modernity's 'Other' and the Transformation of the University.* Pretoria: UNISA Press.

Kinsey, C. 2006. *Corporate Soldiers and International Security: The Rise of Private Military Companies.* London: Routledge.

Kontopoulos, K. 1993. *The Logic of Social Sciences.* Cambridge: Cambridge University Press.

Lugones, M. 2008. 'The Coloniality of Power.' *Worlds & Knowledges Otherwise*, 2 (Spring), pp. 1–17.

Maldonado-Torres, N. 2007. 'On the Coloniality of Being: Contributions to the Development of a Concept.' *Cultural Studies*, 21(2/3) (March/May), pp. 240–270.

Mamdani, M. 1996. *Citizen and Subject: Contemporary Africa and the Legacy of Late Colonialism.* Princeton, NJ: Princeton University Press.

Mamdani, M. 2013. *Define and Rule: Native as Political Identity.* Johannesburg: Wits University Press.

Mazrui, A. A. 1986. *The Africans: A Triple Heritage.* London: BBC Publications.

Mignolo, W. D. 2007. 'Introduction: Coloniality of Power and De-Colonial Thinking.' *Cultural Studies*, 21(2/3), pp. 140–187.

Mignolo, W. D. 2018. 'On Pluriversality and Multipolar World Order: Decoloniality after Decolonization; Dewesternization after the Cold War.' In Bernd Beiter (ed.), *Constructing the Pluriverse: The Geopolitics of Knowledge.* Durham, NC and London: Duke University Press, pp. 90–116.

Mignolo, W. D., & Walsh, C. E. 2018. *On Coloniality: Concepts, Analytics, Praxis.* Durham, NC and London: Duke University Press.

Nandy, A. 1983. *The Intimate Enemy: Loss and Recovery of Self under Colonialism.* New Delhi: Oxford University Press.

Ndlovu-Gatsheni, S. J. 2013. 'The Entrapment of Africa within the Global Matrices of Power: Eurocentrism, Coloniality, and Deimperialization in the Twenty-First Century.' *Journal of Developing Societies*, 29(4), pp. 331–353.

Ndlovu-Gatsheni, S. J. 2015. 'Genealogies of Coloniality and Implications for Africa's Development.' *Africa Development*, XL(3), pp. 13–40.

Ndlovu-Gatsheni, S. J. 2017. 'The Entrapment of the Global South in Global Coloniality.' Keynote Address Delivered at the International Conference on Global Crises, Global Change (GCC): Westminster Undergraduate Conference, Westminster College, United States of America, 30 March to 1 April.

Ndlovu-Gatsheni, S. J. 2019. 'Empire, Decolonization and Development in Africa.' Unpublished Annual Distinguished Hormuud Lecture delivered at the 62nd Annual Meeting of the African Studies Association (ASA), Boston, Massachusetts, United States of America, 23 November.

Newitt, M. 2010. *The Portuguese in West Africa, 1415–1670. A Documentary History.* Cambridge: Cambridge University Press.

Ngugi wa Thiong'o. 1986. *Decolonizing the Mind: The Politics of Language in African Literature.* Oxford: James Currey.

Ngugi wa Thiong'o. 1993. *Moving the Centre: The Struggles for Cultural Freedoms.* Oxford: James Currey.

Ngugi wa Thiong'o. 1997. *Writers in Politics: A Re-Engagement with Issues of Literature and Society.* Oxford: James Currey.

Ngugi wa Thiong'o. 2016. *Secure the Base: Making Africa Visible in the Globe.* London, New York, Calcutta: Seagull Books.

Nimako, K., & Willemsen, G. 2011. *The Dutch Atlantic: Slavery, Abolition and Emancipation*. London: Polity Press.

Quijano, A. 2000. 'Coloniality of Power, Eurocentrism, and Latin America.' *Nepantla: Views from South*, 1(3), pp. 533–580.

Quijano, A. 2007. 'Coloniality and Modernity/Rationality.' *Cultural Studies*, 21(2–3), (March/May), pp. 168–178.

Rist, G. 2019. *The History of Development: From Western Origins to Global Faith: Fifth Edition*. London: Zed Books.

Robinson, C. J. 1983. *Black Marxism: The Making of the Black Radical Tradition*. London: Zed Press.

Rodney, W. 1972. *How Europe Under developed Africa*. London and Dar-es-salaam: Tanzania Publishing House and Bogle-L'Ouverture Publications.

Signe, L., & van de Ven, C. 2019. 'Key to Success for the AfCFTA.' Brookings: Africa Growth Initiative, May.

Sylla, N. S. 2019. 'An Interview with Ndongo Samba Sylla: Confronting Monetary Imperialism in Francophone Africa.' Available: https://africaascountry.com/2019/07/confronting-monetary-imperialism-in-francophon (accessed 22/12/2019).

Terreblanche, S. 2014. *Western Empires, Christianity, and the Inequalities between the West and the Rest*, 1500–2010. Johannesburg: Penguin Books.

Tucker, R. C. (ed.). 1978. *The Marx-Engels Reader*. New York: W. W. Norton.

Wynter, S. 2003. 'Unsettling the Coloniality of Being/Power/Truth/Freedom: Towards the Human After Man, Its Overrepresentation—An Argument.' *The New Centennial Review*, 3(3), pp. 257–337.

6 African Renaissance

Introduction

The leading African intellectual Mahmood Mamdani (1999) posited that 'there can be no African Renaissance without an Africa-focused intelligentsia.' This intervention spoke directly to the idea of the epistemic domain as the first realm that will have to change if Africa is to re-emerge as a reconstituted powerful force in world affairs. Through discourse of Renaissance, Africa is seeking to re-emerge from coloniality and claim its previous status as the cradle of humankind and the home of major human civilizations. With its pre-colonial world class universities in Egypt, Mali, and Morocco, Africa was a leader in the fields of arts, sciences, and technology (see Diop 1974; Gutto 2006; Nabudere 2007). During this second period of human evolution/development, Africa was also home to the mythical Prester John, and the great civilizations of Great Zimbabwe, Mapungubwe, Axum, Carthage, Mali Benin, Congo, Asante Songhayi, and many others were striving. This is why such historians as John Iliffe, in *Africans: The History of a Continent: Third Edition* (2017: 1), posited that 'Africans have been and are the frontiersmen who have colonized an especially hostile region of the world on behalf of the entire human race. That has been their chief contribution to history.' Europe only began to dominate in the third period of human evolution/development, when Europeans emerged, starting in the fifteenth century, inaugurating over 500 years of systemic racial, economic, political, social, and epistemic domination.

The African Renaissance has been one of the most important initiatives aimed at enabling Africa to turn over a new leaf and take charge of its destiny. The concept was popularized by Cheikh Anta Diop in the mid-1940s. However, it should be noted that as early as 1906 Pixley ka Isaka Seme introduced the idea of a 'regeneration' of Africa, and in 1937 Nnamdi Azikiwe of Nigeria engaged with the idea of a 'renascent Africa,' both of which formed a strong background for the unfolding of the idea of the African Renaissance. By the 1990s, President Thabo Mbeki of South Africa made the African Renaissance the hallmark of his continental politics. The 1999 international conference resulted in the publication of a 30-chapter edited volume entitled *African Renaissance: The New Struggle* (1999), with a foreword by President Thabo Mbeki.

This chapter reflects on the African Renaissance from a historical and conceptual perspective. Its entry point is Ngugi wa Thiong'o's work *Something Torn and New: An African Renaissance* (2009b), which opens the canvas on the African Renaissance, contextualizing it perfectly into the broader African struggles against colonialism and imperialism as well as within the terrain of African initiatives to unite Africa and initiate Afro-modernity. To deepen its conceptual and philosophical reflections, this study also draws from the emerging field of decolonial theory. Its key thesis is that if colonialism and coloniality (a continuation of colonial-like relations after the dismantlement of direct colonialism) sought to 'dismember' Africa for imperial strategic purposes, the African Renaissance and decoloniality seek to 're-member' Africans as part of the fulfilment of liberation (Ndlovu-Gatsheni 2015a, 2015b).

According to Ngugi wa Thiong'o (2009b: 4), dismemberment is a 'colonial act,' a 'practice of power, intended to pacify a populace, and a symbolic act, a performance of power intended to produce docile minds.' It is also 'An act of absolute social engineering, the continent's dismemberment was simultaneously the foundation, fuel, and consequence of Europe's capitalist modernity' (Ngugi wa Thiong'o 2009b: 5). Mapping, naming, and owning completed dismemberment under colonialism and coloniality. On the consequences of dismemberment, Ngugi wa Thiong'o (2009b: 28) concluded that 'Dismembered from the land, from labour, from power, and from memory, the result is destruction of the base from which people launch themselves into the world.' African people find it difficult to re-launch themselves into the world because of the invasion of their mental universes by colonialism, which fundamentally 'empty[s] their hard disk of previous memory, and download[s] into them a software of European memory' (Ngugi wa Thiong'o 2009b: 21).

This analysis invites us to reflect on what colonialism is, fundamentally – a question that was posed by Aimé Césaire in 1955. A critical reflection on colonialism takes us to the two schools: the episodic school of colonialism and the epic school of colonialism. In the 'episodic school of colonialism' the entire colonial experience is reduced to a mere 'episode in African history' which did not fundamentally alter its course (see Ajayi 1969). This school arose within nationalist historiography that was ranged against imperial/colonial historiography which denied the existence of African history before the arrival of Europeans (see Falola 2001). The episodic school is countered by the 'epic school of colonialism,' which underscored that colonialism and its current manifestations and operations as 'coloniality' fundamentally and negatively affected the African people on the continent as well as those in the diaspora (Fanon 1968; Ekeh 1983; Mazrui 1986; Ngugi wa Thiong'o 1986, 2009a, 2009b; Césaire 2000; Ndlovu-Gatsheni 2013a, 2013b). If the episodic perspective regarded colonialism as an event, the epic perspective viewed it as a system and a social movement that transformed Africa in a fundamental way. Thus, during its very nascent unfolding, colonial modernity fragmented Africa into two entities, that is, continental Africans and Africans in the diaspora, as it began the process of 'dismembering' the continent. This point is delivered more emphatically by Ngugi wa Thiong'o (2009b: 5):

> The dismemberment of Africa occurred in two stages. During the first of these, the African personhood was divided into two halves, the continent and its diaspora. African slaves, the central commodity in the mercantile phase of capitalism, formed the basis of the sugar, cotton, and tobacco plantations in the Caribbean and American mainland. If we accept that the slave trade and plantation slavery provided the primary accumulation of capital that made Europe's Industrial Revolution possible, we cannot escape the irony that the very needs of that Industrial Revolution—markets for finished goods, sources of raw materials, and strategic requirements in the defence of trade routes—led inexorably to the second stage of dismemberment of the continent.

This initial dismemberment was followed by the Berlin Conference of 1884–1885, which cartographically fragmented Africa into European spheres of influence and reconstituted it into European colonies. Ngugi wa Thiong'o (2009b: 5–6) connected the two processes of dismemberment in these revealing words:

> Just as the slave plantations were owned by various European powers, so post-Berlin Conference Africa was transformed into a series of colonial plantations owned by many of the same European powers. The requirements of the slave plantation demanded the physical removal of human resources from the continent to work on the land stolen from other subject peoples, mainly native Caribbeans and native Americans. The result was an additional dismemberment of the Diasporic African, who was now separated not only from his continent and his labour but also from his very sovereign being. The subsequent colonial plantations on the African continent have led to the same result: division of the African from his land, body, and mind. The land is taken away from its owner, and the owner is turned into a worker on the same land, thus losing control of his natural and human resources. [...] Whereas before he was his own subject, now he is subject to another.

It was indeed the feeling and reality of dismemberment which provoked the drive for the African Renaissance. In his books *Something Torn and New: An African Renaissance* (2009b) and *Re-Membering Africa* (2009a), Ngugi wa Thiong'o correctly defined the African Renaissance as a liberatory process of 're-membering' Africa after centuries of 'dismemberment.' To him

(2009b: 35), it is essentially an encapsulation of re-membering visions, that is, 'the quest for wholeness, a quest that has underlain African struggles since the Atlantic slave trade.' He elaborated, 'Though Ethiopianism and the like preceded these struggles, Garveyism and Pan-Africanism are the grandest secular visions for reconnecting the dismembered' (Ngugi wa Thiong'o 2009b: 35) and further concluded that:

> The African eagle can fly only with his re-membered wings. Re-membering Africa will bring about the flowering of the African renaissance; and Afro-modernity will play its role in the globe on the reciprocal egalitarian basis of give and take, ultimately realising the Garveyism vision of a common humanity of progress and achievement "that will wipe away the odour of prejudice, and elevate the human race to the height of real godly love and satisfaction."
>
> (Ngugi wa Thiong'o 2009b: 98)

If understood from this Ngugian perspective, the African Renaissance emerged concurrently with the unfolding of the Euro-North American-centric modernity and colonial encounters that accompanied it as a form of resistance as well as a vision of liberation. At one level, as articulated by Marcus Garvey (1969: 127), the African Renaissance was expected to 'wipe away the odour of prejudice, and elevate the human race to the height of real godly love and satisfaction.' It was also defined as a restorative initiative that was expected to rebuild black and African pride after centuries of inferiorization and dehumanization. The Black Consciousness Movement (BCM), led by Steve Bantu Biko, was a restorative force, fighting to restore faith in black people's capacity to successfully resist colonial and apartheid oppression while affirming them as the makers of their own history. This point is delivered more clearly by Mabogo Percy More in his recent book, *Biko: Philosophy, Identity and Liberation* (2017: ix), in which he posited that

> in his struggle to offer innovative ways of perceiving, new ways of acting, new ways of thinking, indeed new ways of being-black, new ways of black 'Somebodiness' and new ways of escaping black 'Nobodiness,' Biko evolved a philosophy that went beyond philosophy itself.

Besides the important task of freeing African subjectivity from coloniality, the African Renaissance was also expected to inspire unity among what was known as the 'black race.' However, such works as Kwame Anthony Appiah's *In My Father's House: Africa in the Philosophy of Culture* (1992) and Achille Mbembe's *Critique of Black Reason* (2017) highlighted how the idea of a 'black race' not only emerged as a response to racist discourse but was in fact a reproduction by victims of the racist social classification of human beings. In his critique of the reproduction of a race category by victims of racism, Appiah (1992: 20) argued, 'If we are to escape from racism fully, and from the racialism it presupposes, we must seek other bases for Pan-African solidarity.' Indeed, over time, pan-Africanism as a leitmotif of the African Renaissance matured into a humanist and developmentalist discourse that was opposed to race as an organizing principle of society and the world.

It is not surprising that such scholars-cum-politicians as Pixley ka Isaka Seme of South Africa (1906), Nnamdi Azikiwe of Nigeria (1937), Cheikh Anta Diop of Senegal (1966), and Thabo Mbeki of South Africa (1997) were all committed to an African Renaissance as part of completing the liberatory struggle, which can perhaps be dated as far back as the Haitian Revolution of 1804, and the successful Ethiopian resistance to Italian colonial invasion at the Battle of Adwa in 1896. Seme's award-winning speech, 'The Regeneration of Africa' (1906), suggested that the unity of the African people was necessary if they were to liberate the continent from colonialism and apartheid, and set it on a recovery trajectory for the benefit of its sons and daughters. Seme expressed his pride in being an African within a global context where being black in general and African in particular was consigned to inferiority, and he prophesied a risen African civilization imbued with the spirituality and humanism that had been squandered by European rationality and secularism (see Netshitenzhe 2013; Kumalo 2015).

Azikiwe authored *Renascent Africa* (1968; originally published 1937), in which, like Seme and Garvey, he expressed not only an idea of a new Africa but also his philosophy of black pride and self-reliance. Cheikh Anta Diop's *Towards the African Renaissance: Essays in Culture and Development, 1946–1960* (1966) popularized the concept of the African Renaissance and emphasized the importance of anchoring African development to African history and African culture as well as the necessity of mobilizing Africans on the continent and the diaspora to take charge of inventing their own futures. Concretely, the early phase of the unfolding of the African Renaissance delivered such forces as the civil rights movements in America, the political decolonization of the Caribbean and Latin America territories, the political decolonization of Africa, and the rise of the continental pan-Africanism that gave birth to the Organization of African Unity (OAU) (now the African Union (AU)).

The dismantlement of juridical apartheid settler colonialism in South Africa in 1994 not only marked the realization of Kwame Nkrumah's vision of seeking political kingdom but also provided Africa with two influential leaders, Nelson Mandela and Thabo Mbeki, both of whom strongly believed in the African Renaissance as a restorative force. Soon after becoming the first black president of South Africa, Mandela consistently deployed a progressive pedagogical nationalism that not only was vehemently opposed to racism but always called on the African people to rebuild Africa as a leading site of world civilization. In 1994, standing in Timbuktu (the site of African precolonial civilization), Mandela urged Africans to push forward with the African Renaissance using these words: 'One epoch with its historic task has come to an end. Surely another must commence with its own challenges.

Africa cries out for new birth. Carthage waits the restoration of its glory' (quoted in Ngugi wa Thiong'o 2009b: 130).

Mandela's successor as president of South Africa, Thabo Mbeki, became one of the leading ideologues of the African Renaissance in the twenty-first century. His widely quoted 1996 speech "I am an African" underscored his resolve as an African leader to pursue the African Renaissance as part of a restoration of African people's pride. To him, the African Renaissance was part of defining and adding content to the 'African national democratic revolution' (Mbeki 2015: ix). In mid-1997, he delivered a lengthy speech in the USA, where he posited that 'the African Renaissance is upon us' and elaborated:

> This generation remains African and carries with it an historic pride which compels it to seek a place for Africans equal to all the other peoples of our common universe. It knows and is resolved that, to attain that objective, it must resist all tyranny, oppose all attempts to deny liberty by resort to demagogy, repulse the temptation to describe African life as the ability to live on charity, engage the fight to secure the emancipation of the African woman, and reassert the fundamental concept that we are our own liberators from oppression, from underdevelopment and poverty, from the perpetuation of an experience from slavery, to colonialism, to apartheid, to dependence on alms.
>
> (Mbeki 1997: 1)

At the intellectual level, the hosting of the African Renaissance International Conference from September 28 to 29, 1998, in South Africa, which culminated in the publication of an influential edited volume entitled *African Renaissance: The New Struggle* (1999), formed an important milestone in the interrogation of the meanings, essence, and implications of the African Renaissance for South Africa and Africa in general. Various definitions of the African Renaissance emerged, defining it as an

> expression of democratization's third wave; the mobilization of an identity politics; a campaign to alter local, national, and global principles of political governance, social interchange, and economic exchange; a defence of humanism; an appeal to re-imagine education; and a rallying cry to develop indigenous thought, public culture, and new forms of (post)national political discourse.
>
> (Doxtader 2015: 175)

Despite these wide-ranging interpretations, the AU declared 2013 the year of 'Pan-Africanism and African Renaissance,' and its Agenda 2063 is predicated on a delivery of these goals. To gain a deeper understanding of the African Renaissance, however, it is vital to frame and situate it within the broader trajectories of African liberation struggles and visions of the future.

Historical framing of the African Renaissance

The idea of the African Renaissance must be seen as an ongoing struggle in the midst of an anti-colonial and anti-imperialist struggle as well as a search for a development path and a democratic framework of governance. Five discursive moments of contemporary African history and politics frame the African Renaissance as part of the continent's struggle for freedom. The political decolonization of the twentieth century, which Nkrumah described as the seeking of 'the political kingdom,' formed the first moment. This struggle can be traced as far back as the Haitian Revolution (1791–1804), which produced the first 'black republic' which emerged from the struggles of a people who were not only victims of racism but also said to be slaves by nature (Trouillot 1995). Regarding the significance of the Haitian Revolution, Michael Neocosmos (2016: 78) deleneated two implications: the opening up of 'the universality of humanity, the truth of universal freedom (as opposed to freedom for some and not for others' and the laying out of 'the universal of nationhood among African peoples (the national question) or the right to self-determination, as it became known in the twentieth century).'

One can highlight the continuation of the struggles for political decolonization by considering the significance of William E. B. Du Bois's organization of the Pan-African Congresses, which commenced in 1900 and continued up to 1945. These were some of the concrete initiatives that took place in the form of Africans sitting down to contest and critique Eurocentric global initiatives that excluded Africa from the ordering and reordering of the modern world system (Ndlovu-Gatsheni 2014). It was through the Pan-African Congresses that black people from the rest of the world spoke truth directly to colonial/imperial power and revealed the hypocrisies, conceits, and double standards within the modern world system and global orders. They spoke about all the inimical processes visited on black people, such as enslavement; racism; labour exploitation; colonial violence; and violated rights, including the right to self-determination (Ndlovu-Gatsheni 2014: 23–24).

It was at the Fifth Pan-African Congress, held in Manchester in the United Kingdom in 1945 and attended by African politicians like Kwame Nkrumah of Ghana and Jomo Kenyatta of Kenya, that a direct and emphatic call for an end to colonialism was made. Colonized African people were directly urged to unite and fight for decolonization (Ndlovu-Gatsheni 2014: 24–25). By 1958, Africa could afford to host the All Africa Pan-African Conference not only within the continent but in the independent African state of Ghana, led by an African leader (Kwame Nkrumah), and those present rededicated themselves to the decolonization of the entire African continent. The same Nkrumah who coined the slogan of seeking a political kingdom as the first step in decolonization was by 1965 articulating the problem of 'neo-colonialism,' as a major hindrance to African leaders' attempts to translate hard-won political decolonization into the desperately expected economic decolonization (see Nkrumah 1965). His warning about neo-colonialism and advice about political union as solution still remains powerful and truthful:

> Our essential bulwark against such sinister threats and other multifarious designs of the neo-colonialists is in our political union. If we are to remain free, if we are to enjoy the full benefits of Africa's rich resources, we must unite to plan for our total defence and the full exploitation of our material and human resources, in the full interests of all our peoples. To 'go it alone' will limit our horizons, curtail our expectations and threaten our liberty.
>
> (Nkrumah 1963: vii)

Between 1957 and 1965 Nkrumah had emerged as the leading pan-African voice for immediate continental unity. During this period he published *Africa Must Unite* (1963), which explained the rationale for African political union in very convincing arguments. Nrumah noticed three key problems within the 'political kingdom.' The first was the challenge of forging a pan-ethnic national unity within the newly independent states. This challenge became known as 'nation-building' and 'state-making.' Its enormity was well captured by Liisa Laakso and Adebayo O. Olukoshi (1996: 11–12):

> However, at the heart of the modern nation-state project was the idea, flawed from the outset, of a tight correspondence between the nation and the state whereby each sovereign state was seen as a nation-state of people who shared a common language or culture [...]. This notion of the nation-state stood in direct contradiction to the reality that most states were, in fact, multi-cultural, multi-lingual and multi-religious and that not all ethnic groups (however defined) were sufficiently large or powerful or even willing to achieve a state of their own.

In *Africa Must Unite*, Nkrumah worried about the crisis of internal unity within Ghana since the attainment of political freedom and about the lack of substantive unity at the continental level. He sold the African leaders from the continent a gospel of continental unity as a destiny thrown at them and warned that 'To suggest that the time is not yet ripe for considering a political union of Africa is to evade facts and ignore realities in Africa today' (Nkrumah 1963: 165). He elaborated:

> The greatest danger at present facing Africa is neo-colonialism and its major instrument, balkanization. The latter term is particularly appropriate to describe the breaking up of Africa into small, weak states, since it arose from the action of great powers when they divided up the European part of the old Turkish Empire, and created a number

> of dependent and competing states in the Balkan Peninsula. The effect was to produce a political tinderbox which any spark could set alight.
>
> (Nkrumah 1963: 173)

To Nkrumah, the neo-colonialists and imperialists were ready to go 'fishing in the muddy waters of communalism, tribalism and sectional interests, [and] endeavour to create fictions in national front, in order to achieve fragmentation' (Nkrumah 1963: 173). Thus, the looming neo-colonial strategy of 'balkanization' of Africa and imperial intrusions through neo-colonialism constituted two major challenges that had to be confronted and resolved. To Nkrumah, the creation of a political union of Africa was a necessity, not an option. These challenges undercut both political decolonization and economic decolonization as essential bases for the African Renaissance.

Conceptually speaking, this is constituted by an amalgamation of political decolonization, economic decolonization, cultural decolonization, and epistemic decolonization; it is also clear that such initiatives as Ethiopianism, Garveyism, Negritude, pan-Africanism(s), African personality, Afrocentricity, consciencism, African humanism, African socialism(s), and Black Consciousness Movement (BCM)were all attempts to concretize the African Renaissance (Achebe 1997: 179). Nkrumah's (1964) concept of philosophical consciencism explained the African Renaissance as embracing a synthesis of traditional Africa, Islamic Africa, and Euro-Christian Africa to produce a new ideology for the harmonious growth and development of society. This is how he put it:

> The philosophy that must stand behind this social revolution is that which I have once referred to as philosophical consciencism: consciencism is the map in intellectual terms of the disposition of forces which will enable African society to digest the Western and the Islamic and the Euro-Christian elements in Africa, and develop them in such a way that they fit into the African personality. The African personality is itself defined by the cluster of humanist principles which underlie the traditional African society. Philosophical consciencism is that philosophical standpoint which, taking its start from the present content of the African conscience indicates the way in which progress is forged out of the conflict in that conscience.
>
> (Nkrumah 1964: 79)

To African nationalist thinkers and theorists, the African Renaissance meant a paradigmatic shift from the state of being which colonial subjects characterized by dehumanization, thingification, and depravity, as well as suffering under slavery, imperialism, colonialism, racial-colonial capitalism, apartheid, neo-colonialism, and underdevelopment, towards one that is decolonial, marked by regained sovereign subjectivity and being fully in charge of African futures. It is not surprising that such African leaders and theorists as Frantz Fanon, Leopold Sedar Senghor, Kenneth Kaunda, Julius Nyerere, and Nelson Mandela emphasized the importance of rehumanizing the dehumanized as a central task of the African Renaissance. Kenneth Kaunda defined humanism as a 'philosophy of life' and noted that colonialism 'devalued man' (Kaunda and Morris 1966: 19–21). Kaunda and Morris posited that:

> It was nationalism, of course, which restored our self-confidence, for it taught us what we could do together as men [and women], and only as men [and women]—at no stage in the freedom struggle had we the material power or military might of colonialists. It was humanity in revolt that won us freedom. [...] It was the triumph of a Man-centred society over a Power-centred society. This intense belief in the possibility of Man is a discovery which Africa appears to be making long after the West has discarded it.
>
> (Kaunda and Morris 1966: 21)

In their decolonial-nationalist 'meditations on man,' Kaunda and Morris expressed their conviction that 'only the recovery of a sense of the centrality of Man will get politics back on the right track' and asked, 'How can we humanise our politics in Zambia so that the humblest and least endowed of our citizens occupies a central place in Government's concerns?' (Kaunda and Morris 1966: 41) The dominance of humanist nationalism resulted in various experimentations with African socialism, the most well-known example being that of the '*Ujamaa*' (familyhood) of Tanzania under Julius Nyerere, which sought to provide an escape route from capitalism's idea of happiness based on the 'exploitation of man by man' (Nyerere 1967).

The search for an African Renaissance by African nationalists is further exemplified by such charters and declarations as the Freedom Charter (South Africa), Arusha Declaration (Tanzania), Common Man's Charter (Uganda), and Mulugushi Declaration (Zambia). These were part of nationalist humanist imaginations of a better world, free from racism, exploitation, and oppression. Even if they did not eventually reflect the practical political practices of African leaders, they remain important embodiments of attempts to reconstitute the political in Africa (Ndlovu-Gatsheni 2016a).

The second moment that framed the fossilization of the African Renaissance is economic decolonization, which sought to deal with the emergent problem of 'neo-colonialism' (Nkrumah 1965). The hosting of the Bandung Conference in 1955 and the increasing demands for a New International Economic Order (NIEO) marked the intensification of the struggles for an 'economic' renaissance (see Gumede (2013) on the concept of economic renaissance). Vusi Gumede (2013: 436) understood an African economic renaissance to mean the ability of African people to 'decide on the African economy and the economic system that works for them.' The Bandung

Conference offered a venue in which to decide not only on the economic but also on the political system that would work for Africa and Asia (Wright 1956). A 12-point economic cooperation agenda identified development as an urgent priority for Afro-Asian states. African and Asian leaders seemed to have realized that the development they urgently wanted could not be attained within a modern world system that was racially hierarchized and Euro-North American-centric. Thus, political decolonization needed to be expanded in order to grapple with a global system that remained asymmetrical in its power configuration. This is why the participants at the Bandung Conference were deeply troubled by their limited participation in the international institutions that had been established to govern world affairs (Abdulgani 1964).

One can safely argue that while the Bandung Conference seems to have correctly identified 'global coloniality' as a major hindrance to the achievement of development in Africa and Asia, it did not successfully delink with nationalist, bourgeois, nation-centric ideas or conventional economic ideas (Ndlovu-Gatsheni 2013b). Three objectives drove the Bandung spirit: non-alignment in the age of the Cold War; elimination of all forms of colonialism and racism; and, finally, modernization and economic development (Mayall 1990). The idea of non-alignment spoke to an aspiration for a new international norm that gave smaller and less powerful states the right to develop and orchestrate an autonomous path to the future. The issue of equality of states was stressed, including rising concerns about the under-representation of African and Asian states on the United Nations Security Council. The Bandung spirit also articulated the problem of international economic injustices (Krasner 1981). It laid a strong basis for the crystallization of a Third World coalition in the United Nations, which, in 1964, constituted the United Nations Conference on Trade and Development (UNCTAD).

The Non-Alignment Movement (NAM), which had originally been formed at a summit in Algiers in 1971, was another forum used to push for autonomous economic development and sovereign political trajectory. NAM included Latin American states which had gained political independence far earlier than Asian and African colonies. These states had been active within the United Nations in pushing the agenda of reforming the international economic and political system. At the Cairo Economic Conference of 1962, the Afro-Asian and Latin American states had already pointed out that the more dangerous division of the world was the North-South divide, which took the form of 'haves' and 'have-nots,' rather than the ideologically informed East-West divide that preoccupied the Western powers (Nesadurai 2005: 12).

The resolutions of the first NAM Summit, held in Belgrade in Yugoslavia in 1961, and the Cairo Summit of 1962 are credited for putting pressure on the United Nations to establish UNCTAD as an agency to address Third World development issues. The problem was that UNCTAD played only a marginal role in global economic governance as the USA and other industrial powers rejected any role for the body in trade negotiations (Taylor 2003). At the time of its launch, the Latin American economist Raúl Prebisch was pushing forward the dependency thesis to explain the problem of development in the Third World. He was appointed UNCTAD's first secretary general. Informed by dependency ideas, UNCTAD's demands included greater access to industrial countries' markets, greater self-reliance amongst the Third World countries, the right to nationalize assets, and democratization of all binding international decision-making based on the principle of 'one-nation, one vote'(Gosovic 1972).

These demands were informed by Prebisch's decolonial diagnosis of Third World underdevelopment in terms of its structural dependency on a capitalist core that controlled all levers of international decision-making and profitable economic activity. The proposals were rejected by industrial powers. However, Third World leaders did not give up the fight for a reformed international system. The period from 1973 to 1980 was dominated by the demand for an NIEO. Following the oil crises of 1971 and 1973, the Third World coalition united to push further for this through the G77 – a coalition of developing countries. The NIEO was informed by the dependency ideas which emphasized the decolonization of global coloniality that favoured the industrial powers and disadvantaged those countries that had emerged from colonialism. It called for a restructuring of global structural regimes underpinning unequal trade and other economic interactions (Cox 1979: 257).

The more radical members of the G77 demanded restitution based on the notion that the industrialized powers owed something to the South as compensation for slavery and colonialism (Cox 1979). In the spirit of the NIEO, African leaders adopted the African Declaration on Cooperation, Development and Economic Independence in 1973, which articulated Africa's strategy for gradual disengagement from the world economy through the escalation of national and continental self-reliance. This was followed by The Revised Framework of the Principles for the Implementation of New International Economic Order in Africa of 1976. It was produced by the United Nations Economic Commission for Africa (UNECA) and became the intellectual and theoretical foundation for the drafting of the Monrovia Strategy for the Economic Development of Africa of 1979, which emphasized collective self-reliance, economic integration of African economies, investment in science and technology as the backbone of Africa's development process, self-reliance in food production, and a commitment to achieve modern African economies by the year 2000 (Baah 2003).

The intensification of the African demand for an NIEO was resisted by the industrial powers as part of a communist conspiracy, as irrational, and as too revolutionary. Consequently, very little headway was made simply because the powerful and dominant wanted to stay powerful and dominant. The small concession made was the adoption in 1975 of the Charter of

Economic Rights and Duties of States at the United Nations General Assembly, which, to a minor extent, included the 'rights and duties of all states to aid the economic development of other states along the path chosen by its government' (Murphy 2005). But the overall picture is that proposals and demands from the Global South suffered rejection from the powerful industrialized nations of Europe and North America. The lack of strong unity in the Third World coalition also contributed to the failure and collapse of the NIEO. Samir Amin had this to say about its demise:

> So, in the end, the battle for the NIEO was lost. As well as the failure being noted, the causes have to be studied. Are they purely circumstantial (in the economic crisis)? Can they be attributed to "tactical errors" by the Third World (its own divisions and weaknesses)? Or do these circumstances and weaknesses show the impossibility of autocentric development at the periphery of capitalist system?
>
> (Amin 1990: 56–57)

The NIEO was soon eclipsed by the era of hegemonic neoliberalism that was ushered in by the Anglo-American leaders Margaret Thatcher and Ronald Reagan in the late 1970s. But African leaders continued to try and forge ahead with African development initiatives, even within a context dominated by a developing hegemonic merchant system that carried imperiality and coloniality. This takes us to the third moment that framed the African Renaissance.

The third moment of the crystallization of the African Renaissance comprised the postcolonial struggles for popular democracy, ranged against long-standing single-party and military dictatorships, as well as the austerity measures imposed by international financial institutions such as the World Bank and the International Monetary Fund (IMF). At the centre of political and economic decolonization stood an elephant in the room, which Thandika Mkandawire (2011) termed the Truman version of development. This was an imperialism-driven version of development, cascading from the imperial/colonial idea of Europe and North America being entrusted by modern history with the task of developing the Third World in its image (Truman 1949). At the centre of the Truman version of development is what Fantu Cheru termed 'the imperial project,' informed by geo-political considerations and the Global North's political and economic power calculations as well as a consistent rhetoric of humanitarianism that conceals coloniality (Cheru 2009: 275–278).

As Africans were pushing for African Renaissance, it was inevitable that the Truman version of development would lock horns with the Bandung decolonial version of development cascading from the Bandung Conference of 1955. The latter articulated development as liberation and a human right that has to be fought for by those who have been colonized (Mkandawire 2011). What has sustained the hegemonic Truman version of development is the imperial 'development merchant system (DMS) driven by the Bretton Woods Institutions (BWIs). DMS embraced the financing of the implementation of exogenous development agenda in Africa' (Adedeji 2002: 4). What David Slater (2004: 223) termed the 'imperiality of knowledge' constituted by the 'interweaving of geopolitical power, knowledge and subordinating representation of the other' is part of DMS. Effectively, DMS maintains coloniality long after the dismantlement of administrative colonialism.

A consortium of IMF, the World Bank, the World Trade Organization (WTO), international non-governmental organizations (IGOs), and multinational corporations (MCs) constituted DMS. It sustained and advanced a 'Bretton Woods Paradigm' of development as part of a continuation of the Truman version (Therien 1999: 723–742). It is this reality that led the African scholar and activist Yash Tandon to write a book entitled *Trade Is War: The West's War against the World* (2015), in which he posited that:

> It is not war in the ordinary sense of the term—war with bombs and drones—but trade in the capitalist-imperial era is as lethal, and as much of a "weapon of mass destruction," as bombs. Trade kills people; it drives people to poverty; it creates wealth at one end and poverty at another; it enriches the powerful food corporations at the cost of marginalising poor peasants, who then become economic refugees in their own countries or who (those who are able-bodied) attempt to leave their countries to look for employment in the rich countries of the West—across the Mediterranean from Africa to Europe, across the Mexican border with the USA, across the seas from South Asia to Australia.
>
> (Tandon 2015: 7)

However, the spirit of the African Renaissance has continued to enable Africans to craft counter-hegemonic development initiatives and strategies. These initiatives include the formation of the OAU in 1963; the demand for an NIEO; the crafting of the African Declaration on Cooperation, Development and Economic Independence of 1973; the Revised Framework of the Principles for the Implementation of New International Economic Order in Africa of 1976; the Lagos Plan of Action for the Economic Development of Africa of 1980; the African Priority Programme for Economic Recovery of 1986; the African Alternative Framework to Structural Adjustment Programme for Social Economic Recovery and Transformation of 1989; the African Charter for Popular Participation for Development of 1990; the United Nations New Agenda for Development of Africa of 1991; and the New Partnership for African Development (NEPAD) of 2001 (Adesina et al. 2006).

The OAU, working closely with the UNECA, continued to produce consciously inward-looking pan-African development plans which sought to articulate a comprehensive and unified strategy to reduce dependence on external powers. The plans were predicated on the decolonial philosophy of self-reliance and self-improvement. The Lagos Plan of Action (LPA) of 1980 emerged within this context. At the centre of the plan was not complete delinking but strategic disengagement from those features of the international economic system that were keeping Africa dependent, underdeveloped, weak, and poor (Ikome 2007). The LPA was a comprehensive initiative consisting of 13 chapters, covering all sectors of the African economy and informed by detailed objectives that included alleviation of poverty among Africans, diversification of productive economic capabilities, internalization of forces of supply and demand, and mobilization of Africans for production. Much like the Bandung Conference, the LPA identified Africa's development as structural, hindered by a hostile external environment. It was informed by both dependency ideas and the spirit of pan-Africanism.

The LPA has been criticized for articulating a one-sided cause for the development crisis in Africa. It identified a hostile external environment without paying equal attention to internal problems, which are equally important in understanding the issues with African development. The emphasis on a hostile external environment led the LPA to focus too much attention on trade and ignore such internal constraints as the lack of serious commitment by African leadership to the development of the African continent and its people (Onimonde et al. 2004). Corruption and authoritarianism were not clearly identified as internal constraints to development. The LPA is said to have been conceived as a top-down project that ignored other important sectors capable of driving African development. More importantly, the LPA identified problems and offered some solutions but without any financial commitment (Ikome 2007). Crucially, the LPA document 'demonstrated both a disturbing lack of imagination and a low level of consciousness of the character of the option of self-reliance' (Amin 1990: 59).

But even if the LPA was an authentically African development initiative, it was destined to suffer from a lack of financial support and delegitimization by forces of coloniality. What Adedeji identified as a DMS worked actively to destabilize any African development initiative, so as to push an exogenous initiative that did not threaten the hegemony of the West. The LPA, despite its declared self-reliance paradigm and its robust criticism of the colonial and neo-colonial heritage, 'could not escape the conventional methodology closely associated with the conventional strategy of peripheral capitalist development' (Amin 1990: 59). Amin posed the question:

> Should development be conceived in accordance with the demand of the international order, or conversely, is it necessarily in conflict with it. Can the international order be transformed and "adjusted" to the priority demands for Third World development, or conversely can the latter only be the result of the reverse "adjustment"?
>
> (Amin 1990: 60)

What must be highlighted is that, under the leadership of Adedeji, UNECA spent most of the late 1970s and 1980s confronting the impositions of Bretton Woods institutions while at the same time pushing for economic pan-Africanism founded on African ideas and priorities. Adedeji retired in 1991 as Executive Secretary of UNECA. A vacuum immediately emerged in the realm of pan-African ideas and pan-African economic policies. This is why Adedeji said:

> Unfortunately, the ECA appears to have thrown in the towel since my departure from Addis Ababa in 1991. [...] the ECA has abandoned ship, leaving behind the theoreticians, prophets, and marabouts of development, who, together with the Bretton Woods institutions, constitute the Development Merchant System (DMS). These actors constitute the 'sellers' of the DMS, while African political regimes are 'buyers.' Both have profited and are profiting from this trade, while the mass of Africa's 800 million people constitute the permanent underdogs and losers of this system. If African countries are ever to have the space to develop their own national development strategies and forge their own futures, the ECA must once again become involved in development. The commission has little alternative but to resume the struggle for achieving increasing measures of self-reliance, self-sustainability, democratically determined development, a regime of good governance, and the acceleration of the process of regional integration with an increasing realization of collective regional self-reliance.
>
> (Adedeji 2009: 345–346)

What must be also noted is that the LPA was launched in the midst of the rise of neoliberalism and the Washington Consensus, and the end of Adedeji's term of office in 1991 coincided with the dominance of neoliberal ideas. The formation of the African Leadership Forum (ALF) by Nigeria's Olusegun Obasanjo and its resultant crafting of the Kampala Declaration of 1990, together with its notions of the African 'calabashes' of Security, Stability, Development, and Cooperation of Africa (CSSDA), did not succeed in passing the torch of pan-Africanism and acted as an anchor for African Renaissance within the context of aggressive neoliberal encroachments and invasions of African policy and development (see Khadiagala 2010: 380).

The 1980s and 1990s witnessed the ascendance and consolidation of the neoliberal model of development informed by post-Keynesianism. This post-Keynesianism became known as the Washington Consensus, which carried anti-state philosophies and a strong belief in the free reign of markets, privatization, and deregulation. The Berg Report of 1981 introduced the philosophy and practice of structural adjustment programmes (SAP). As a result of their implementation, African states lost what little control they had over development policy. African development became driven from outside, with devastating consequences for the African people and their leaders. Thandika Mkandawire argued, 'For Africa the 1980s and 1990s was a period of wanton destruction of institutions and untrammelled experimentation with half-baked institutional ideas. The result was "unconstructive destruction" in its most institutionally debilitating form' (Mkandawire 2003: 10).

The consequences of SAPs included the removal of the state from driving development, exacerbation of internal inequalities and worsening poverty, rehabilitation of coloniality, and loss of policy space by African leaders. Instead of the BWIs accepting responsibility for drawing Africa deeper into crisis through the introduction of SAPs, the World Bank produced a 1989 document entitled *From Crisis to Sustainable Growth*, in which they blamed a lack of good governance and policy reform for the economic crisis and lack of development in Africa in the 1980s. In 1994 the World Bank produced another report entitled '*Adjustment in Africa*,' in which the issues of sound macroeconomic and structural management were defended as prerequisites for growth and poverty reduction in Africa. Lack of development and economic growth was explained in terms of poor policy choices by African leaders, inefficiency, and corruption. Structural barriers in the international political economy were not identified as a cause of underdevelopment. The African postcolonial state was identified as the major culprit inhibiting development in Africa (Fukuyama 2004).

An African consensus emerged that SAPs were a disaster for the development of the continent. By the late 1980s, an alternative to SAPs was being sought through UNECA, which culminated in the production and adoption of the African Alternative Framework to Structural Adjustment Programmes for Socio-Economic Recovery and Transformation of 1989. Through this, Africans rejected SAPs, offering well-reasoned arguments for this rejection (Tomori and Tomori 2004). However, the initiative was not taken seriously, and its recommendations fell on deaf ears.

By the beginning of the 2000s, Africa, like the rest of the world, was experiencing a millennial spirit of renewal. This period witnessed the rise of the so-called new African leaders, who were thought to be less corrupt and fully committed to the economic renewal of the continent. These new leaders committed themselves to enabling Africa to claim the twenty-first century as the African century for development. The African Renaissance received a new boost as President Mbeki of South Africa worked actively with like-minded leaders to deliver African development and political renewal. The common slogan was 'African solutions to African problems' (Ferim 2013). Valery Ferim (2013: 143) articulated this rational in these words:

> The principle of 'African solutions to African problems' thus implies a resurgence of African renaissance and a zeal to combat the tyrannical forces of neo-colonialism. In addition, it indicates a commitment by African leaders to retake control of the continent and be instrumental in influencing the socio-political and economic affairs of the region. Also,

> African solutions to African problems is a recognition of the fact that African societies are different—their colonial history is unique, its societies heterogeneous, and its challenges daunting. Hence, there is (or at least there should be) an African model for development that is different from the Western path.

The flagship projects for the new leaders of Africa became the NEPAD that was adopted in 2002 and the African Peer Review Mechanism (APRM). Across the globe, there was a feeling of optimism that the twenty-first century would indeed be an African century, in which Africa would be allowed to drive its own development with support from the developed countries of the North. This mood made some Africans oblivious to coloniality as an obstacle to development. NEPAD was sold to the African people as a vehicle to carry then to a better future. Unlike the LPA, which focussed mainly on external structural barriers as responsible for the failure to achieve a developed Africa, NEPAD highlighted such factors as bad governance, corruption, and conflicts. African leaders committed themselves to resolving the internal bottlenecks through APRM and dedication to democratic governance. The drivers of NEPAD seemed to be convinced of the possibilities of a mutually beneficial partnership between poor African countries and the industrialized and rich countries of the North.

The G8 pledged to fully support NEPAD; many questioned why it would do this when, throughout the postcolonial period, the industrialized countries of the North had opposed African development initiatives. Is NEPAD not part of those spurious neo-colonial partnerships that hide the realities of structural inequalities? Is it part of Africa's indigenous/endogenous development agenda, or is component of DMS but masquerading as an African development initiative? It would seem that NEPAD falls neatly within the discourse of partnerships that commenced with such initiatives as the Lomé Conventions rather than with the Bandung decolonial version of development. The Lomé Conventions were part of the sustenance of coloniality long after the end of direct colonial administrations. Critiquing the whole notion of partnerships between Europe and Africa in general and economic partnership agreements (EPAs) in particular, Serges Djoyou Kamga (2014: 247) depicted EPAs as another tool in the scramble for Africa and highlighted the fact that they hindered the achievement of African regional integration.

Despite African leaders' making commendable efforts towards institution building, including launching the Pan-African Parliament (PAP) as part of the concretization of the African Renaissance, there was still no agreement on the establishment of what became known as the United States of Africa (AU 2006). African leaders fell back into the debates of the 1960s, discussing whether this should be a gradual or an immediate process. At the Ninth Ordinary Session of the Assembly of AU Head of States and Government held at Accra in Ghana from 1 to 3 July 2007, they deliberated on the proposal to establish the 'United States of Africa' with an appointed president, a central bank, and pan-African ministers. This proposal never took off. Then President of Libya Muammar al-Gaddafi pushed for an immediate declaration of the 'United States of Africa.' The outcome was the Accra Declaration, signed on 3 July 2007, which called for an acceleration of the 'economic and political integration of the African continent, including the formation of a Union Government for Africa with the ultimate objective of creating a United States of Africa' (AU 2007). However, nothing has happened since to further this aspect of African Renaissance. The untimely exit of Mbeki from the political stage and the equally untimely assassination of Gaddafi compounded the trials and tribulations of the African Renaissance project. It became leaderless, just as it had after the untimely removal of Nkrumah from power in 1966.

Unfortunately, President Thabo Mbeki, who had emerged as the most able articulator of the African Renaissance, became embroiled in the complex politics of South Africa and increasingly lost popularity at home. His critics argued that he behaved like a philosopher king, disconnected from the people and being aloofness. Two of his interventions exacerbated his unpopularity (Glaser 2010). The first was his HIV/AIDS policy, under which he was accused of being an HIV/AIDS denialist at a time when many people were succumbing to the virus and dying. The second was his 'quiet diplomacy' approach, particularly with regard to the Zimbabwean crisis. As a result, he was accused of protecting a dictator (President Robert Mugabe) who was said to be brazenly violating people's rights and trampling on democracy.

This gave a bad name to the whole idea of 'African solutions for African problems' as a leitmotif of the African Renaissance (Glaser 2010). Mbeki was not even able to finish his second term of office as president of South Africa – he was 'recalled' by his own political party (the ruling African National Congress (ANC)). All these developments weighed heavily on the project of the African Renaissance, resulting in a nightmare of a situation. It was Mbeki's political fate that led Khadiagala (2010: 384) to posit that 'role models with some inkling of conceptual conviction and courage, probity and legitimacy do not often prevail in African continental leadership, while the less remarkable, but street-wise 'thinkers' survive to make discordant noises that parade as ideas.'

The remaining members of what Khadiagala (2010: 383) termed the 'renaissance coalition' soon attracted political scandals. Obasanjo tried to engineer a third presidential term in Nigeria. President Bouteflika of Algeria successfully altered the constitution and secured a third term, which he won in 2009. President Wade of Senegal 'used the past 11 years in power to decimate the democratic institutions' (Khadiagala 2010: 383). Colonel Muammar al-Gaddaffi's democratic standing had long been dented by overstaying in power, and his physical elimination by NATO forces deprived Africa of a committed pan-Africanist.

Conclusions

After a lull in the pan-African initiatives of the early 2000s, two major movements took place which cannot be ignored in any reflection on the African Renaissance. The first is the Afro-Arab Spring that broke out in 2011, targeting once again the long-standing dictatorial regimes in Tunisia, Egypt, and Libya, which had survived the second and third waves of democratization that engulfed sub-Saharan Africa in the late 1980s and early 1990s. The second is the outbreak of the Rhodes Must Fall (RMF) movement in South Africa in 2015, which demanded epistemological decolonization. Where does the African Renaissance sit within these two movements? Charles Villa-Vicencio, Erik Doxtader, and Ebrahim Moosa's edited volume *The African Renaissance and the Afro-Arab Spring: A Season of Rebirth?* (2015) tried to link the 'Afro-Arab Spring' with the African Renaissance, concluding that a mere change of 'season' was not enough to amount to a renaissance: 'Spring is a fragile season. It can be delayed by a hard winter and pre-empted by a fiery summer' (Doxtader 2015: xxxii).

But in an extended foreword to the book, Thabo Mbeki reiterated the central objectives of the African Renaissance as creating the necessary space for the people of Africa to determine their destiny as well as build a democratic Africa. To him, the 'Arab Reawakening' will only be 'a genuine renaissance if it is the product of the conscious activity of the African masses across their various racial, ethnic, class, gender, and other social divides' (Mbeki 2015: ix). Mbeki outlined five benchmarks that can be used to measure the quality of the 'Afro-Arab Spring' as a renaissance: (a) a re-assertion of the right of the African masses to determine their destiny and recover their democratic right to govern; (b) a resumption of the struggle for the victory of the national democratic revolution; (c) a rebellion against the abuse of power by ruling elites in order to enrich themselves at the expense of the people; (d) an affirmation of the determination of the African masses to ensure that the national wealth is used to end poverty and underdevelopment, and to bridge the disparities in income, wealth, and opportunity; and finally (e) confirmation of the determination of the masses of the African people to gain their human dignity and their commitment to rely on their native intelligence and labour to realize their all-round development (Mbeki 2015: xi). Mbeki gave the 'Afro-Arab Spring' the benefit of the doubt and hoped it would deliver substantive popular democratic revolution. However, the movement was hijacked by the military and the fundamentalist Islamic formations, which drained its popular democratic content and diluted its liberatory thrust.

What is intriguing is Mbeki's fifth benchmark for a genuine African Renaissance, which emphasized reliance 'on their native intelligence and labour to realize their all-round development.' This seems to speak to epistemic freedom as an essential pre-requisite for the realization of a genuine African Renaissance (see Ndlovu-Gatsheni 2018). This links the Afro-Arab

Spring with the RMF movements that broke out in 2015 and 2016 in Mbeki's own country, South Africa, which were spearheaded by university students. The demand for cognitive justice which permeated these revolutionary student movements seems to speak to the need for an intellectual renaissance that deliberately invests in the building of necessary 'native intelligence' in a country and a continent where epistemological decolonization has not yet been achieved (Ndlovu-Gatsheni 2018). What was sparked by the existence of a statue of the leading British imperialist Cecil John Rhodes at the centre of the University of Cape Town (UCT) quickly morphed into Fees Must Fall, Outsourcing Must Fall, and many other demands (Ndlovu-Gatsheni 2016b). These included a critical questioning of the neoliberal education in which knowledge is commodified and arguments for changing institutional cultures deemed to be racist, patriarchal, and sexist; decolonizing the curriculum, which, the students argued, was Eurocentric and irrelevant; and agitating for an end to the exploitative 'outsourcing' and casualization of workers (see Ndlovu-Gatsheni 2016b, 2018; Ndlovu-Gatsheni and Zondi 2016).

Taken together, the Afro-Arab Spring and the RMF movements indicated that there was and still is a noticeable determination among African people, especially youth and students, to exercise their 'native intelligence' and agency to push for a genuine African Renaissance. The two events not only connected the powerful and persuasive call for an African Renaissance that emerged at the end of apartheid colonialism in the southern tip of the African continent (South Africa) in the 1990s and the popular revolts that rocked North Africa in 2011 but also revealed how South Africa, as the geo-political site from which the African Renaissance call was made, is itself engulfed by revolutionary student movements demanding the completion of the decolonization struggle. It would seem that a genuine African Renaissance won't be achieved through elite pacts and declarations but through popular struggles for deimperialization, decolonization, and democratization.

References

Abdulgani, R. 1964. *Bandung Spirit: Moving on the Tide of History*. Jakarta: Prapanga.

Achebe, C., in Moore-Gilbert, B. 1997. *Postcolonial Theory: Contexts, Practices, Politics*. London: Verso.

Adedeji, A. 2002. *From the Lagos Plan of Action to the New Partnership for African Development and from the Final Act of Lagos to the Constitutive Act: Wither Africa*? Paper presented at the African Forum for Envisioning Africa, Nairobi, Kenya, 26–29 April.

Adedeji, A. 2009. 'The United Nations Economic Commission for Africa.' In A. Adekeye (ed.), *From Global Apartheid to the Global Village*. Durban: University of KwaZulu-Natal Press, pp. 334–358.

Adesina, J. O., Graham, Y., & Olukoshi, A. (eds.). 2006. *Africa and Development Challenges in the New Millennium: The NEPAD Debate*. Dakar: CODESRIA Books.

Ajayi, J. F. A. 1969. 'Colonialism: An Episode in African History.' In L. H. Gann and P. Duignan (eds.), *Colonialism in Africa, 1870–1960, Vol. 1*. Cambridge: Cambridge University Press, pp. 497–509.

Amin, S. 1990. *Maldevelopment: Anatomy of a Global Failure*. Tokyo: United Nations University Press.

Appiah, K. A. 1992. *In My Father's House: Africa in the Philosophy of Culture*. New York: Oxford University Press.

AU (African Union). 2006. *Study on an African Union Government: Towards the United States of Africa*. Addis Ababa: African Union.

AU (African Union). 2007. *Declaration of the Assembly of Heads of States and Government (Accra Declaration)*. Accra: Ghana.

Azikiwe, N. 1968. *Renascent Africa*. London: Frank Cass.

Baah, A. 2003. 'History of African Development Initiatives.' Paper Presented at the African Labour Research Network Workshop, Johannesburg, South Africa, 22–23 May.

Césaire, A. 2000. *Discourse on Colonialism*. New York: Monthly Review Press.

Cheru, F. 2009. 'Development in Africa: The Imperial Project versus the National Project and the Need for Policy Space.' *Review of African Political Economy*, 120, pp. 275–278.

Cox, R. 1979. 'Ideologies and the New International Economic Order: Reflections on Some Recent Literature.' *International Organization*, 33(2), pp. 257–308.

Diop, C. A. 1966. *Towards the African Renaissance: Essays in Culture and Development, 1946–1960*. New York: Karnak House.

Diop, C. A. 1974. *The African Origins of Civilization: Myth or Reality?* New York: Lawrence Hill Books.

Doxtader, E. 2015. 'The Potential of an African Assertion: Once More, in the Name of a Renaissance.' In C. Villa-Vicencio, E. Doxtader and E. Moosa (eds.), *The African Renaissance and the Afro-Arab Spring: A Season of Rebirth?* Cape Town: UCT Press, pp. 171–192.

Doxtader, E., Villa-Vicencio, C., & Moosa, E. 2015. 'Introduction: Beginning Again? The Quest of a Continent.' In C. Villa-Vicencio, E. Doxtader and E. Moosa (eds). *The African Renaissance and the Afro-Arab Spring: A Season of Rebirth?* Cape Town: UCT Press, pp. xvii–xxxiv.

Ekeh, P. 1983.*Colonialism and Social Structure: University of Ibadan Inaugural Lecture*, 1980. Ibadan: Ibadan University Press.

Falola, T. 2001. *Nationalism and African Intellectuals*. New York: University of Rochester Press.

Fanon, F. 1968. *The Wretched of the Earth*. New York: Grove Press.

Ferim, V. 2013. 'African Solutions to African Problems.' In M. Muchie, P. Lukhele-Olorunju and O. Akpor (eds.), *The African Union Ten Years After: Solving African Problems with Pan-Africanism and the African Renaissance*. Pretoria: Africa Institute of South Africa, pp. 143–155.

Fukuyama, F. 2004. *State Building: Governance and World Order in the Twenty-First Century*. London: Profile Books.

Garvey, M. 1969. *The Philosophy and Opinions of Marcus Garvey, or, Africa for Africans, Vol. 2*. New York: Arno Press.

Glaser, D. (ed.). 2010. *Mbeki and After: Reflections on the Legacy of Thabo Mbeki*. Johannesburg: Wits University Press.

Gosovic, B. 1972. *UNCTAD: Conflict and Compromise*. Leiden: A. W. Sifthoff.

Gumede, V. 2013. 'African Economic Renaissance as a Paradigm for Africa's Socio-economic Development.' In K. Kondlo (ed.), *Perspectives on Thought Leadership for Africa's Renewal*. Pretoria: Africa Institute of South Africa, pp. 436–457.

Gutto, S. B. O. 2006. 'Towards a New Paradigm for Pan-African Knowledge Production and Application in the Context of the African Renaissance.' *International Journal of African Renaissance-Multi-, Inter-and Transdisciplinarity*, 1(2), pp. 306–323.

Ikome, F. N. 2007. *From LPA to NEPAD: The Political Economy of African Regional Initiatives*. Midrand: Institute for Global Dialogue.

Iliffe, J. 2017. *Africans: The History of a Continent: Third Edition*. Cambridge: Cambridge University Press.

Kamga, S. G. 2014. 'Economic Partnerships Agreements: Another Tool for the Scramble for Africa or a Viable Undertaking for the Continent's Development.' In M. Muchie, V. Gumede, P. Lukhele-Olorunju and H. T. Demissie (eds.), *Unite or Perish: Africa Fifty Years after the Founding of the OAU*. Pretoria: Africa Institute of South Africa, pp. 247–262.

Kaunda, K. D., & Morris, C. M. 1966. *A Humanist in Africa: Letters to Colin M. Morris from Kenneth D. Kaunda President of Zambia*. Nashville, TN: Abingdon Press.

Khadiagala, G. M. 2010. 'Two Moments in African Thought: Ideas in Africa's International Relations.' *South African Journal of International Affairs*, 17(3) (December), pp. 375–386.

Krasner, S. 1981. 'Transforming International Relations: What the Third World Wants and Why.' *International Studies Quarterly*, 25(2), pp. 119–148.

Kumalo, S. 2015. 'Ex Africa Semper Aliquid Novi! Pixley Ka Isaka Seme, the African Renaissance and the Empire in Contemporary South Africa.' *Alternation Special Edition*, 14, pp. 190–211.

Laakso, L., & Olukoshi, A. O. 1996. 'The Crisis of the Post-Colonial Nation-State Project in Africa.' In A. O. Olukoshi and L. Laakso (eds.), *Challenges to the Nation-State in Africa*. Uppsala: Nordic Africa Institute, pp. 7–39.

Makgoba, W. M. (ed.). 1999. *African Renaissance: The New Struggle*. Cape Town: Mafube & Tafelberg.

Mamdani, M. 1999. 'There Can Be No African Renaissance without an Africa-focused Intelligentsia.' In M. W. Makgoba (ed.), *African Renaissance: A New Struggle*. Johannesburg and Cape Town: Mafube Publishing and Tafelberg Publishers, pp. 125–134.

Mayall, J. 1990. *Nationalism and International Society*. Cambridge: Cambridge University Press.

Mazrui, A. A. 1986. *The Africans: A Triple Heritage*. London: BBC Publications.

Mbeki, T. 1997. Address by Executive Deputy President Thabo Mbeki, to Corporate Council on Africa's 'Attracting Capital' Summit, April 19. Available: www.sahistory.org.za/archive/address-executive-deputy-president-thabo-mbeki-corporate-council-africas-attracting-capital-. South African History Online.

Mbeki, T. 2015. 'Foreword: The Arab Reawakening: An African Renaissance Perspective.' In C. Villa-Vicencio, E. Doxtader and E. Moosa (eds.), *The African Renaissance and the Afro-Arab Spring: A Season of Rebirth*. Cape Town: UCT Press, pp. ix–xv.

Mbembe, A. 2017. *Critique of Black Reason*. Durham, NC: Duke University Press.

Mkandawire, T. 2003. *Institutions and Development in Africa*. Paper presented at the Cambridge Journal of Economics Conference on Economics for the Future, 17–21 September.

Mkandawire, T. 2011. 'Running While Others Walk: Knowledge and the Challenge of Africa's Development.' *Africa Development*, 26(2), pp. 1–36.

More, M. P. 2017. *Biko: Philosophy, Identity and Liberation*. Cape Town: HSRC Press.

Murphy, C. N. 2005. *Global Institutions, Marginalization and Development*. London: Routledge.

Nabudere, D. W. 2007. 'Cheikh Anta Diop: The Social Sciences, Humanities, Physical and Natural Sciences and Transdisciplinarity.' *International Journal of African Renaissance Studies-Multi-, Inter and Transdisciplinarity*, 2(1), pp. 6–34.

Ndlovu-Gatsheni, S. J. 2013a. *Coloniality of Power in Postcolonial Africa: Myths of Decolonization*. Dakar: CODESRIA Books.

Ndlovu-Gatsheni, S. J. 2013b. *Empire, Global Coloniality and African Subjectivity*. New York: Berghahn Books.

Ndlovu-Gatsheni, S. J. 2014 'Pan-Africanism and the International System.' In T. Murithi (ed.), *Handbook of Africa's International Relations*. London: Routledge, pp. 21–29.

Ndlovu-Gatsheni, S. J. 2015a. 'Decoloniality as the Future of Africa.' *History Compass*, 13(10), pp. 485–496.

Ndlovu-Gatsheni, S. J. 2015b. 'Decoloniality in Africa: A Continuing Search for a New World Order.' *Australasian Review of African Studies*, 36(2), pp. 22–50.

Ndlovu-Gatsheni, S. J. 2016a. *The Decolonial Mandela: Justice, Peace and the Politics of Life*. New York: Berghahn Books.

Ndlovu-Gatsheni, S. J. 2016b. 'Why Are South African Universities Sites of Struggle Today?' *The Thinker: Pan-African Quarterly for Thought Leaders*, 4(70), pp. 52–61.

Ndlovu-Gatsheni, S. J. 2018. *Epistemic Freedom in Africa: Deprovincialization and Decolonization*. London: Routledge.

Ndlovu-Gatsheni, S. J., & Zondi, S. 2016. 'Introduction: The Coloniality of Knowledge: Between Troubled Histories and Uncertain Times.' In S. J. Ndlovu-Gatsheni and S. Zondi (eds.), *Decolonizing the University, Knowledge Systems and Disciplines*. Durham, NC: Carolina Academic Press, pp. 3–24.

Neocosmos, M. 2016. *Rethinking Freedom in Africa: Towards a Theory of Emancipatory Politics*. Johannesburg: Wits University Press.

Nesadurai, H. E. S. 2005. *Bandung and the Political Economy of North–South Relations: Sowing the Seeds for Re-visioning International Society*. Working Paper No. 95, Institute of Defence and Strategic Studies, Singapore, December.

Netshitenzhe, J. 2013. *The Vision of Seme 107 Years On: Is Civilization Still a Dream and Is the Regeneration of Africa Possible?* Inaugural Pixley Ka Isaka Seme Lecture, Columbia University, 29 October.

Ngugi wa Thiong'o. 1986. *Decolonizing the Mind: The Politics of Language in African Literature*. Oxford: James Currey.

Ngugi wa Thiong'o. 2009a. *Re-Membering Africa*. Nairobi: East African Educational Publishers Ltd.

Ngugi wa Thiong'o. 2009b. *Something Torn and New: An African Renaissance*. New York: Basic Civitas Books.

Nkrumah, K. 1963. *Africa Must Unite*. London: PANAF Books.

Nkrumah, K. 1964. *Consciencism: Philosophy and Ideology for De-colonization*. New York: Monthly Review Press.

Nkrumah, K. 1965. *Neo-Colonialism: The Highest Stage of Imperialism*. London: PANAF.

Nyerere, J. K. 1967. *Freedom and Unity*. Dar es Salaam: Oxford University Press.

Onimonde, B. et al. 2004. *African Development and Governance Strategies in the 21st Century*. London: Zed Books.

Seme, P. I. 1906. 'The Regeneration of Africa by Pixley ka Isaka Seme.' Available: www.anc.org.za/content/regeneration-Africa.

Slater, D. 2004. *Geopolitics and the Post-Colonial: Rethinking North–South Relations*. Malden, MA: Blackwell.

Tandon, Y. 2015. *Trade Is War: The West's War against the World*. New York: OR Books.

Taylor, I. 2003. 'The United Nations Conference in Trade and Development.' *New Political Economy*, 8(3), pp. 409–418.

Therien, J. P. 1999. 'Beyond the North–South Divide: Two Tales of World Poverty.' *Third World Quarterly*, 20(4), pp. 723–742.

Tomori, S. O., & Tomori, O. W. 2004. 'Revisiting African Alternative Framework to Structural Adjustment Programme for Socio-Economic Recovery and Transformation in contemporary Nigeria.' In B. Onimonde et al. (eds.), *African Development and Governance Strategies in the 21st Century*. London: Zed Books, pp. 32–67.

Trouillot, M.-R. 1995. *Silencing the Past: Power and the Production of History*. Boston, MA: Beacon Press.

Truman, H. 1949 [1964]. *Public Papers of the Presidents of the United States: Harry S. Truman*. Washington, DC: United States Government Printing Office.

Villa-Vicencio, C., Doxtader, E., & Moosa, E. (eds.). 2015. *The African Renaissance and the Afro-Arab Spring: A Season of Rebirth?* Cape Town: UCT Press.

Wright, R. 1956. *The Colour Curtain: Report on the Bandung Conference*. London: Dobson Books.

7 African humanities

Introduction

Without the humanities there is no society. The humanities are the soul of human life. They give human life taste and meaning. At the centre of the humanities are spiritualities, history, arts, cognitions, traditions, customs, values, ethics, identity, and culture as the ingredients and elements of human life. In 1989, the leading African novelist Chinua Achebe of Nigeria was invited to the 26th anniversary of the Organization for Economic Cooperation and Development (OECD) in Paris, France, which was dominated by European, American, Canadian, and Australian economists and bankers, and decided to speak on the theme 'Africa Is People' (Achebe 2009). The veteran novelist was provoked by the European bankers and economists' speaking in abstract economic theories, models, and formulas, and more specifically by how, in their discussions, Africa emerged as a laboratory for their fine theories. This is the challenge he threw at his hosts:

> Here you are, spinning your fine theories, to be tried out in your imaginary laboratories. You are developing new drugs and feeding them to a bunch of laboratory guinea pigs and hoping for the best. I have news for you. Africa is not fiction. Africa is people, real people. Have you thought of that? You are brilliant people, world experts. You even have the very best intentions. But have you thought, really thought, of Africa as people?
>
> (Achebe 2009: 157)

In addition to being a novelist Achebe was an African humanist. The question of the human pre-occupied him as he reflected on human and world affairs. In a published chapter in *The Education of a British-Protected Child* (2009) he elaborated on the theme 'Africa Is People' this way:

> 'Africa is people' has another dimension. Africa believes in people, in cooperation with people. If the philosophical dictum of Descartes 'I think, therefore I am' represents a European individualistic ideal, the

> Bantu declaration 'Umuntu ngumuntu ngabantu' represents an African communal aspiration: 'A human is human because of other humans.' Our humanity is contingent on the humanity of our fellows. No person or group can be human alone. We rise above the animal together, or not at all. If we learned that lesson even this late in the day, we would have taken a truly millennial step forward.
>
> (Achebe 2009: 166)

Being the cradle of humankind might be the source of Africa's emphasis on collective and compositional humanity. My entry point into the subject of African humanities is the complex issue of contestations over being human and indeed the denial of the humanity of African people. Remember that, historically speaking, the unfolding of the European Renaissance, Protestant Reformation, Enlightenment, Euromodernity, enslavement, mercantilism, colonialism, neo-colonialism, neoliberalism, and indeed globalization – as complex historical, discursive, and epistemological processes – resulted in the colonization of knowledge, time, space, and the very notion of being human. At the centre of the humanities, as a field of study, lurks the contested idea of the human – the very question of being human and its meaning. The core subject of the humanities constitutes the state of being human. Because of the colonization of knowledge and being human itself, the humanities became haunted by a difficult onto-epistemic question. Poul Holm, Arne Jarrick, and Dominic Scott, in *Humanities World Report 2015* (2015: 3), highlighted the difficulties of the humanities, noting that it is 'a notoriously difficult question' mainly because to say 'that the humanities study the human—is clearly too superficial, because the medical sciences and psychology also study "the human," as do the social sciences.' What must be made clear is that the humanities are not merely reducible to the study of the human but were actively deployed in the making/invention of the human. This will be made clear in the second section of this chapter, which is dedicated to the question of what constitutes the state of being human. To Lisa Lowe and Kris Manjapra (2019: 29), 'The humanities could be instead a way of thinking, reading, writing, and critically reflecting on the plasticity of the human; the human not as fixed form, but as shifting relation itself.'

In *The Humanities in Africa: Knowledge Production, Universities, and the Transformation of Society* (2016: xi), the leading African historian Toyin Falola said this about the humanities: 'There is no distance between object and subject. The Humanities concern intimate knowledge of ourselves and the lives we live as humans, not the natural world of things or animals.' However, in the African humanities, the Cartesian dualisms are not constitutive of the concept of being human. This is why Ngugi wa Thiong'o, in *Decolonizing the Mind: The Politics of Language in African Literature* (1986: 87), defined decolonization as 'the search for a liberating perspective within which to see ourselves clearly in relationship to ourselves and to other selves in the universe.' The idea of 'other selves' is important in understanding the African humanities. The human is not the only 'self' in the universe; it is in a state of becoming, not being.

It is for this reason that Jean Comaroff and John L. Comaroff, in *Theory From the South Or, How Euro-America Is Evolving Toward Africa* (2012: 51–52), question whether 'the autonomous person [was] a European invention.' Their answer, based on an anthropological study of the Tswana people of southern Africa, was yes because the Tswana imaginings of being-in-the world is defined not only by social fluidity but also by continuous self-construction premised on 'the foundational notion of being-as-becoming.' The concept of 'incompleteness' as constitutive of African conceptions of being is also highlighted by Francis B. Nyamnjoh in *Drinking from the Cosmic Gourd: How Amos Tutuola Can Change Our Minds* (2017: 2), in which he stated that:

> Such conceptions of incompleteness could enrich the practice of social science and the humanities in Africa and globally. [...] [I]ncompleteness as social reality and form of knowing generative of and dependent on interconnections, relatedness, open-endedness and multiplicities is both exciting and inspiring, at personal, group and collective, political and scholarly levels. Incompleteness harbours emancipatory potentials and inspires unbounded creativity and hopefully a reclamation of more inclusionary understandings of being human and being in general. [...] Africa is incomplete without the rest of the world, and the rest of the world is incomplete without Africa; and both are incomplete without the natural and supernatural worlds.

Decolonizing the humanities in general and making a case for the African humanities in particular cannot be attained without the depatriachization of modern knowledge. In *The Invention of Women: Making Sense of Western Gender Discourses* (1997: x) the leading African sociologist and feminist Oyeronke Oyewumi made a convincing case for a decolonial paradigm shift away from Eurocentric biological determinist thinking, which privileges 'body-reasoning and 'bio-logic,' and its consequent invention and imposition of gender discourses on African societies, which, in the process, distort history and ways of knowing which are different from those of Europe. Using the empirical study of the Yoruba people of Nigeria in West Africa, Oyewumi (1997: 10) developed this powerful thesis:

> In fact, the categorization of women in feminist discourses as a homogenous, bio-anatomically determined group which is always constituted as powerless and victimized does not reflect the fact that gender relations are social relations and, therefore, historically grounded and culturally bound. If gender is socially constructed, then gender cannot behave in the same way across time and space. If gender is a social construction, then we must examine the various cultural/architectural

> sites where it was constructed, and we must acknowledge that variously located actors (aggregates, groups, interested parties) were part of the construction. We must further acknowledge that if gender is a social construction, then there was a specific time (in different cultural/architectural sites) when it was 'constructed' and therefore a time before which it was not. Thus, gender, being a social construction, is also a historical and cultural phenomenon. Consequently, it is logical to assume that in some societies, gender construction need not have existed at all.

Oyewumi (1997: xii) boldly stated that the 'human body need not be constituted as gendered' and that the 'precolonial Yoruba society' proved that 'body-type was not the basis of social hierarchy: males and females were not ranked according to anatomic distinction.' This is an important part of decolonizing the humanities, with a specific focus on its patriarchization through the process of gendering. This chapter contributes to the subject of decolonizing the humanities from a conceptual and theoretical vantage point. Decolonizing the humanities is fundamental to liberating the conceptions of the human from the Euro-Cartesian notion of 'being' as a 'self-made, self-conscious,' 'rights-bearing individual' and a 'complete' emerging from 'an onto-Manichean colonial line' (see Comaroff and Comaroff 2012: 52–53; Ndlovu-Gatsheni 2013; Maldonado-Torres 2017: 117). This chapter therefore begins with the complex question of what it means to be human because this is at the core of humanities. Taking into account the complex and inextricable entwinement of ontology and epistemology in the invention of the humanities as a field of study as well as research and the realities of colonization and colonialism, the chapter posits that any effort towards the decolonization of the humanities is fundamentally part of the broader casting of light on those people whose being has been questioned, whose ways of lives have been dismissed, and whose knowledge had been museumized.

What constitutes the state of being human?

The Caribbean intellectual Sylvia Wynter (1984, 2003) directly tackled the question of the human (defined as Man) as a European invention and highlighted its problems. Her intervention, through the concepts of 'Man 1' and 'Man 2,' provides a detailed philosophical, historical, and anthropological analysis of the making of the modern, dominant 'Euro-American White Bourgeois ethnoclass' (Wynter 1984; see also Cornell and Seely 2016: 122). Wynter depicted 'Man 1' as the invention of the European Renaissance, which coincided with the weakening of Christian theological hegemony and the emergence of modern Europe. During the age of Christian theological hegemony God was the omnipotent fountain of knowledge, and the mastery of theological texts was the only way of gaining knowledge (Cornell and Seely 2016: 122).

Being human was defined as being a 'True Christian Self' rather than 'Untrue Christian Others' (such as pagans, idolaters, infidels, witches, and all 'Enemies-of Christ,' who were legitimate targets of violence and killing) (Wynter 1984; Cornell and Seely 2016: 123). According to Wynter (1984), the 'order of things' in the Foucauldian sense began to change in the fourteenth and fifteenth centuries, when such European thinkers as Petrarch and Pico revived pre-Christian Greco-Roman philosophers like Cicero in their inauguration of *studia humanitis* (the humanities). This was a 'heretical' intervention in the God-centred view of the world. It was also an epistemic break. What was born was 'Man 1' (as secular-political subject/*homo politicus*) (Cornell and Seely 2016: 123). From this emerged the European 'Age of Discovery,' enabled by the rise of the Copernican and Newtonian scientific revolutions (Wynter 2003: 280). What was paradigmatic was the shift from the conception of humanity as 'fallen' and subject to the whims of God to the rise of 'Man 1' as the 'self-inventing Master who can understand and control Nature through Reason' (Cornell and Seely 2016: 124): 'The birth of Man 1, then, is a radical epistemological, ontological, and metaphysical shift which has profound implications for the ways in which Europeans viewed non-Europeans' (Cornell and Seely 2016: 124).

Enslavement and colonialism is traceable to this epistemic shift in Europe. This is why Wynter (2003: 266) wrote:

> In the wake of the West's reinvention of its True Christian Self in the transumed terms of the Rational Self of Man 1 [...] it was to be the peoples of the militarily expropriated New territories (i.e., Indians), as well as the enslaved people of Black Africa (i.e., Negroes), that were made to reoccupy the matrix slot of Otherness—to be made into the physical referent of the idea of the irrational/subrational Human Other, to this first degodded (if still hybridly religio-secular) 'descriptive statement' of the human in history, as the descriptive statement that would be foundational of modernity.

The next paradigmatic shift was occasioned by the European Enlightenment from the sixteenth through to the eighteenth centuries, which embraced the emergence of racial capitalism accompanied by bourgeois revolutions, the formation of the modern nation-state, and the upsurge of liberal philosophy of the 'Rights of Man.' Here was born what Wynter (2003: 282) termed 'Man 2' (biocentric *homo economicus*). What emerged from this and its implications for Africa is well captured by Cornell and Seely (2016: 126–127):

> What Wynter allows us to see with her painstaking genealogy of European Man is that the liminalization of all colonized peoples is part and parcel of the very thinking of European reason, science, and technology, including the modern conceptions of nature, life, the human, and species being.

The birth of Man 2 represented the emergence of the four 'horsemen of the apocalypse: racism, slavery, white supremacy and capitalism' (see Horne 2018: 256). Throughout this unfolding of the European conception of the human and the inimical processes of dehumanization, contestations over the meaning of being human continued within Europe and beyond, complicating the current liberal notion of a celebrated linear development of human rights. Nelson Maldonado-Torres (2017) traces the contestation of the conception of the human to the time of Pico della Mirandolla Giovanni's (1956[1886]) 'Oration on the Dignity of Man' (*Oratio de hominis dignite*), which, if read in conjunction with Wynter (2003), constitutes a manifesto of the European Renaissance and the birth of 'Man 1.' The age of 'Oration' is followed by the age of 'Declarations' (*Declaration of the Rights of Man/ Declaration of Independence*). Maldonado-Torres (2017: 121) informs us that:

> Between 'oration' and the 'declarations' one finds that multiple other modes of writing or genres were used in the effort to clarify the new emerging concepts of the human. They included the 'meditations' and the 'discourse' (as in Descartes' *Meditations on First Philosophy* and Descartes' *Discourse on Method* as well as Rousseau's *Discourse on the Origins of Inequality* and *Discourse on Arts and Sciences*), the 'essay' (as in John Locke's *An Essay Concerning Human Understanding*) and the 'treatise' (as in Locke's *Two Treatise on Government* and David Hume's *Treatise on Human Nature*), among others.

What is even more important is how the European conceptions of being human continued even into the *Universal Declaration of Human Rights* in 1948, provoking contestations by such black intellectuals as Aime Cesaire (1950), Frantz Fanon (1953), and many others, who fought for decolonization of this idea and conceptions of what it means to be human. In European thought, however, the contestations only crystallized within what became known as the 'great chain of being,' with artists and philosophers debating and positing the place of the human in this chain. At the beginning of the contestations over being human, the initial concern was how to make a distinction between the animal and the human. This grew into the search for a distinction between the divine and the human. During the colonial encounters and colonial conquest the contestations became very complex, with religious criteria classifying people with souls and others without souls kicking in. Within the broader discursive terrain of Euromodernity arose the discourses of rapture and difference, further complicating and accentuating the contestations of the question of being human. Ideas began to emerge of 'modern' versus 'pre-modern,' with the former claiming to be the embodiment of being human and the later relegated to a sub-human category. With the onset of so-called 'effective colonialism' other criteria of being human emerged, ranging from civilization to development. Such categories as 'native' were invented to signify people who had been thrown out of civilization and then branded as tribes living in accordance with ossified and unchanging customs and traditions. In *Citizen and Subject: Contemporary Africa and the Legacy of Late Colonialism* (1996) and *Define and Rule: Native as Political Identity* (2013), the leading African political scientist Mahmood Mamdani focussed on the making of colonial governmentality and the invention of such complex political subjectivities as 'native.' According to him (2013: 2–3)

> Unlike what is commonly thought, native does not designate a condition that is original and authentic. Rather as in Maine, the native is the creation of the colonial state: colonized, the native is pinned down, localized, thrown out of civilization as an outcast, confined to custom, and then defined as its product.

Mamdani's argument suggests that, inevitably, struggles over nationhood and citizenship cannot be fully comprehended without understanding how African humanities emerged and developed from the margins of being denied existence into a problematic recognition.

Discussing the birth of the humanities as a field of study Immanuel Wallerstein, in *The Uncertainties of Knowledge* (2004), delves into the birth of the bimodal categorization of knowledge, resulting in what C. P. Snow (1965) depicted as the 'two cultures.' Between 1750 and 1850 science and philosophy were separated. The humanities were born out of the reorganization of the faculty of philosophy in the eighteenth century. At the same time science was gaining a lot of prestige, already at the expense of the humanities. Boaventura de Sousa Santos (2017: 28) termed the focal area of the humanities the 'social physics' (the study of social phenomena/science of society/study of the human). Still, to understand the birth of the disciplines we have to turn to the French historian of science Michel Foucault and his *The Order of Things: An Archaeology of Human Sciences* (1970: 344–345):

> The epistemological field traversed by the human sciences was not laid down in advance [...]. They appeared when man constituted himself in Western culture as both that which must be conceived of and that which is to be known. There can be no doubts, certainly, that the historical emergence of each of the human sciences was occasioned by a problem, a requirement, an obstacle of a theoretical or practical order: the new norms imposed by industrial society upon individuals were certainly necessary before psychology, slowly, in the courses of the nineteenth contort, could constitute itself as a science: and the threats that, since the French Revolution, have weighed so heavily on the social balances, and even on the equilibrium established by the bourgeoisie, were no doubt also necessary before a reflection on the sociological type could appear.

As mentioned above, the 'coloniality of being' complicated the very definition of being 'human' as it became bifurcated into the *anthropos* (deficient human beings rationally and ontologically) and the *humanitas* (complete human beings rationally and ontologically) (Mignolo 2011; Ndlovu-Gatsheni 2013). I must repeat that, historically speaking, the unfolding of the European Renaissance, Protestant Reformation, Modernity, Enlightenment Reason, racism, enslavement, imperialism, colonialism, neo-colonialism, neoliberalism, and globalization – as complex historical, discursive, and epistemological processes – contributed to the colonization not only of time and space but also of the very notion of being human/human subjectivities as well as the humanities. The colonization of the humanities fundamentally began with the epistemic invasion of the mental universe of a people who were colonized. The primacy of knowledge in this colonization is highlighted by Walter D. Mignolo and Cathrine E. Walsh (2018: 135):

> What matters is not economics, or politics, or history, but knowledge. Better yet, what matters is history, politics, economics, race, gender, sexuality, but it is above all knowledge that is intertwined in all these praxical spheres that entangles us to the point of making us believe that it is not knowledge that matters but really history, economy, politics, etc. Ontology is made of epistemology. That is, ontology is an epistemological concept; it is not inscribed in the entities the grammatical nouns name.

If colonization of the humanities entailed a re-articulation of ontology in a Eurocentric and colonial way, then decolonization of the humanities should include a liberation of ontology in decolonial ways. Cathrine Odora Hoppers and Howard Richards (2012: 8) posited that 'The casting of light at last onto subjugated peoples, knowledges, histories and ways of living unsettles the toxic pond and transforms passive analysis into generative force that valorises and recreates life for those previously museumised.' They continued, 'The task for rethinking thinking is therefore precisely this: to recognise the cultural asphyxiation of those numerous "others" that has been the norm, and work to bring other categories of self definition, of dreaming, of acting, of loving, of living into the commons as a matter of universal concern' (Hoppers and Richards 2012: 8). What Hoppers and Richards (2012) termed rethinking thinking is a strategy of decolonizing knowledge.

As background to the complexities of the development and 'disciplining' of modern knowledge, it is important to state that, as the modern world system emerged and unfolded in the fifteenth century, knowledge underwent bimodal division into ideographic epistemology (humanities) and nomothetic epistemology (natural sciences) (Wallerstein 2004: 19). By the nineteenth century, it had undergone a 'trimodal division' into 'natural,' 'humanities,' and 'social' sciences (Wallerstein 2004: 21). By the end of twentieth century and the beginning of the twenty-first, the age of uncertainty of knowledge set in as the modern world system experienced a systemic and epistemic crisis. Modernity's promise that through science all problems facing humanity would be solved had not materialized; instead modernity created more modern problems without offering modern solutions (Escobar 2004).

Two new debates in the disciplinary knowledge emerged in the 'natural' sciences known as 'Complexity Studies' and in 'humanities' termed 'Cultural Studies' (Wallerstein 2004: 21). Both changes challenged previous certitudes and determinisms in both 'natural' sciences and 'humanities,' and highlighted uncertainties, inderteminance, and instability in knowledge. What came under scrutiny was the notion of 'scientism,' that is, 'the claim that science is disinterested and extra-social, that truth claims are self-sustaining without reference to more general philosophical assertions, and that science represents the only legitimate mode of knowledge' (Wallerstein 2004: 13). The resurgent and insurgent of decolonization of knowledge is, therefore, emerging within a context in which all sciences were increasingly understood as 'social,' the scientific model of knowledge is itself being questioned, and 'knowledge of knowledge of things' is under critique at a planetary level (Santos 2017: 41).

What is emerging poignantly from the above analysis is that if the colonization of knowledge was an epistemic project that was highly imaginative, conceptual, and theoretical, then the decolonization of the humanities has to be epistemic and equally imaginative, conceptual, and theoretical. This approach is supported by other decolonial scholars, such as Mignolo and Walsh (2018: 136), who wrote, 'what is the praxis that lead(s) to decolonizing knowledge and being? I do not see another way of responding to this question than by saying that the praxis has to be theoretical.'

Provincializing and deprovincializing

Provincializing and deprovincializing are strategies of decolonizing in general. Provincializing arises from the reality of the overrepresentation of a province of the world in knowledge, education, and social theory. That province is Europe. Deprovincializing is meant to address the problem of marginalization, decentredness, and dismemberment in the knowledge domain. The ultimate goal, decolonially speaking, is to put all onto-epistemic traditions in a non-dominant and equal position for the purposes of enriching human life in its diversity. The decolonial task of the 'provincializing' of Europe arose as a direct response to a problem which John Headley (2008) celebrated as the 'Europeanization of the world.' Headley (2008: 8) defended the spread and imposition of European civilization on other civilizations as a 'unique gift' 'bequeathed to the world,' ignoring the genocides, epistemicides, linguicides, culturecides, and alienations that resulted from it. Instead of grappling with these evils, Headley posed them as a 'paradox' rather than part of the imperial logic of domination:

> But the paradox is trumped by another, even more astonishing—that the civilization that in its colonialism and imperialism gave us the most

> savage, inhuman treatments of indigenous populations, not to mention the ultimate inhumanity of Auschwitz, was the same that promoted the idea of a common humanity and programs of human rights accompanied subsequently by a myriad of private organizations that continue to address poverty, hunger, disease, and multifarious needs throughout the globe. Yet perhaps this is not a paradox at all but can be understood as integral to the complexity and varieties of the human animal.
>
> (Headley 2008: 4)

On the one hand, Headley sought to naturalize the evils of imperialism and colonialism, but, on the other hand, he sought an intellectual escape route by stating that 'The present study, however, refuses to become entangled in this ongoing debate or mired in confronting counterclaims of other civilizations to a comprehensive understanding of humankind or to the value and role of political dissent by means of diversity' (Headley 2008: 4–5). Thus, for him, the European Renaissance and Protestant Reformation constituted the first current in the unfolding of the idea of a common humanity and, eventually, that of today's concept of universal human rights. In short, he sought to provide a good story of the 'Europeanization of the world' through a refusal to listen to the victims of this very process.

What is clear is that Headley's Eurocentric historical rendition of the 'origins of human rights and democracy' leaves no space for grappling with the reality of 'coloniality' as a constitutive element in the 'Europeanization of the world.' One has to turn to Latin American scholars such as Anibal Quijano (2000) and Walter D. Mignolo (2000) to understand coloniality as a name for 'the transhistoric expansion of colonial domination and the perpetuation of its effects in contemporary times' (see, specifically, Morana et al. 2008: 2).Without the reality of coloniality, the problem of decolonizing the humanities would not have arisen in the first place. Coloniality is a system of social classification of human beings based on the idea of race, and it extended to the control of labour and subjectivity, which enabled the 'practices and policies of genocide and enslavement, the pillage of life and land, and the denials and destruction of knowledge, humanity, spirituality, and cosmo-existence' to perpetuate (Mignolo and Walsh 2018: 16).

Provincializing Europe is inevitably a confrontation with global coloniality (Ndlovu-Gatsheni 2013). It is a decolonial process of the 'de-Europeanization' of the world. De-Europeanization is part of deimperialization, which is necessary for decolonization to succeed. Kuan-Hsing Chen (preface 2010) articulated deimperialization as requiring the former empires to engage in a re-examination of 'their own imperialist histories' and accept 'the harmful effects those histories have had on the world.' Ngugi wa Thiong'o (1993: xvi–xvii) articulated it in terms of 'moving the centre in two senses at least': geographically and culturally, from Europe and North America 'to a multiplicity of spheres in all the cultures of the world' and, class-wise, socially, and within all modern nations, from 'the dominant social stratum, a male bourgeois minority.' He elaborated on the logic of this double-movement of the centre: 'Moving the centre in the two senses—between nations and within nations—will contribute to the freeing of world cultures from the restrictive walls of nationalism, class, race and gender' (Ngugi wa Thiong'o 1993: xvii).

This is necessary because European thought, which is often rendered as 'Eurocentrism,' is overrepresented in modern disciplinary knowledge, modern education, modern global normativity, modern conceptions of human subjectivity, global cartography and architecture of power, and social theory. At the same time, six modern European languages – Italian, Spanish, Portuguese, English, French, and German – continue to be dominant in the mediation of modern knowledge across the globe. This reality led Mignolo (2010: xxv–xxvi) to argue that 'What constitutes the West more than geography is a linguistic family, a belief system and an epistemology.' Even the very idea and a philosophy of human history continues to reflect European Renaissance thought, Enlightenment reason, and Cartesianism (Ndlovu-Gatsheni 2018). With all this evidence, the overrepresentation of Europe is self-evident. This has provoked various calls for the 'provincialization' of Europe as a solution to this overrepresentation – some of the calls are postcolonial and anti-colonial nationalist, and others are decolonial.

The work of the African historian Cheikh Anta Diop (1954, 1974a, 1974b) represented the anti-colonial nationalist position and formed the earliest Afrocentric intellectual and academic interventions, which directly confronted Eurocentrism and laid the foundation for the decentring of racism in modern scholarship in general and modern humanities in particular. Diop dedicated his entire scholarship to the recovery of the heritage of African people, beginning by claiming Egypt as an African civilization. The Palestinian intellectual Edward W. Said's *Orientalism* (1978) was another important work and was a critique not only of the dominance of Europe in conceptions of history, politics, power, and culture but also of its role in the creation of the paradigm of difference by defining, naming, and characterizing other civilizations while building its own occidental identity.

Dipesh Chakrabarty, a historian, postcolonial theorist, and active member of the Indian Subaltern Studies, posed some of the key questions regarding the ubiquity of the mythical figure of Europe, particularly in terms of how it has been etched into epistemes of social sciences and humanities. In a new preface to his celebrated book *Provincializing Europe: Postcolonial Thought and Historical Difference* (2008: i), Chakrabarty underscored the reality of the overrepresentation of Europe in Indian life:

> The legacy of Europe—or British colonial rule, for that is how Europe came into our lives—was everywhere: in traffic rules, in grown-ups' regrets that Indians had no civic sense, in the games of soccer and cricket, in my school uniform, in Bengali-nationalist essays and poems critical of social inequality, especially of the so-called caste-system, in implicit and explicit debates about love-match versus arranged marriages, in literary societies and film clubs. In practical, everyday living 'Europe'

was not a problem to be consciously named or discussed. Categories or words borrowed from European histories had found new homes in our practices.

After explaining how Europe had 'Europeanized' Indian ways of life and knowledge, Chakrabarty set out to claim European ideas as universal:

> To 'provincialise' Europe was precisely to find out how and in what sense European ideas that were universal were also, at one and the same time, drawn from very particular intellectual and historical traditions that could not claim any universal validity. It was to ask a question about how thought was related to place. Can thought transcend places of their origin? Or do places leave their imprint on thought in such a way as to call into question the idea of purely abstract categories?
>
> (Chakrabarty 2008: xiii)

The question, which emerges and is directly relevant to the task of decolonizing the humanities, is how did Enlightenment reason become integral to human sentiment outside Europe, and how did it embed itself within the humanities as a field of study across the world? What has to be done to disentangle the victims of Europeanization from the normative frameworks introduced by Enlightenment reason? Chakrabarty's take is that we must not advance the project of 'provincializing' Europe in the form of 'postcolonial revenge.' He argues:

> European thought is at once both indispensable and inadequate in helping us to think through the experiences of political modernity in non-Western nations, and provincializing Europe becomes the task of exploring how this thought—which is now everyone's heritage and which affects us all—may be renewed from and for the margins.
>
> (Chakrabarty 2008: 16)

Thus, the challenge in decolonizing the humanities is determining how to get beyond Eurocentric thinking and histories. How do those people who experienced epistemological colonialism represent themselves in human history? The difficulty, as Chakrabarty (2008: 28) states it is that 'That Europe works as a silent referent in historical knowledge.' His closing remarks on the subject of 'provincializing' Europe are typical of postcolonial rather than decolonial thought: 'provincializing Europe cannot ever be a project of shunning European thought'; he proceeds to posit that 'For at the end of European imperialism, European thought is a gift to all of us. We can talk of provincializing it only in an anticolonial spirit of gratitude' (Chakrabarty 2008: 255).

But 'provincializing' Europe in a decolonial sense has never been associated with anything akin to an 'anticolonial spirit of gratitude.' Rather decoloniality cascaded from the reality of what Mignolo (2000) termed a 'colonial wound,' not 'gratitude.' Its departure point is simple: Europe is not the world, it is a province of the world. But through imperialism, colonialism, neo-colonialism, globalization, and other 'imperial designs,' it moved itself to the centre of the world. This imperial/colonial move resulted in the marginalization, subjugation, and displacement of other provinces. In decoloniality, European thought has never been a 'gift.' Rather it is a carrier of 'colonial matrices of power' (Mignolo 2000; Mignolo and Walsh 2018). The best decolonial strategy is to delink from these matrices by whatever and all means necessary. It is within this context that the strategy of 'deprovincialising Africa' becomes important. Deprovincializing what was provincialized (dismembered, marginalized, and peripherized) becomes very necessary as a component of decolonization. In a practical decolonial sense, the concepts of 'provincializing' and 'deprovincialising' take us directly to what Lewis R. Gordon (2011) described as the 'shifting of the geography of reason' (from Europe and North America to Africa and the Global South) as well as the 'biography of reason' (from dead white men to African thinkers and thinkers from the Global South who were and are not necessarily white and male). This is an important move in the process of decolonizing the humanities because it restores the denied epistemic virtue that was thrown away as well as the denial of being of the colonized. All this is done in order to attain epistemic freedom.

The primacy of epistemic freedom

The recognition that all human beings were born into valid and legitimate knowledge systems is the beginning of the decolonization of the humanities through the assertion of epistemic freedom (Mudimbe 1994; Ndlovu-Gatsheni 2018). Today's struggles for epistemic freedom across the world are ranged against existing and resilient cognitive injustices, cascading from colonialism and maintained by an uneven global intellectual division of labour. Cognitive injustice speaks to the failures in the domain of knowledge to recognize the different ways of knowing by which diverse people across the human globe make sense of the world and provide meaning to their existence (Santos 2014). Thus, cognitive injustice is basically a social injustice that cascades from the denial of the humanity of other people and by extension the refusal to recognize their epistemic virtue (Ndlovu-Gatsheni 2018).

Tracing the origins of cognitive injustices, Ngugi wa Thiong'o (1986) underscored how the metaphysical empire unfolded in terms of the invasion of the mental universe of colonized people. He elaborated that this invasion amounted to the removal of the hard disks of previous African knowledge and memory, and the downloading into African minds of the software of European knowledge and memory (Ngugi wa Thiong'o 2009). The key consequences of these processes have been epistemicides (killing of existing endogenous knowledges), linguicides (killing of existing indigenous languages and the imposition of colonial languages), culturecides (killing of indigenous cultures and introducing cultural imperialism), and alienation (exiling of indigenous people from their languages, histories, cultures, and even themselves) (Ndlovu-Gatsheni 2018). The critical question which arises is whether it is possible for the knowledge of a people to really die. Did colonialism and coloniality ever succeed in eliminating existing knowledges? It is these questions that led Mignolo and Walsh (2018: 191) to problematize the concept of epistemicides by saying that colonialism could kill people, but it could not kill ideas.

Just as some people survived genocides, the colonized survived epistemicides; however, the fact that some people survived does not render either of these concepts unproblematic. In the same manner the 'resurgences and 're-existence' initiatives and struggles flourishing across the Global South and directly confronting Eurocentrism should not be used to deny the colonial intention and practice of epistemicides and genocides. Genocides are always preceded by epistemicides. Although indigenous languages survived linguicides, and African cultures and arts survived cultural imperialism, the fact that the languages and knowledges of the indigenous and colonized people are still struggling to fully recover from coloniality indicates the depth of the colonial practices of epistemicides and linguicides.

The existence of a resilient, uneven intellectual division of labour which engenders what Paulin Hountondji (1997) termed epistemic dependence makes the case for epistemic freedom even stronger today. Europe and North America have remained the centre from which what is considered valid and scientific knowledge cascades and circulates to the rest of the world. In this uneven division of labour, Africa in particular and the Global South in general exist as sites for the hunting and gathering of raw data (Hountondji 1997, 2002). Europe and North America remain the key sites of a professional processing of data for the purposes of the formulation of social theories. These theories are voraciously consumed in Africa. What are considered to be prestigious and international peer-reviewed journals that easily earn African scholars recognition and promotion are based in Europe and North America. All of these are clear hallmarks of intellectual/academic dependence that provoke the resurgence of struggles for epistemic freedom in the twenty-first century.

These struggles are ranged against the present-day neoliberal illusions of a magnanimous liberal empire that has delivered a global economy of knowledge which every human enjoys. At the centre of the so-called global economy of knowledge is resilient Eurocentrism. In a fundamental sense, struggles for epistemic freedom were and are a direct response to the denial of humanity itself (coloniality of being), which automatically resulted in the denial of knowledge and epistemic virtue from those who became victims of colonialism (Maldonado-Torres 2007; Ndlovu-Gatsheni 2018). The success of colonialism and coloniality in the domain of knowledge was and is always dependent on winning some of the colonized people to its side to the extent that they then speak and write as though they were located on the racially privileged side of the colonial matrices of power (Grosfoguel 2007). This confused mentality is nourished by the seductive aspects of coloniality, particularly its masquerading as a civilizing enterprise when in reality it was a death project. But to gain a deeper comprehension of the challenges of decolonizing the humanities, it is important to historically situate it within the long-standing struggles for epistemological decolonization.

African struggles for epistemic freedom

The struggles for epistemological decolonization are traceable to early African-educated elites, like Edward Wilmot Blyden of Sierra Leone, James Africanus Beale Horton of Sierra Leone, and J. E. Casely Hayford of Ghana. These educated Africans agitated and fought for the establishment of universities in Africa from as early as the 1860s and 1870s (Ashby 1964). It was these people who toyed with the idea of an 'African university' (rooted in African cultural and intellectual soil and climate). They were opposed to the colonial regimes imposing the 'university in Africa' as a transplant from Europe and North America. According to Eric Ashby, Blyden advocated for an African university that was free from the grip of the 'despotic Europeanizing influences which had warped and crushed the Negro mind' (Ashby 1964: 12–23; see also Blyden 1882). Blyden became the leading advocate, if not the pioneer, of the philosophy of 'African personality,' which he did not want Western education to destroy. Rather, he wanted it to be nurtured as part of the restoration of African cultural self-respect.

The philosophy of 'African personality' was predicated on five key issues: the separate and unique destiny of black people from Europeans, the development of a distinctive African mentality, religion's place of pride in African thought and life, the inherent socialist/communal nature of African society, and the strong idea of 'Africa for Africans' (Frankel 1974). Blyden was opposed to modern Western civilization because he saw it as a carrier of 'race poison,' harking back to the Greek and Latin civilizations as classics that could nourish Africa intellectually without racism (Ashby 1964: 13). He was also the earliest advocate to promote African languages, African songs, and African oral traditions as part of higher education. His decolonial ideas were echoed by Reverend James Johnson of Sierra Leone, who argued for a higher education institution that would 'Leave undisturbed our particularities' (Wandira 1977: 40).

What happened to these early struggles and demands for an African university is analogous to what happened to the person who cried for a fish and was given a snake instead. In the first place, the colonial regimes argued for a sound African secondary education as an essential pre-requisite and foundation for African university education. Second, the early educational institutions established in Africa, such as Fourah Bay College in Sierra Leone (1876), emerged as 'colleges' of overseas universities (Ashby 1964).

Third, the colonial regimes continued to turn a blind eye to the expansion of higher education for Africans, leaving the missionaries to concentrate on the primary and secondary sectors. As argued by Mazrui, mission education inaugurated the first form of African intellectual dependency and acculturation/'cultural schizophrenia' through by young Africans from their parents and enclosing them in mission boarding schools (Mazrui 1978: 27). Colonial education at whatever level amounted to the desocialization of Africans as well as their miseducation.

Nationalism, Africanization, and deracialization

African nationalism was underpinned by what Shiera S. el-Malik and Isaac A. Kamola (2017) termed the 'African anticolonial archive.' This carried the promise of a re-socialization and re-education of African people after centuries of desocialization and miseducation. It is an archive that embodied African utopic aspirations, their trials and tribulations, and their triumphs and possibilities set against the background of colonialism and imperialism. It is therefore not surprising that the dawn of African political independence in the 1960s was accompanied by intensified struggles to Africanize the university in Africa into an African university. At its deepest level, this struggle entailed formulating a new philosophy of higher education grounded in a deep appreciation of African histories, cultures, ideas, and aspirations as well as a fundamental redefinition of the role of the university.

It was in the 1960s that the idea of an African developmental university emerged. Such a university was expected to be truly African and to play an active role in nation-building, socio-economic development, and promoting African consciousness (Nyerere 1966: 219).Thus, on another level, the 1960s constituted the 'golden age' of the African higher education sector. Not only did the institutions of higher learning multiply, but the Africanization agenda was embraced by leading scholars, such as Cheikh Anta Diop, who dedicated his entire career to producing Africa-centred knowledge and challenging the myths created by imperial colonial historiography (Diop 1974, 1981). A vibrant and respected African Nationalist School emerged at the University of Ibadan in Nigeria, led by historians such as Kenneth Onwuka Dike, Jacob Ade Ajayi, John Omer-Cooper, and many others, who contributed immensely to the Africanization of history as a discipline as well as to the African nation-building project (Ifemesia 1988; Falola 2001: 224). African music, arts, and cultures flourished during the heydays of anti-colonial nationalism, and African intellectuals-cum-politicians and activists were very productive ideologically (see Table 7.1).

The formation of the Association of African Universities (AAU) in Rabat in Morocco in 1967 revealed the continued commitment of African leaders and African intellectuals to decolonizing and Africanizing universities in Africa, and to making these truly African universities. But unlike the

Table 7.1 Summary of African ideological production

Ideology	*Core issues*
1 Negritude	Africanness, black consciousness, black being, African personality, African identity, black identity, recovery and restoration of Africanity from rootlessness
2 Garveyism	Blackism on a world scale, black consciousness, return to Africa, black self-reliance, black republic, black self-improvement, black racial pride
3 Pan-Africanism	Black consciousness, African unity, Africa self-determination, decolonization, black power, African diaspora uniting with continental Africans, countering racism, building African institutions
4 African nationalism	Black territorial consciousness, territorial independence, self-determination, deracialization, Africanization, catching-up, indigenization, decolonization
5 African humanism	Restoration of human dignity, will to live, paradigm of peace, ethics of living together, anti-classism, anti-racism, rehumanization
6 African socialism	African communalism, anti-classism, anti-capitalism, anti-exploitation of some human beings by others, egalitarianism, self-reliance
7 African renaissance	Rebirth of Africa, Africa regeneration, rebuilding African institutions, African unity, pan-Africanism, black consciousness, African solutions to African problems

Source: Drawn by the author.

nationalist political leaders, African intellectuals never tired of defending so-called 'international standards.' The AAU expressed adherence to world academic standards and development of a higher education in the service of Africa, and was in favour of linking the African spirit of the university with the pan-African spirit embodied by the Organisation of African Unity (Yesufu 1973b: 5). At its first general conference, held in Kinshasa, Zaire, in September 1969, the AAU's chosen theme – 'The University and Development' – was revealing of the envisaged role of the university.

A 1972 AAU workshop, themed 'Creating the African University: Emerging Issues in the 1970s,' which ran from 10 to 15 July in Accra, Ghana, demonstrated that the struggle for an African university was continuing even within the context of African economies beginning to collapse. The workshop's purpose was to formulate a new philosophy of higher education and develop institutions of higher education that were truly African, drawing 'inspiration from Africa, and intelligently dedicated to her ideas and aspirations' (Yesufu 1973b: 5). Importantly, the workshop delegates agreed that tinkering with imported ideas was not enough, and what was needed was a fundamental re-conceptualization of the idea of the university in Africa. There was clear agreement among the members of the AAU that the African university must be a developmental one. However, Wandira raised critical concerns about what he termed the 'Yesufu University Model,' emerging from the 1972 AAU workshop. Throughout the colonial and 'postcolonial' period African intellectuals intensified anti-colonial/decolonial intellectual production, targeting the various aspects of racism, patriarchy, and colonialism embedded in knowledge (see Table 7.2).

Table 7.2 Summary of African intellectual production

Intellectuals/academics	*Issues/concerns*
Africa's long history pre-dating colonialism 1 Cheikh Anta Diop, Theophilus Obenga, Molefe Kete Asante, Jacob Ade Ajayi	Egyptian civilization, precolonial African history, African civilizations, African agency, African inventions
How Africa grappled with African, Islamic, and Western cultures and interventions 2 Edward Blyden, Kwame Nkrumah, Ali A. Mazrui	African personality, intersections, and synthesis of African, Islamic, and Western/Christian civilizations/cultures/heritages; Concienscism; triple heritage (hybridity)
How Europe underdeveloped Africa and maintained its grip over the continent 3 Kwame Nkrumah, Samir Amin, Walter Rodney, Dani Nabudere, Bade Onimode, Patrick Bond	Slavery, colonialism, neo-colonialism, unequal exchange, unequal development, maldevelopment, underdevelopment
How Europe invaded the mental universe of Africa/colonization of African minds 4 Frantz Fanon, Albert Memmi, Ngugi wa Thiong'o, Chinweizu, V.Y. Mudimbe, Claude Ake	Black existentialism, wretched of the earth, colonizer-colonized relations, colonial language, colonial education, colonial library, imperialism of social science, neo-colonialism
How Europe ruled Africa and its implications for postcolonial reform 5 Frantz Fanon, Albert Memmi, Mahmood Mamdani, Issa G. Shivji, Achille Mbembe	Legacy of late colonialism, native question, colonial governmentality, political subjectivity, national question, define and rule, nationalism, decentralized despotism, direct rule, indirect rule

(Continued)

Intellectuals/academics	*Issues/concerns*
How Africa governed itself after dismantlement of direct colonialism 6 Achille Mbembe, Mahmood Mamdani, Issa G. Shivji, Adebayo Olukoshi, Ibbo Mandaza, Dani Nabudere, Brian Raftopoulos	Ideology, class, constitutionalism, postcolony, authoritarianism/ commandment, vulgarity, repression, looting, violence, national question, nation-building, state-making, neo-colonialism, democracy, human rights, labour and workers, civil society
Conceptions of African social formations, especially gender relations and womanhood 7 Ifi Amadiume, Oyeronke Oyewumi, Nkiru Nzegwu, Amina Mama, Rudo Gaidzanwa, Patricia MacFadden	Colonial invention of gender, sexism, matriarchy, religion, culture, knowledge, feminism, African philosophy, subjectivity, family, motherhood, patriarchy, misogyny, violence against women
African struggles for development and African national projects 8 Claude Ake, Thandika Mkandawire, Adebayo Olukoshi, Paul Tiyambe Zeleza, Tukumbi Lumumba-Kasongo, Dzodzi Tsikata, Rudo Gaidzanwa, Sam Moyo, Fantu Cheru	African nationalism, national question, African state, African nation-state project, structural adjustment programmes, African development plans, African developmental states, governance, social policy, land question, land tenure, agrarian reform
African transcendental identity 9 Paul Tiyambe Zeleza, Archie Mafeje	African combative ontology, national question, nationalism, humanism
Changing higher education landscape and crisis 10 Paul Tiyambe Zeleza, Adebayo Olukoshi, Mahmood Mamdani	Africanization, internationalization, curriculum, autonomy, excellence, indigenization, academic freedom, privatization knowledge economy, knowledge dissemination

Source: Drawn by the author.

Even though the African economies were hit by crisis in the 1970s, and despite the fact that some notorious dictators like Idi Amin had ascended to power, African intellectuals and academics continued to fight for intellectual spaces, this time outside the declining universities. The formation of the Council for the Development of Social Science Research in Africa (Codesria) in 1973 is a case in point. With the support of donor funding, Codesria emerged as a research council that became a comfortable home for exiled academics like Thandika Mkandawire from Malawi and Archie Mafeje from South Africa. It also became a home for radical left-leaning intellectuals like Samir Amin from Egypt, Mahmood Mamdani from Uganda, Sam Moyo from Zimbabwe, Issa Shivji from Tanzania, and many others. In the words of Mamdani (2016: 78), Codesria 'was a ready-made forum for public intellectuals.'

What distinguished Codesria was the intense public debates it generated on topical issues affecting Africa, such as African politics and the problem of political authoritarianism, African political economy, dependency, democracy, gender and the emancipation of women, the agrarian question and land reform, neoliberalism and structural adjustment programmes, higher education, economic and social development, and the national question and constitutionalism. What also distinguished Codesria was its 'nondisciplinary' orientation (Mamdani 2016: 78–79). Codesria produced some of the most groundbreaking research, some of which directly confronted Eurocentrism (the mother and father of epistemological colonization). For example, the work of Samir Amin (2009) confronted Eurocentrism directly, while that of Archie Mafeje directly and consistently challenged anthropology as a handmaiden of colonial knowledge. It was actually Codesria which published two of the most influential volumes on the university in Africa: *African Universities in the Twenty-First Century: Volume 1: Liberalization and Internationalization* (2004) and *African Universities in the Twenty-First Century: Volume 2: Knowledge and Society* (2004). To its credit, Codesria has maintained a clear oppositional position to imperialism, colonialism, and neo-colonialism. It is still a vibrant intellectual space, and one can only hope that it builds on its unparalleled intellectual work to directly address the topical issue of the decolonization of the universities and the epistemological question.

The 1980s and 1990s became crisis years for the university in Africa, and attempts to create an African university collapsed. New factors intervened to deepen the crisis. For example, the World Bank introduced a negative attitude towards universities, discrediting them as agencies of development and public institutions worthy of government and international support. Instead, the World Bank (1986) prioritized secondary education. The idea of creating African universities died as the powerful international forces of neoliberalism and global finance posited that Africa had no need for universities and that what was taught there was irrelevant to the needs of the global market and national development (Olukoshi and Zeleza 2004). But instead of the university in Africa dying, it was forced to mutate into a 'corporate university' in the 1980s and 1990s. Markets became the major agents of coloniality.

The fall and revival of African humanities

When the modern world was invaded by what became known as the Washington Consensus underpinned by neoliberal philosophies, humanities that had flourished in the 1960s and early 1970s fell. The 'corporate university' that emerged from the invasion of institutions of higher education by a coloniality of markets with its privileging of business models has become averse not only to humanities but also to critical thinking in general (Gordon 2006: 5). What distinguished the corporate university in the words of Lewis R. Gordon (2006: 9–10) was the rise of the 'academic managerial class' using 'corporate analogs' as the basis of its governing institutions. Gordon (2006: 10) elaborated that the rise of this 'academic managerial class has been, perhaps the most catastrophic development in the modern university.' The catastrophic aspect of this phenomenon is multidimensional. First, this academic managerial class, according to Gordon (2006: 10), is 'unlike past scholars who so happened also to administrate' because it 'no longer has knowledge as part of its telos.'

Worse still, this academic managerial class 'has folded onto itself as the object of its own preservation and the result is its proliferation' (Gordon 2006: 10). Gordon characterizes the composition of this academic managerial class as one 'consisting of failed academics and scholars whose credentials do not extend beyond their doctorates' and who practise the 'sociology of revenge and entrenched resentment toward productive and influential scholars' (Gordon 2006: 10). It is this academic managerial class that 'seeks inspiration from the corporate world primarily because of a form of decadence of the imagination in which corporate management is equated with management itself' (Gordon 2006: 10–11). It is within this context of a decadent corporate university presided over by an equally decadent academic managerial class that many scholars found themselves in the midst of what Mamdani (2007) termed the 'market place.'

The advent of the Rhodes Must Fall (RMF) and Fees Must Fall (FMF) movements in South Africa in 2015 and 2016 as heirs to the long-standing struggles for an African university and epistemic freedom in Africa resulted in the revival of the humanities. These movements, which were spearheaded by university studies, demanded not only free education but also the decolonization of the universities. They made clear demands, such as the decommissioning of colonial/apartheid iconographies; the restoration of African indigenous languages in teaching, learning, and research; and the changing of alienating institutional cultures that bred patriarchy, sexism, racism, elitism, and other forms of exclusion and discrimination, and they also picked up the labour issue of the casualization of workers and demanded that they be given secure employment (Ndlovu-Gatsheni 2018). Taken together, these demands amounted to the re-humanization of the people who had been dehumanized. The question of being human and its meaning once again became a major subject of scholarly reflection within the universities (Jansen 2017; see Chinguno et al. 2017 on the student voices). Table 7.3 provides a summary of the key demands of the Rhodes Must Fall movement.

Leading scholars like Falola (2016) have also picked up the issue of the importance of African humanities. In a rather poetic style, Falola articulated the importance and function of African humanities this way:

> When your mind is in turmoil, and your emotions become fragile, you call on us.
> When you have bad dreams, and see witches pursuing you, you call on us.

Table 7.3 Summary of the key demands of Rhodes Must Fall movement

Demand	*Elaboration*
1 Idea of the university	• Free from Eurocentrism and colonialism • Anchorage on African soil • Responsive to African aspirations • Non-elitist • Promotion of education as public good • De-corporatization
2 Iconography	• Decommissioning of offensive colonial/apartheid symbols and statues • Renaming, taking into account African realities and histories
3 Funding of education	• De-corporatization • Accessibility of education • Free, quality, and relevant education • De-commodification of knowledge
4 African languages	• Removal of colonial languages • Use of indigenous African languages in learning, teaching, and research • Multilingualism as recognition of African linguistic realities
5 Institutional cultures	• End racism • End patriarchy and sexism • End alienating elitist and foreign cultures • End culture of corporatization
6 Knowledge, curriculum, and pedagogy	• Africa-centred education that is globally competitive • Banish Eurocentrism • Relevance of education • Changing demographics of teachers (by gender and race) • Use of African languages • Privileging of African indigenous knowledges • Democratized pedagogies
7 Outsourcing of labour	• Liberation of poor black/African workers from exploitative and precarious 'casualization' • Rehumanizing of black/African workers through insourcing

Source: Drawn by the author.

> When there are conflicts to resolve, you call on us.
> When peace breaks down, you call on us.
> When you are seeking leaders and the understanding of leadership qualities you call on us.
> When you arrive home in the evening to relax or you want to spend weekend in the comfort of your home, we give you films (the almighty Nollywood films!) based on the stories we invent for you.
> When you look elegant in your attire, you benefit from our creativity.
> When you are sick, you go to the doctor for treatment, but the healing words come from us.
> We give you the humanism to cope.
> When you die, and the doctors have been paid, the hospitals have collected their money, we do the celebration of life for you.
> We pray for your body to rest in peace.
> What else do you want from us, I ask?
>
> (Falola 2016: 86–87)

The truth of the matter is that without the humanities there is no humanity (humanism) in its individual and collective sense (Falola 2016: 86)

Conclusion

What emerges poignantly from this chapter is that the struggle to decolonize the humanities is fundamentally a re-humanizing process after centuries of the dehumanization of those people who underwent enslavement, colonialism, patriarchization, capitalism, and apartheid. What has galvanized this necessary struggle for re-humanization is the definitive entry of the descendants of the enslaved, colonized, and racialized people into the modern academies in large numbers. These people, whose very being has been subjected to numerous questions and doubts, are proclaiming loudly to the world not only that they were born into valid and legitimate knowledge systems but also that their lives matter. The prospects not only for the decolonization of the humanities but also for them to take their rightful place as the most needed and relevant knowledge are very bright today because there is a resurgent and insurgent decolonization/decoloniality across the world whose call is to re-humanize the dehumanized. The humanities offer the medium of rehumanization.

References

Achebe, C. 2009. *The Education of British-Protected Child*. London: Penguin Books.
Amin, S. 2009. *Eurocentrism: Modernity, Religion, and Democracy: A Critique of Eurocentrism and Culturalism*. Second Edition. New York: Monthly Review Press.

Ashby, E. 1964. *African Universities and Western Tradition.* Cambridge, MA: Harvard University Press.

Blyden, E. W. 1882. *The Aims and Methods of a Liberal Education for Africans: Inaugural Address Delivered by Edward Wilmot Blyden, LLD., President of Liberia College, January 5, 1881.* Cambridge, MA: Harvard University Press.

Cesaire, A. 1950 [2000]. *Discourse on Colonialism.* Translated by Joan Pinkham. New York: Monthly Review Press.

Chakrabarty, D. 2008. 'Preface to the 2007 Edition: Provincializing Europe in Global Times.' In D. Chakrabarty (eds.), *Provincializing Europe: Postcolonial Thought and Historical Difference: New Edition with a New Preface By the Author.* Princeton, NJ and Oxford: Princeton University Press, pp. i–xxi.

Chen, K. H. 2010. *Asia as Method: Towards Deimperialization.* Durham, NC and London: Duke University Press.

Chinguno, C., Kgoroba, M., Mashibini, S., Masilela, B. N., Maubane, B., Mthombeni, A., & Ndlovu, H. 2017. *Rioting and Writing: Diaries of Wits Fallists.* Johannesburg: Society, Work and Development Institute.

Comaroff, J., & Comaroff, J. L. 2012. *Theory from the South Or, How Euro-America Is Evolving Toward Africa.* Boulder, CO and London: Paradigm Publishers.

Cornell, D., & Seely, S. D. 2016. *The Spirit of Revolution: Beyond the Dead Ends of Man.* Cambridge: Polity Press.

Diop, C. A. 1954. *Nation, Negres et Culture.* Paris: Presence Africaine.

Diop, C. A. 1974a. *The African Origin of Civilization: Myth and Reality.* New York: Lawrence Hill Books.

Diop, C. A. 1974b. *Precolonial Black Africa.* New York: Lawrence Hill Books.

Diop, C. A. 1981. *Civilization or Barbarism: An Authentic Anthropology.* Chicago, IL: Lawrence Hill Books.

El-Malik, S. S., & Kamola, I. A. (eds.). 2017. *Politics of African Anticolonial Archive.* London and New York: Rowman & Littlefield International.

Escobar, A. 2004. 'Beyond the Third World: Imperial Globality, Global Coloniality and Anti-Globalization Social Movements.' *Third World Quarterly*, 25(1), pp. 207–230.

Falola, T. 2001. *Nationalism and African Intellectuals.* Rochester, NY: University of Rochester Press.

Falola, T. 2016. *The Humanities in Africa: Knowledge Production, Universities, and the Transformation of Society.* Austin, TX: Pan-African University Press.

Fanon, F. 1953 [2008]. *Black Skins, White Masks.* New York: Grove Press.

Foucault, M. 1970. *The Order of Things: An Archaeology of Human Science.* London: Tavistock.

Frankel, M. Y. 1974. 'Edward Blyden and the Concept of African Personality.' *African Affairs*, 73(292), pp. 277–289.

Giovanni, P. D. M. 1956. *Oration on Dignity of Man.* Chicago, IL: Gateway Editions.

Grosfoguel, R. 2007. 'The Epistemic Decolonial Turn; Beyond Political-Economy Paradigms.' *Cultural Studies*, 21(2–3), (March/May), pp. 211–223.

Gordon, L. R. 2006. *Disciplinary Decadence: Living Thought in Trying Times.* Boulder, CO and London: Paradigm Publishers.

Gordon, L. R. 2011. 'Shifting the Geography of Reason in an Age of Disciplinary Decadence.' *Transmodernity*, 1(2) (Fall), pp. 95–102.

Headley, J. 2008. *The Europeanization of the World: On the Origins of Human Rights and Democracy*. Princeton, NJ and Oxford: Princeton University Press.

Holm, P., Jarrick, A., & Scott, D. 2015. *Humanities World Report 2015*. New York and London: Palgrave Macmillan.

Hoppers, C. O., & Richards, H. 2012. *Rethinking Thinking: Modernity's 'Other' and the Transformation of the University*. Pretoria: UNISA Press.

Horne, G. 2018. *The Apocalypse of Settler Colonialism: The Roots of Slavery in Seventeenth-Century North America and the Caribbean*. New York: Monthly Review Press.

Hountondji, P. J. (ed.). 1997. *Endogenous Knowledge: Research Trails*. Translated by Ayi Kwesi Armah. Dakar: CODERIA Book Series.

Hountondji, P. J. 2002. *The Struggle for Meaning: Reflections on Philosophy, Culture, and Democracy in Africa*. Athens: Ohio University Research in International Studies Africa Series No. 78.

Ifemesia, C. (ed.). 1988. *Issues in African Studies and National Education: Selected Work of Kenneth Onwuka Dike*. Awka: K.O. Dike Centre.

Jansen, J. 2017. *As By Fire: The End of the South African University*. Cape Town: Tafelberg.

Lowe, L., & Manjapra, K. 2019. 'Comparative Global Humanities after Man: Alternatives to the Coloniality of Knowledge.' *Theory, Culture and Society*, 36(5), pp. 23–48.

Maldonado-Torres, N. 2007. 'On Coloniality of Being: Contributions to the Development of a Concept.' *Cultural Studies*, 21(2/3), pp. 240–270.

Maldonado-Torres, N. 2017. 'On the Coloniality of Human Rights.' *Revista Critica De Ciencias Sociais*, 144, Dezembro, pp. 117–136.

Mamdani, M. 1996. *Citizen and Subject: Contemporary Africa and the Legacy of Late Colonialism*. Princeton, NJ: Princeton University Press.

Mamdani, M. 2007. *Scholars in the Market Place: The Dilemmas of Neo-Liberal Reform at Makerere University, 1989–2005*. Dakar: CODESRIA Books.

Mamdani, M. 2013. *Define and Rule: Native as Political Identity*. Johannesburg: Wits University Press.

Mamdani, M. 2016. 'Between the Public Intellectual and the Scholar: Decolonization and Some Post- Independence Initiatives in Higher Education.' *Inter-Asia Studies*, 17(1), pp. 56–98.

Mazrui, A. A. 1978. *Political Values and the Educated Class in Africa*. Berkeley and Los Angeles: University of California Press.

Mignolo, W. D. 2000. *Local Histories/Global Designs: Coloniality, Subaltern Knowledges and Border Thinking*. Princeton, NJ: Princeton University Press.

Mignolo, W. D. 2010. 'Foreword: Yes, We Can.' In H. Dabashi (ed.), *Can Non-Europeans Think?* London: Zed Books, pp. viii–xliii.

Mignolo, W. D. 2011. *The Darker Side of Western Modernity: Global Futures, Decolonial Options*. Durham, NC and London: Duke University Press.

Mignolo, W. D., & Walsh, C. E. 2018. *On Coloniality: Concepts, Analytics, Praxis*. Durham, NC and London: Duke University Press.

Mudimbe, V. Y. 1994. *The Idea of Africa*. Bloomington and Indianapolis: Indiana University Press.

Morana, M., Dussel, E., & Jauregui, C. A. 2008. 'Colonialism and Its Replicants.' In M. Morana, E. Dussel and C. A. Jauregui (eds.), *Coloniality At Large: Latin America and the Postcolonial Debate*. Durham, NC and London: Duke University Press, pp. 1–20.

Ndlovu-Gatsheni, S. J. 2013. *Empire, Global Coloniality and African Subjectivity*. New York and Oxford: Berghahn Books.

Ndlovu-Gatsheni, S. J. 2018. *Epistemic Freedom in Africa: Deprovincialization and Decolonization*. London and New York: Routledge.

Ngugi wa Thiong'o. 1986. *Decolonizing the Mind: The Politics of Language in African Literature*. Oxford: James Currey.

Ngugi wa Thiong'o. 1993. *Moving the Centre: The Struggle for Cultural Freedoms*. Oxford: James Currey.

Ngugi wa Thiong'o. 2009. *Something Torn and New: An African Renaissance*. New York: Basic Civitas Books.

Nyamnjoh, F. B. 2017. *Drinking from the Cosmic Gourd: How Amos Tutuola Can Change Our Minds*. Mankon, Bamenda: Langaa Research & Publishing CIG.

Nyerere, J. K. 1966. *Freedom and Unity/Uhuru Na Umoja*. Dar-es-Salaam: Oxford University Press.

Olukoshi, A. and Zeleza, P. T. 2004. 'Introduction: The Struggle for African Universities and Knowledges.' In P. T. Zeleza and A. Olukoshi (eds.). *African Universities in the Twenty-First Century*. Dakar: CODESRIA Book Series, pp. 1–18.

Oyewumi, O. 1997. *The Invention of Women: Making an African Sense of Western Gender Discourses*. Minneapolis and London: University of Minnesota Press.

Quijano, A. 2000. 'Coloniality of Power, Eurocentrism, and Latin America.' *Nepantla: Views from South*, 1(3), pp. 533–580.

Said. E. W. 1978. *Orientalism*. New York: Vintage Books.

Santos, B. de. S. 2014. *Epistemologies of the South: Justice against Epistemicide*. London and Boulder, CO: Paradigm Publishers.

Santos, B. de S. 2017. *Decolonizing the University: The Challenges of Deep Cognitive Justice*. Newcastle upon Tyne: Cambridge Scholars Publishing.

Snow, C. P. 1965. *The Two Cultures, and a Second Look*. Second Edition. Cambridge: Cambridge University Press.

Wallerstein, I. 2004. *The Uncertainties of Knowledge*. Philadelphia, PA: Temple University Press.

Wandira, A. 1977. *The African University in Development*. Johannesburg: Ravan Press.

Wynter, S. 1984. 'The Ceremony Must Be Found: After Humanism.' *Boundary*, 212/213(3/1), pp. 19–70.

Wynter, S. 2003. 'Unsettling the Coloniality of Being/Power/Truth/Freedom: Towards the Human, After Man, Its Overrepresentation—An Argument.' *CR: The New Continental Review*, 3(3), pp. 257–337.

Yesufu, T. M. 1973a. 'Emerging Issues of the 1970s.' In T.M. Yesufu (ed.), *Creating the African Emerging Issues in the 1970s*. Ibadan: Oxford University Press, pp. 37–81.

Yesufu, T. M. 1973b. 'Introduction.' In T. M. Yesufu (ed.), *Creating the African University: Emerging Issues in the 1970s*. Ibadan: Oxford University Press.

Zeleza, P. T., & Olukoshi, A. (eds.). 2004a. *African Universities in the Twenty-First Century: Volume 1: Liberalization and Internationalization.* Dakar: CODESRIA Books.

Zeleza, P. T., & Olukoshi, A. (eds.). 2004b. *African Universities in the Twenty-First Century: Volume II: Knowledge and Society.* Dakar: CODESRIA Books.

8 Conclusion

Turning over a new leaf

The present time is haunted by deficits of convincing and appealing utopic registers of the future. This is why you find European philosophers like Slavoj Zizek preaching the apocalyptic gospel of the end times, if they aren't calling for the defence of lost causes. Does this mean that the search for the future must gaze back into the past, with the past becoming the future? The second important utopic register is that which worships at the altar of technology/the cult of technology and its successful digitalization of human minds, resulting in a future ruled by machines. Does this mean that the search for the future must be predicated on the possibility of the posthuman? The Fanonian decolonial call for Africa to turn over a new leaf is today intersecting with calls for Africa to adapt to the Fourth Industrial Revolution (4IR), the signature of which is known as the 'Silicon Valley.' One wonders whether the 4IR and the Silicon Valley are not part of what Fanon termed the 'European game.' Technology is identified by Samir Amin as one of the key element of the five monopolies that underpin the world capitalist system. Europe and North America, now joined by China, continue to control technology, including weapons of mass destruction. To pose these questions must never be taken to mean that there are 'neo-Luddites' and 'counter-Fourth Industrial Revolution revolutionaries' opposed to technology. The die-hard technology worshippers (both within and outside Africa) who speak the language of artificial intelligence (AI), 'smart,' and 'data-driven' are very quick to raise the red flag against those who critique the ideas of technology as the solution to African problems of development. The key issue of epistemological colonization does not feature in their debates on how technology would be a panacea for African problems. Global asymmetrical power relations underpinned by coloniality are also ignored as Africa is urged to adapt to technology. The reality is that Africans have never been strangers to technology. In fact, they were active inventors of technology which enabled them to emerge from foraging/hunting and gathering ways of living to sedentary civilizations.

The shift from Stone Age to Iron Age was part of African endogenous revolutionary self-improvements and betterment of life. Africans were indeed the frontiersmen and women of humankind who tamed and effectively used hostile environments. The Nile Valley, for example, became one of the earliest centres of underground mining and indeed the earliest industrial hub of its kind known anywhere in the world. Rock paintings found in the southern African region vividly capture human symbolic behaviour during the microlithic period. Pottery and grinding-stones are evidence of food production and processing. Thus, for Africa to successfully turn over a new leaf, there is a need to appreciate its history of innovation and creativity. The earliest evidence of metalworking in Africa comes from southern Egypt in the late fifth millennium BC.

The problem with current dominant discourses of industrial revolutions is that they ignore the *longue durée* of African inventions and industrial changes, even prior to colonization. Such African scholars as Cheikh Anta Diop, Theophilus Obenga, Molefi Kete Asante, and others have consistently called our attention to early African civilizations, especially the celebrated Egyptian civilization. Their ideas have crystallized into an influential school of thought known as Afrocentricity. The key message from these Afrocentric scholars is that Africa has a very strong basis from which to build as it turns over a new leaf from a pupil waiting to be educated by teachers from other civilizations into a teacher and inventor of technologies and civilizations. This thinking is capable of repositioning Africa correctly in relation to the Fourth Industrial Revolution.

It is to be ahistorical and Eurocentric to privilege only the four industrial revolutions in which Europe and North America played a leading role, and ignore the long history of human inventions of technologies and civilizations which pre-date the nineteenth century. The privileged four industrial revolutions are: (i) The First Industrial Revolution, which is said to have been enabled by the creative utilization of water and steam power; (ii) The Second Industrial Revolution, which is said to have been made possible by and driven by the discovery of electricity, which enabled mass production; (iii) The Third Industrial Revolution, which is said to be predicated on the use of electronics, information technology, and the internet, and which has enabled the digitization of production, distribution, and services; and (iv) The Fourth Industrial Revolution, which is currently upon us and is characterized by the use of AI: machines so intelligent that they are able to identify human problems and make decisions similar to those made by humans. It is said that we have entered the exciting and brave new world of the 'internet of things' (IOT), which includes the use of crypto-currencies known as Bitcoin.

There are a few problems with the above rendition of the four industrial revolutions as simply driven by technological development (a depoliticized technicist thesis). It is this problematic rendition of modern industrial revolutions which makes their advocates give credit to such individuals as Copernicus and Isaac Newton, naming them as the trail blazers in scientific revolutions. What is ignored is how these modern scientific revolutions were enabled by the invasion and exploitation of African material and human resources. For example, the First Industrial Revolution was enabled partly by technology and partly by an exploitation of resources (material and human) by the leading mercantilist powers. The invasion of the Americas (dubbed the New World) in 1492 enabled Europe to exploit people, material resources, and indeed epistemic theft for its own benefit and development. The enslavement of African people for over 400 years played no small part in enabling the First Industrial Revolution to take place in Britain. Britain became a major colonial power (an empire) through the exploitation of other parts of the world.

What is also ignored by those celebrating the first, second, and third industrial revolutions is why Africa became an object of these revolutions rather than an active player. Did colonial conquest and colonial domination not disrupt the chosen and natural trajectory of African self-improvement (known as development)? As mentioned throughout this book, even the decolonization of the twentieth century did not enable Africa to turn over a new leaf – from being an object of global designs – to become an independent/genuinely sovereign people with autonomous agency to shape Africa's future and determine its destiny. Turning to the Fourth Industrial Revolution, the problem now is that Africa is being coerced into preparing and adapting to a revolution in which it has not played a conscious role. Of course, there are possibilities of benefits as well as risks, akin to boarding a plane whose destination the passengers do not know.

Ideally, human beings must arrive consciously in this exciting and brave new world, marked by the rule of machines and technologies, including lifeless robots (the robotic revolution), with both eyes open. The idea of a sudden 'arrival' of a Fourth Industrial Revolution begs the big question: from where? In other words, technologies are made for the people, not the people for technology. Thus, it is not to be against technology to reveal that technology has never been neutral and objective; it has always mirrored and reflected societal issues, including inequalities and injustices. Simple access to technology is determined by power and economic dynamics. One does not become an opponent of technology and the Fourth Industrial Revolution by alerting the world to the fact that 'mining' people for data is overtly tantamount to reducing human beings to raw material. These critiques should not succumb to the overwhelming voices of tech enthusiasts. We must openly explore the possibilities of 'digital'/'data' colonization without rejecting technology. Africans must maintain vigilance against what Chinweizu termed a 'cargo mentality of development,' whereby they wait for technology from somewhere else and only prepare for and adapt to it!

What is proposed here is that there is need to turn over a new leaf and that this must be led by an 'actually existing' Africa, represented by its majority population of peasants and workers, not the minority educated and Westernized elites prone to mimicry and dependence on anything coming from the global north. How would the 'actually existing' Africa leverage on digital technologies and artificial intelligence for its chosen trajectory of turning over a new leaf from colonial entrapment and poverty? If this Africa is to prepare for the Fourth Industrial Revolution, what exactly must it do? Should 'actually existing' Africa not get its infrastructure in order first, particularly its energy capacity because any of the benefits from the Fourth Industrial Revolution needs a stable supply of electricity?

The second priority area is connected to infrastructure development in order to enable internet connectivity which reaches peasants who do not live in urban areas. This speaks to the long-standing issues of bridging the urban-rural divide that was deliberately created by colonialism for the purposes of maintaining a reservoir (reserves) of cheap labour. Thus, at the centre of any infrastructure development project must be the development of reliable and affordable mobile telecommunications infrastructure.

The starting point for Africa is to grow the 'Decolonial Tree of Knowledge' (DTK) through the transformation of the existing education sector. African schools, colleges, and universities have remained Eurocentric and indeed outward-looking. The education they offer is still not relevant enough to Africa. From its very introduction, modern Western education was meant to service the empire, not African people. The African nationalist project's Africanization and indigenization projects of the 1960s and 1970s did not successfully transform the education sector. The idea of Africa as a pupil to be taught by Europe was a colonial project which turned Africa into an object of development rather than an active subject. Thus, the idea and reality of Africa as lagging behind the rest of the world in the knowledge sector is a deliberate colonial invention. This is why the advocates of the Fourth Industrial Revolution still argue as though Africa is a mere object of technology dumping rather than an inventor of technology. A different mindset and consciousness of the African people as craftsmen and craftswomen is an essential pre-requisite for Africa benefiting from the fruits of the Fourth Industrial Revolution. The education sector is a key site and indeed a catalytic force in its turning over a new leaf. There are indeed clear signs that African leaders are conscious of the fundamental role of the education sector in enabling this development. The African Union (AU)'s 2011 launch of the Pan-African University (PAU) to advance its vision and agenda by 2063 is a promising move. PAU's intellectual agenda is informed by strategic objectives of development set out by the AU. A clear privileging of STEM (Science, Technology, Engineering, and Mathematics) drove the structuring of PAU curriculum resulting in the introduction of new fields of study such as those of petroleum, agriculture, water, minerals, and space, the humanities and the social sciences were not ignored. Studies of African history, gender, regional integration, migration, policy, and governance are part of the PAU curriculum. However, PAU has been weakened from its inception by the failure of its founders to unthink the Eurocentric-Enlightenment-inspired epistemologies that plunged Africa into its present crisis. The AU leaders themselves are not aware that the dominant but exhausted Eurocentric epistemologies which brought about the present crisis cannot be the same factors that take Africa into the future.

Thus, what remains a key challenge is transforming the numerous universities in the different territories of Africa to help them produce knowledge and skills that the continent can use in its drive towards turning over a new leaf. Most of these 'universities in Africa' have not made a radical shift into being genuinely 'African universities' that serve African people while remaining globally competitive. They have retained their colonial identity as part of a hegemonic Westernized global university system servicing the Euro-North American-centric modern world system and its shifting global orders. Even many of the universities, which were a gift of African nationalism, were born Western-centric, though some carried African indigenous names. I repeat that such nationalist-inspired initiatives as deracialization, indigenization, and Africanization did not successfully result in epistemological decolonization. Of course, the leadership of the 'universities in Africa' changed from European to Africa. The teaching staff changed as more African scholars entered the university service. Access to higher education increased for African students. Taken together, these processes took the format of inclusion into the 'European game,' with very minor changes. What is needed is a change to the rules of the game as Africa takes its rightful driving seat in African development.

It is no wonder that, between 2015 and 2016, South African students burst into the public arena with the catchy slogan 'Rhodes Must Fall,' openly challenging the colonial and patriarchal institutional cultures of South African universities. Modern South Africa has always been an important part of colonial imaginaries, dubbed the 'little Europe' at the southern tip of the African continent. Its universities had not managed to delink from the colonial imaginaries. Thus, what began as Rhodes Must Fall, targeting the presence of the statue of Cecil John Rhodes, spread into other demands, such as 'Fees Must Fall,' and embraced decolonization as a clarion call for decolonial change. The demands for the decolonization of South African universities by students demonstrate an upsurge in epistemological consciousness necessary for Africa's drive to turn over the leaf. In *Epistemic Freedom in Africa: Deprovincialization and Decolonization* (2018), Sabelo J. Ndlovu-Gatsheni made a very strong and convincing case for epistemological decolonization and epistemic freedom. Epistemic freedom was offered as a foundational basis of all other freedoms, including political, economic, and cultural freedoms.

Meanwhile, it is always gratifying that amid a plethora of challenges, the African people continue to forcefully turn over a new leaf in many arenas. For example, the Western African region continues to make Africans proud by taking bold and revolutionary pan-African steps, such as the introduction of a common passport and agreeing on a common currency (ECO). The idea of a common currency for the Western African region dates back some 30 years. ECOWAS is a union of 15 African states, which represent a total population of 385 million. The proposed currency is expected to facilitate increased trade and lower transaction costs amongst the 385 million

Western Africans. It is also hoped that a single currency will enable the region to collectively deal with monetary shocks cascading from the global designs of the powerful northern powers. Of course, to reap the fruits of a common currency is also to be dependent on the intensification of infrastructure development and industrialization across the region.

The downside is that such erstwhile colonial powers as France (which since the 1960s has been benefiting from monetary imperialism through CFA) have demonstrated their eagerness to hijack the currency initiative by working with the president of Ivory Coast, Alasane Quattara. In December 2019, the French president Macron and Quattara announced that the eight West African countries that have been suffering from CFA monetary imperialism would adopt ECO as new currency and that the ECO would be pegged at the same level as the euro, thus taking the initiative away from ECOWAS and causing confusion among the West African states. What this proves is that as Africa fights to turn over a new leaf, the agents of global coloniality are always attentive and ready to counter and hijack the initiatives so as to keep Africa within the ambit of a Euro-North American-centric world system. One even wonders if the ECO initiative is indeed a decolonial initiative or just a mimicry of the European Union and its euro. There is no sign of different knowledge and economic thought in the discussions on the new monetary zone. It is still a bourgeois project without a clear involvement of the African people.

The other important initiative consonant with Africa's efforts to turn over a new leaf is the emerging consensus and the actual signing of the agreements on the African Continental Free Trade Area (AfCFTA) by 54 African states, excluding Eritrea. If this initiative is fully grounded in Nkrumah's vision and underpinned by a decolonial consciousness, it has the potential to create continental economic autonomy and power. However, in the discussion leading to the AfCFTA, there is a lot of old-style economism, with its privileging of economic growth via increased trade as the solution to Africa's problems. There is also an emphasis on monetary benefits, with AfCFTA envisaged to enable Africa to leverage on its 1.3 billion people to create a $3 billion economic zone. What is disturbing is the neoliberal language of African people being defined as a market. While economic strength is needed for Africa to turn over a new leaf from neo-colonial dependency to economic autonomy, there is a lot of work to be done to avoid repeating the same mistakes that undercut the NEIO in the 1960s and 1970s. The position of Africa in the capitalist global economy is an invidious call for decolonization and decorporatization as the basis for a better African future.

The fact that since the 1960s, 14 former French colonies in Western and Central Africa had been saddled with French monetary imperialism makes the demands for decolonization/decoloniality very urgent. The mounting consciousness among Africans regarding this monetary imperialism was graphically demonstrated to the whole world by anti-CFA franc Franco-Benin activist Kemy Seba, who publicly set fire to a 5,000 CFA note in

Senegal. Increasingly, the colonial arrangement called 'Francafrique,' symbolizing France's continued maintenance of neo-colonial relations, has fallen under heavy criticism.

It would seem that under the pressure of their citizens, the ruling elites of the usually complacent Francophone Africa would be left with no option but to turn over a new leaf and delink from the erstwhile colonial power's monetary imperialism/monetary slavery, which would compel them to pay what is known as 'colonial tax.' When that day comes, Kwame Nkrumah, Julius Nyerere, Thomas Sankara, and Colonel Murmur al-Gaddafi will be smiling approvingly from their graves as they see Africa turning over a new leaf at last. What makes this struggle promising is that even West African artists have composed and recorded a song entitled 'seven minutes against the CFA franc,' rapping and singing in Wolof, Bambara, English, and French, and directly calling for an end to France's monetary imperialism. France's current attempts to hijack the ECO monetary initiative in order to continue monetary imperialism has to be confronted, together with its African elite allies, like President Quattara of the Ivory Coast.

What is clear is that Africa is fighting to turn over a leaf within a context in which the once triumphant liberal democracy is coming under very heavy criticism. The rise to power of racist and xenophobic populists, reminiscent of the interwar years of fascism and Nazism, in the USA, Brazil, and other parts of the world has badly de-legitimized liberal democracy. While Africans have continued to fight for democracy and to consolidate existing democracies, the question of what exactly democracy is continues to demand a definition beyond the rituals of elections every five years. Do the intensifying struggles for decolonization/decoloniality deepen or threaten liberal democracy? Decolonization/decoloniality is more amenable to social democracy, with its emphasis on social justice. Epistemological decolonization is about the democratization of knowledge by way of recognizing the diverse ways of knowing through which different people make sense of the world. At issue here is the question of cognitive justice, which is an essential pre-requisite for social justice. In short, decolonization/decoloniality calls for substantive democracy free from classism, patriarchy, epistemicides, culturecides, linguicides, economic extroversion, and racism.

Finally, Africa is fighting to turn over a new leaf within a global context at a time when the ideas of 'revolutions' have been substituted by reformist and problematic ideas of 'transitions.' The idea of 'transitions' kicked in during the neo-liberal triumphalism of the 1990s. They emerged within what became known as the 'third wave of democracy' on a global scale and in Africa became known as the struggles for 'second liberation' – this time from one-party state life presidencies and military juntas. Liberal democracy became the rallying call. That spirit of 'transitions' manifested in what became known as the 'Arab Spring,' which rocked North Africa and the Middle East. What has recently compromised the potentialities of civil society-driven 'transitions' have been the military interventions in civil politics in Egypt, Zimbabwe, Algeria, and Sudan. The military hijacked people power by taking over from the deposed dictators or imposing other dictators.

These recent political developments on the African continent have alerted us to the realities of the ever-present danger of the intervention of military forces during the 'interregnum,' in which the old dictator is forced to exit the political stage, and the democratic forces are not capable of defending their gains and immediately form a new government. Of course, in the examples of Egypt, Zimbabwe, Algeria, and Sudan, there are complex nuances peculiar to each case. For example, in Zimbabwe, the civil society was demobilized by the time the military removed the long-standing authoritarian Robert Mugabe from power in November 2017. In such a situation, the military had their cake and ate it too. But what is very clear from this book is that the terrain to turn over a new leaf in Africa will never be an event – it is a painstaking process of trials, tribulations, setbacks, and triumphs. It is clear, as stated by Samir Amin, that only the African people will make it possible for Africa to turn over a new leaf. For this to be possible 'bad faith,' as defined by Lewis Gordon, must fall. *Amandla!*

Index

K Nkrumah & J Nyerere:

three

- the institutionalisation of a right to self-determination at the United Nations
- the formation of regional federations
- the demand for New International Economic Order